DR. STRANGEMITTEN'S
Shrunken Heads
PLAY
RULES
QUIT
A GAME FROM
KEWLBOX.COM
PRIVACY STATEMENT
LEGAL INFO
Copyright © 2004 by Blockdot, Inc. All Rights Reserved.
Hey Fred!

Alexander Isley Inc.
Designers
Throwing Cheese
Since 1988

Design Aces

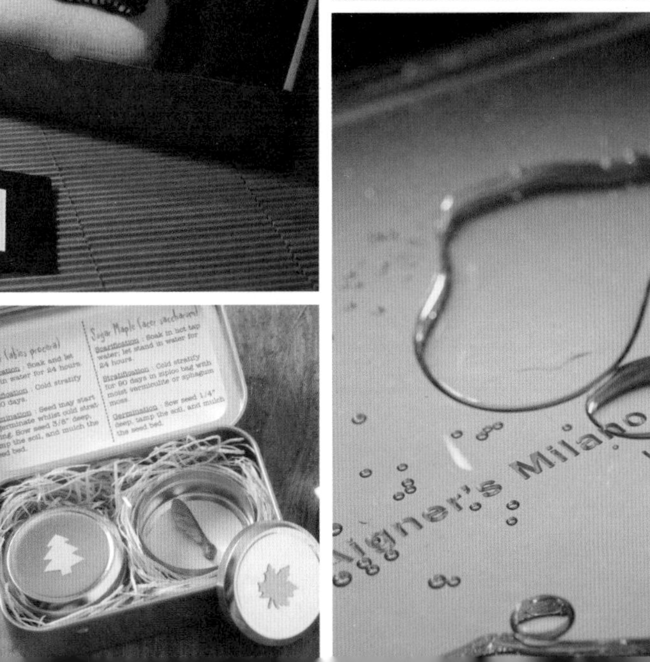

ORANGEBOX
LEMONBOX

ROME & GOLD CREATIVE
JOIN US
TICKETS FOR TWO!

GRAPHIC WORKSHOP

INNOVATIVE PROMOTIONS *THAT* WORK

GRAPHIC WORKSHOP

INNOVATIVE PROMOTIONS *THAT* WORK

A *Quick* Guide to the Essentials of Effective Design

LISA L. CYR

ROCKPORT PUBLISHERS
GLOUCESTER MASSACHUSETTS

First published in the United States of America by
Rockport Publishers, a member of
Quayside Publishing Group
33 Commercial Street
Gloucester, Massachusetts 01930-5089
Telephone: (978) 282-9590
Fax: (978) 283-2742
www.rockpub.com

Library of Congress Cataloging-in-Publication Data
Cyr, Lisa. L.
Graphic workshop, innovative promotions that work : a quick guide to the essentials of effective design / Lisa L. Cyr.
p. cm.
ISBN 1-59253-219-5 (hardback)
1. Commercial art—United States—History—21st century—Case studies. 2. Graphic arts—United States—History—21st century—Case studies. 3. Sales promotion—Case studies. I. Title.
NC998.5.A1.C97 2006
741.6068'8—dc22 2005027583

ISBN 1-59253-219-5

10 9 8 7 6 5 4 3 2 1

Design: Stoltze Design
Layout: Leslie Haimes

Printed in China

I would like to thank all of the creative firms, designers, photographers, animators, and artists who have shared their work and vision. Their ability to consistently push boundaries in search of a higher ground is inspirational. I'd also like to thank my editor, Kristin Ellison, who has always been a champion for truly creative endeavors, for allowing me the opportunity to showcase extraordinary talent. Many kudos to Clifford Stoltze, the designer of the book, for his consistent ability to lift design to a fine art form. Last, I want to thank my family for their ongoing support, and God for giving me the gift of expression and the desire to share it with others. This book is dedicated to my most creative endeavor, my daughter, Michaela.

"Whatever you can do, or dream you can, begin it. Boldness has genius, power, and magic."

—Goethe

Contents

Introduction

A NEW PARADIGM

Over the last two decades, the world has seen enormous change. Technological innovation has made it ever so easy to disseminate information to a global audience almost instantaneously. With this immediate accessibility, however, the floodgates have opened to mediocrity in communications; almost anyone can now enter the arena with the aid of electronics. In the quick-fix-get-the-job-done-and-the-work-out philosophy of the twenty-first century, we are seeing more and more ready-made, convenience-based, and overtly cost-conscious creative work enter into the culture. This time-is-of-the-essence reality has opened a market for corporate-controlled stock image banks, royalty-free design, and off-the-shelf identity systems. They are cheap, readily accessible, and allow for a quick turnaround. It seems that the speed and the cost for which things are done is becoming ever more important, oftentimes trumping quality and leading to the creation of an almost homogenized aesthetic. Just because we have the tools to produce faster than ever before does not mean we should discount quality and the time it takes to develop something truly original and distinctive. Producing work that is constantly compromised will come back to bite the industry as time goes on.

As visual communicators, it is our role to lead. We need to eradicate the complacency that exists, educating clients of the importance of producing creative work with imaginative content that speaks to the culture in ways that inspire and motivate. To take charge of our industry and our destiny, we need more than ever to innovate and experiment, working outside our comfort zone and limitations to move forward. We have to be willing to strive for greatness every time, refusing to compromise and settle for the mundane. By continuing to question the existing paradigm, we can begin to discover new solutions and opportunities for our work to move and grow. In the days of speed and haste, our patience and ongoing commitment to excellence will serve as a working model for the next generation of communicators, a brilliant reminder of the importance and virtues of integrity, hard work, and creative vision.

Chapter One

"It is always best to be true to who you are and the kind of work you like to do, attracting clients who value and respect what you bring to the table."

—Matt Ralph, Plainspoke

IMAGE AND BRAND-BUILDING PROMOTIONS

Oftentimes creatives enter the marketplace not truly knowing or understanding their brand. They spend years working on project after project, finding the work all-consuming, the assignments uninspiring, and the clients difficult, to say the least. Many spend their careers trying to be what they think others want, constantly shifting and moving with no clear direction. "A good sea captain would never set out on a long ocean voyage without first plotting the course and knowing the ports he wants to visit. The same fundamentals apply in our business," observes Richard Klingle-Watt of Blu Concept. "To thrive, not just merely survive, you must take an honest look at what kinds of projects you love to do, what you're really good at doing, and where you want to go, adjusting your course accordingly." To have a viable and rewarding career, it is important to know your brand before you begin to market yourself. "Our personality is best defined as being thoughtful, serious about what we do, and a little anal-retentive about production details and quality. We are not over-the-top zany, and any attempt at projecting that would mislead clients and result in the wrong client-to-studio match," shares Matt Ralph of Plainspoke. "It is always best to be true to who you are and the kind of work you like to do, attracting clients who value and respect what you bring to the table." Having a clear understanding of your unique vision, philosophy, and approach, whether you are a firm or freelancer, is essential to building a healthy and successful business for the long term.

When it comes to new business development, actively pursue relationships with clients who share your vision. Being selective in your approach attracts work that will feed your brand, building recognition and market value as time goes on. "The ideal client for Belyea is excited about messaging and design, enjoys partnering with our team, and has a real budget to produce a premium product. When we work with companies that are a good fit, we all win," notes principal Patricia Belyea. "The creative team enthusiastically delivers materials that build our client's brand, and Belyea produces one more example of our expertise, which ultimately builds our brand." When you take on work that you are sincerely passionate about, it creates leverage for other rewarding projects with like-minded clients. "By targeting a select group, we've been able to grow the business on our terms, one great client at a time," adds Klingle-Watt. "This strategy is still working for us today." True success has nothing to do with the amount of work you engage in. Instead, it's the quality and kind of work that you attract that ultimately matters the most. Whether your company is new and embarking on a launch or a seasoned firm looking to maintain market position, a distinctive brand-building promotion can prove to be very effective in calling attention to what you have to uniquely offer.

Signature Look

OBJECTIVE Illustrator Sterling Hundley was looking for a one-of-a-kind, well-crafted vessel to carry his work—one that would capture the attention of art buyers who receive hundreds of solicitations each week.

AUDIENCE The primary target audience was select editorial publications. Since the inaugural launch, the illustrator has also used the promotional vehicle to promote his work to a more diverse range of markets, including advertising and book publishing.

CONCEPT To attract the eye of busy art directors, the packaging of Hundley's work needed to be extraordinary—something that would stand out and command attention. The illustrator chose to use his visual skills and technical abilities to produce a distinctive, highly tactile presentation case sure to spark curiosity and interest. Once opened, a series of custom-labeled panels provides a consistent framework for the illustrator's signature style. Postcards, featuring recent works, were sent as follow-ups.

MESSAGE Sterling Hundley is a quality illustrator with a unique vision. Come take a look at what he can do.

RESPONSE The intriguing package has made a memorable first impression with everyone who has received it—a must in a highly competitive business such as illustration.

Firm Sterling Hundley, illustrator
Creative Direction Sterling Hundley
Design Anna Eidelman and Boris Churashëv
Illustration Sterling Hundley
Printing Epson Stylus Photo 1280 (images on board, business card, and labels) and Zooom Printing (postcards)
Special Techniques Dremel tool (imprint on cover)
Manufacturers Richmond Metal (metal) and Siewers Lumber & Millwork (wood)

"Ultimately, I want an art director to remember the work as professional and well-crafted, and I strive to carry that message throughout every aspect of what I do. I feel that by tying together all the separate pieces of my self-promotion with a common thread of design and identity, clients see consistency. A solid brand creates confidence in the work that you are delivering."

—Sterling Hundley, illustrator

fig. 1.1

The aluminum presentation case is accented with a signature attachment that is made by hand using a Dremel tool on a zinc etching plate. The dark tones are created with etcher's ink, which is rubbed and tooled using the end of a brush. Two coats of Crystal Clear spray seal the ink to the plate.

fig. 1.2

Postcards, in two formats, are offset-printed in four-color process on a coated cardstock and custom labeled to add a matte finish to the overall glossy surface.

fig. 1.3

The sides and interior of the custom box are made of rosewood and stained basswood. The entire box is assembled using screws, washers, rivets, and contact cement. It is bound together using hinges cut to a custom size.

fig. 1.4

Helvetica Neue, Mrs Eaves, and Trade Gothic are the primary fonts used throughout the entire package and identity.

fig. 1.5

The matching business card is made of a sheet of etcher's aluminum, heavyweight vellum, and burgundy cardstock. It is imprinted digitally using an inkjet printer.

fig. 2.1

Inside the brand-building box are a series of illustrated works that can be customized easily to a client's specific buying needs.

fig. 2.2

The artwork is digitally printed on Epson matte paper and adhered to board using a spray adhesive. A custom label wraps around the back, listing the illustrator's contact information.

Learn the Rules

Firm Rule29
Creative Direction Justin Ahrens
Design/Illustration Justin Ahrens
Copywriting Rule29 and Terry Marks
Photography Brian MacDonald and Justin Ahrens
Printing O'Neil Printing
Bindery Roswell Bookbinding
Manufacturers Uline (foam sleeve and box)

"This promotion has really helped us engage in deeper conversations with clients who have been using us for the same type of jobs over and over. It has allowed us to talk to them again from the ground floor."

—Justin Ahrens, Rule29

OBJECTIVE After celebrating five successful years in business, Rule29 wanted to share their unique insight and approach with clients in a promotional endeavor that would answer the frequently asked question, "What is rule twenty-nine or, for that matter, rules one through twenty-eight?" It was time for the design firm to formally put the mystery to rest and share their rules for success, so they teamed up with creative collaborator Terry Marks, who really drove the piece.

AUDIENCE The elegant promotional book was distributed to existing and prospective clients, primarily CEOs and marketing executives. One thousand were created in all.

CONCEPT The brand-building book, appropriately titled *Rules 1–28*, makes Rule29's unique namesake purposeful, revealing certain truths by which the firm navigates its business. The plush cover and decorative foil-stamped graphics entices recipients to open the book, while the engaging and thought-provoking copy keeps their interest piqued from page to page. "Making creative matter" is the tagline used throughout.

MESSAGE Come explore the firm's axioms for success, twenty-nine rules to live and work by.

RESPONSE As a result of this promotional endeavor, Rule29 has received tremendous feedback. Relationships with long-term clientele reached new heights, sparking further, more elaborate collaboration. In regards to new business, the piece attracted prospects who share the same synergy and vision, a key component to success.

fig. 1.1 The promotion is distributed in a sturdy white corrugated cardboard box with a custom-designed label.

fig. 1.2 The piece is protected inside the box by a foam sleeve. A custom label, printed on label stock in PMS 648 and PMS 688, keeps it closed.

fig. 1.3 A special thank-you card, printed in four-color process plus satin aqueous varnish on Topkote gloss 100 lb. text, is also inserted in the package.

fig. 2.1

The powder blue, suede-covered book is foil-stamped in white. The decorative details and color scheme are intrinsic to the Rule29 brand.

fig. 2.2

The 5 1/4" x 5 1/4" (13.5 x 13.5 cm) book is perfect-bound with a royal blue ribbon bookmarker.

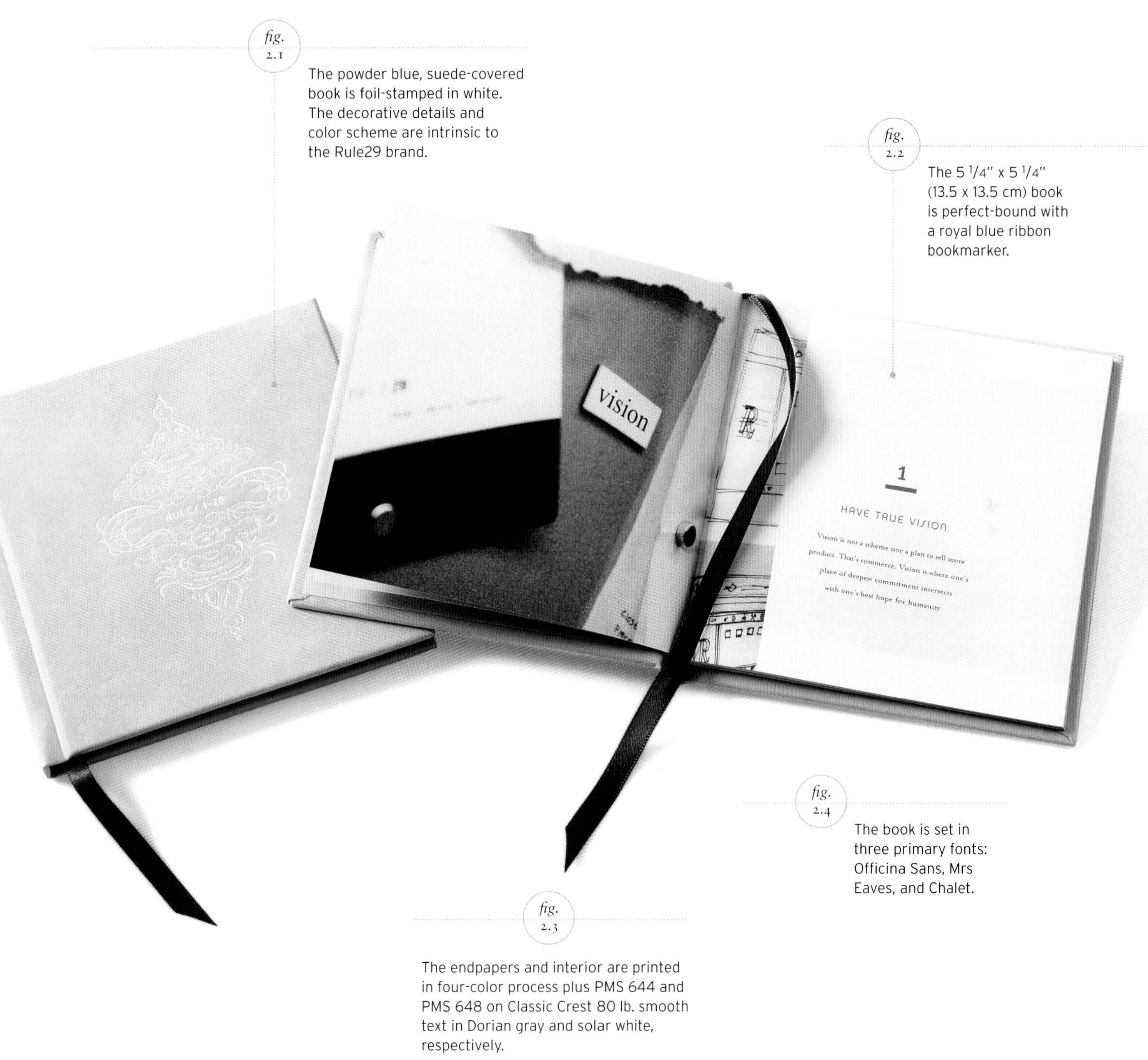

fig. 2.4

The book is set in three primary fonts: Officina Sans, Mrs Eaves, and Chalet.

fig. 2.3

The endpapers and interior are printed in four-color process plus PMS 644 and PMS 648 on Classic Crest 80 lb. smooth text in Dorian gray and solar white, respectively.

Taking Flight

Firm Finchworks
Creative Direction Frances Vandal and Denice Killian
Design/Illustration Frances Vandal
Printing Lexmark C912 inkjet printer
Manufacturers The Paper Company (specialty papers), Rubber Stampede (rubber stamp and ink), A.C. Moore (circular box), Kreinik Metallics (cord), Michaels (bird, eggs, and raffia), and Zucker Feather Products (feathers)

"Because the name Finchworks does not readily say graphic design and marketing communications, our initial promotional package serves to explain the rationale behind our name, our mission, and our personality."

—Frances Vandal, Finchworks

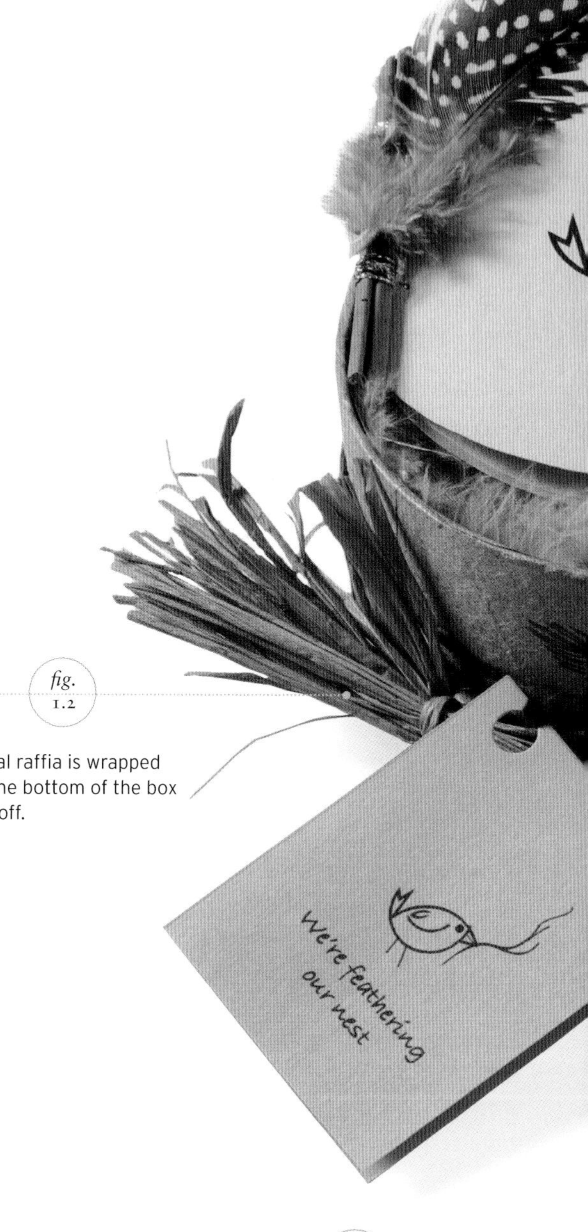

fig. 1.2

Additional raffia is wrapped around the bottom of the box and tied off.

fig. 1.3

A custom hangtag, digitally printed on yellow cardstock and attached with brown embroidery thread, communicates the overall "feathering our nest" theme.

OBJECTIVE Finchworks, a newly formed creative design firm consisting of two twenty-year veterans in the field, wanted to create a memorable promotional package to introduce their new venture to the marketplace.

AUDIENCE The target audience for the inaugural promotional initiative was prospective clientele, including art directors, marketing communications managers, and creative directors. The piece was also distributed to past clients and business acquaintances. Forty promotions were produced.

CONCEPT The name Finchworks was derived from the partners' fondness and affection for the zebra finches that they raise as a hobby. The hardworking, industrious, and very prolific birds perfectly encapsulate the firm's spirit. To introduce their brand to the marketplace, the firm chose to produce a distinctive, multitextural promotional ensemble. The package is distributed in a square box wrapped with yellow beaded specialty paper and a custom label. The handcrafted introductory package was followed up with personal phone calls.

MESSAGE The newly formed partnership is feathering their nest.

RESPONSE The Finchworks brand-building piece has garnered a lot of excitement, creating a buzz in the community.

fig. 1.4

Inside the decorated box, a small feather boa in soft beige tones is layered and formed to create a nest.

fig. 1.1

A yellow finch figure is attached firmly to the top of the circular box by piercing two holes into the lid and threading through thin wire, twisting it in place. Raffia is wrapped several times around the base of the bird, tied off, and trimmed. Two tiny plastic eggs are glued into place to reinforce the nesting idea. A label digitally imprinted with the firm's logo is applied to the inside cover, masking the wire tie.

fig. 1.5

The handcrafted promotional package is covered with crinkled brown kraft paper applied with Modge Podge matte medium and a sponge brush. Graphics of a bird feather are rubber-stamped on the outside of the package for visual interest.

fig. 1.6

The mini booklet, digitally printed on yellow cardstock for the cover and Arctic 60 lb. white bond for the inside pages, is hand-trimmed, sewn, and cleverly bound using gold thread with sticks and a feather.

Passion for Details

OBJECTIVE Huber&Co Design wanted to create a distinctive, detail-oriented promotional piece that would provide insight into the concepts behind the wide range of work they do.

AUDIENCE The promotion was sent to prospective clientele, mostly corporate brand managers and marketing directors. Five hundred were distributed.

CONCEPT The design firm chose to produce an elongated booklet that boasts many subtle details. The perforated graphic accent on the cover, the metal fastener binding, the transparent bellyband, and the vellum overlays each provide a certain refined elegance to the brand-building piece.

MESSAGE Huber&Co Design has a passion for detail.

RESPONSE The design firm received a lot of positive feedback from prospects, landing a few choice accounts.

Firm HUBER&CO DESIGN

Creative Direction ANTON HUBER

Design ANTON HUBER

Printing/Bindery WERKSTATT HÖEFLICH

Manufacturers METAL FASTENER (LOCAL OFFICE SUPPLY OUTLET)

"Most of our work is about developing one strong, simple idea created with passion and a sense for detail."

—Anton Huber, Huber&Co Design

fig. 1.1

The portfolio-based promotion, printed on Roemerturm Samat 280 gsm cover and 150 gsm text for the inside, is bound using a metal fastener.

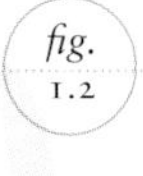

fig. 1.2

The vertical perforation on the cover serves as a graphic accent to the horizontally oriented piece.

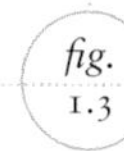

fig. 1.3

A bellyband, made of Fedrigoni 250 gsm translucent paper, wraps the piece shut.

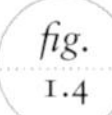

The primarily warm color scheme uses three colors: PMS 412, PMS 1545, and PMS warm gray 2.

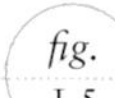

Throughout the promotional booklet, translucent pages with descriptive copy overlay photo-driven case studies, making a connection between the initial concept and the final piece.

Trade Gothic and Garamond Amsterdam are the fonts used throughout.

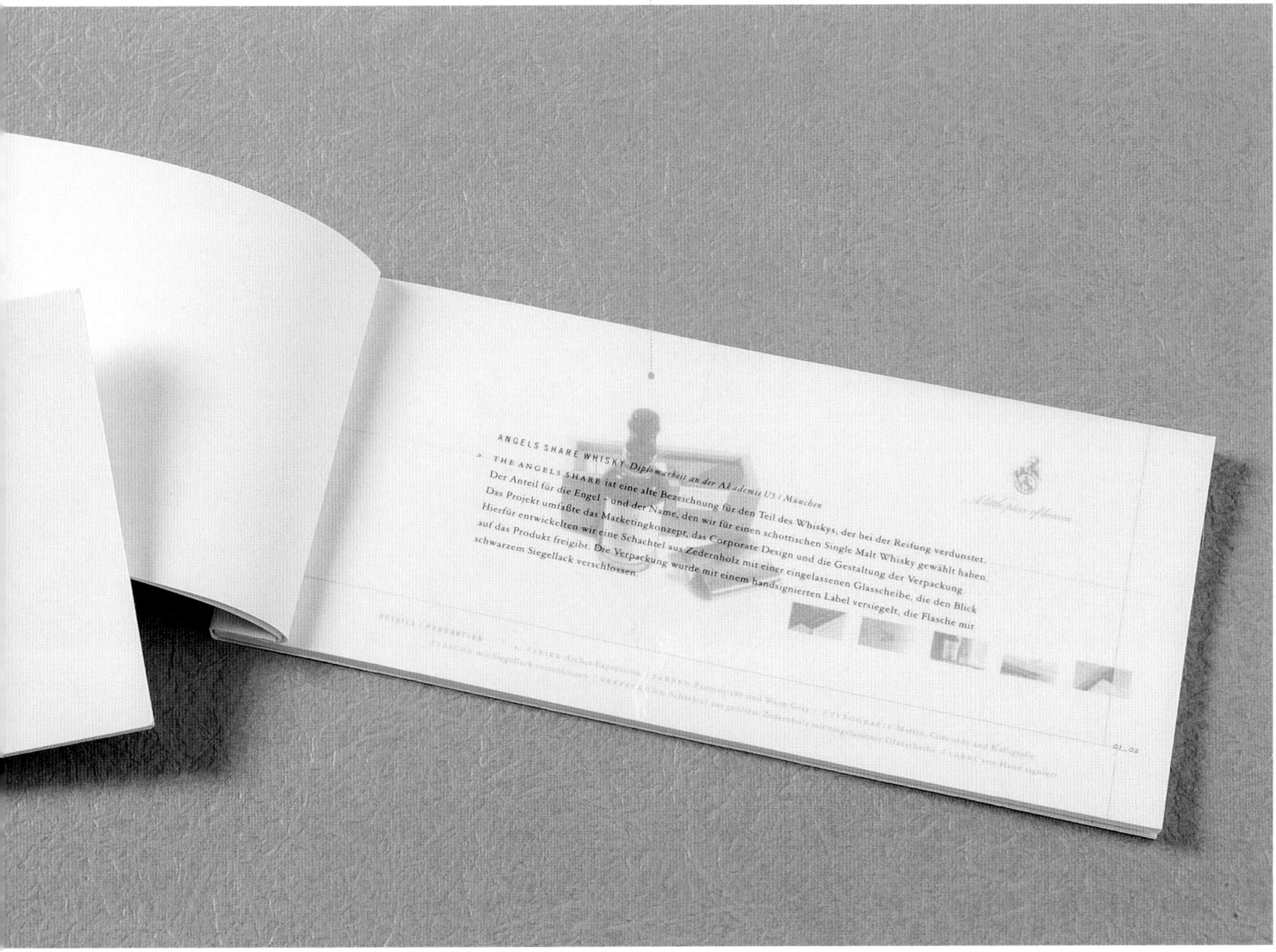

Peel Away

Firm H, Strategic Graphic Design
Creative Direction Winnie Hart
Design Winnie Hart and Gaby Tillero
Photography Sara Essex
Printing Franklin Southland
Manufacturers Office Depot (box and inflatable pen)

"We applied the same principles to develop an identity piece for H as we would use for any client. The metaphor of an orange to represent our Hthink process simplifies the message by making it tangible."

—Winnie Hart, H

OBJECTIVE H was looking to create a promotion that would communicate their unique approach to branding and positioning.

AUDIENCE The brand-based promotion was distributed to existing and prospective clientele. One thousand pieces were produced. The firm plans to continue with the project.

CONCEPT The promotion asked clients to question the effectiveness of their current approach to marketing. Using the metaphor of an orange to represent a business and its products, the design firm demonstrated how a company could distinguish itself by identifying its unique selling position and communicating it clearly and effectively through great design to a targeted audience. Oranges, shown in various forms, assist in illustrating the firm's internal strategic planning and development process called Hthink. The promotion is distributed in a 7" x 8 1/2" x 1 1/2" (18 x 21.5 x 4 cm) corrugated cardboard box with a custom label. An email campaign was used as a follow-up.

MESSAGE Think H when it comes to branding.

RESPONSE The firm received a 10 percent rate of response from the reply card and dozens of emails, resulting in three new business relationships.

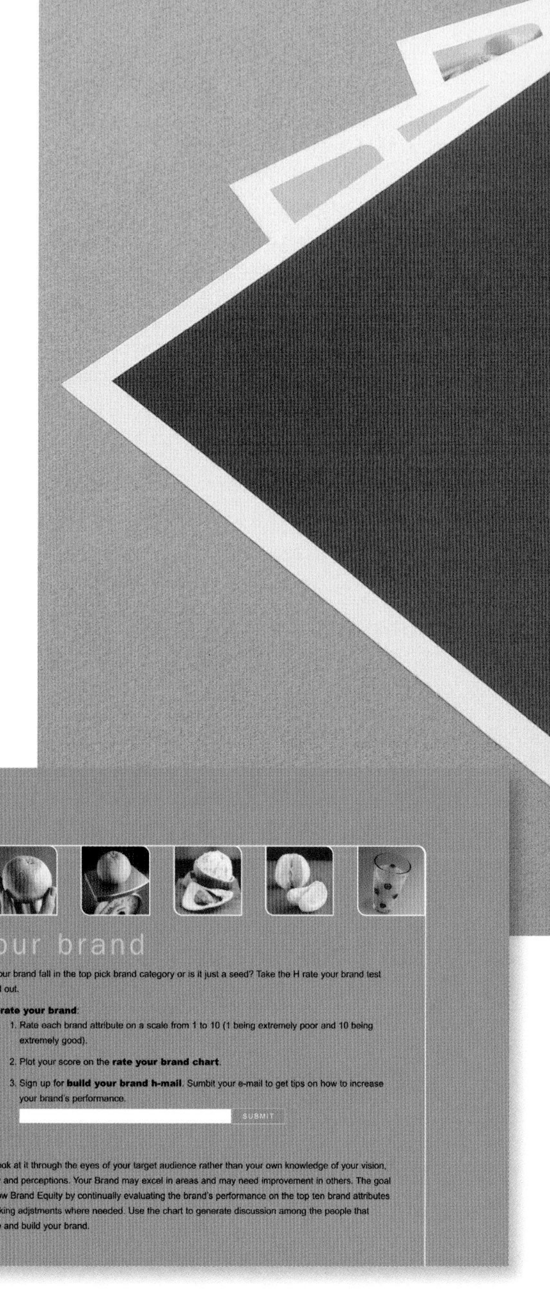

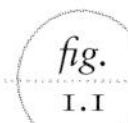

A brand chart, available on the firm's website www.thinkh.com, is a self-evaluation form the design firm uses to mirror back a client's concept of its brand. The orange theme is carried throughout.

fig. 2.1

The fonts Helvetica, Franklin, and Platelet are used throughout.

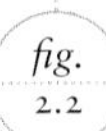
fig. 2.2

The promotional cards, printed in four-color process plus PMS 718 on 120 lb. Utopia Silk cover, are sent in a series as well as individually in envelopes. Dull varnish is used to protect the heavy coverage of ink.

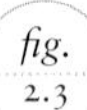
fig. 2.3

An inflatable vinyl pen, enclosed inside an elongated, tentlike structure called a pen pod, is used as an interactive add-on, motivating recipients to respond to the enclosed business reply card.

Escape from the Ordinary

OBJECTIVE Double Image Studio, a team of two photographers, wanted a distinctive promotional package that would speak to their diverse, multicultural expertise. The[Box] was brought in to capture the perfect setting for the studio's worldly photography.

AUDIENCE The target audience was creative directors, art directors, designers, and art buyers working for advertising agencies and corporations throughout the United States. Two hundred promotional packets have been produced to date.

CONCEPT Double Image Studio's photographic vision features slice-of-life scenes from all over the world. To carry their global message, the design firm employed the look and feel of an airline ticket. Every detail from the studio's profile, capabilities, and client list to the presentation of images is formatted to resemble a travel itinerary and ticket. With a selection of ten cards from which to choose, the staple-bound ticket can be customized easily to the recipient's buying needs. The promotion is followed up with a custom case study–based brochure that features a project taken on by the studio. The initiative is part of a rebranding campaign that includes a new set of portfolios, postcards, e-cards, and a new website.

MESSAGE Double Image Studio has a unique way of looking at the world.

RESPONSE The promotion has allowed the photographic studio to get their foot in the door to not only show their work but also to bid on many exciting projects.

Firm the[Box]
Creative Direction Anna Eidelman and Boris Churashëv
Design Anna Eidelman and Boris Churashëv
Photography Nicholas Timmons and Susan Delgado
Printing/Bindery Digital Banana (brochure and pocket envelope), Epson 1280 inkjet (business card), and Epson R2400 (case study brochure)
Client Double Image Studio

"Do you know that feeling when the airline ticket for your vacation arrives in the mail? You are excited. You open the envelope and see yourself escaping from the ordinary. That is the feeling that Double Image Studio brings to every project."

—Boris Churashëv, the[Box]

The case study brochure is digitally printed in-house on Moab Entrada Fine Art 190gsm in bright white.

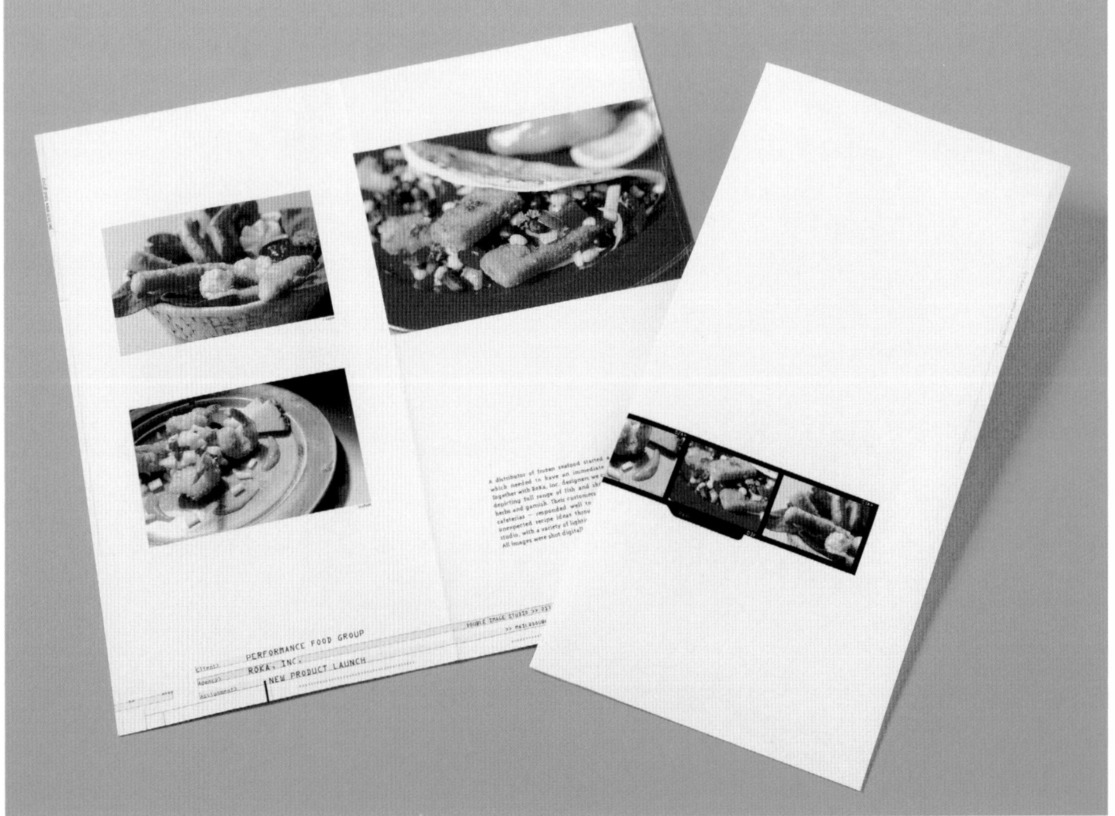

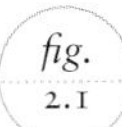

Triplex, Double Image Studio's brand font, is used along with OCRA and Letter Gothic, chosen for their resemblance to type used in airline tickets.

The brand-building promotion is digitally printed on Mega 80 lb. dull coverstock and fits nicely into a pocket envelope, printed on Mega 100 lb. gloss text stock.

fig. 2.3

Modeled after an airline ticket, the die-cut, perforated, and staple-bound brochure features worldly photographic images printed on a selection of ten cards, making it easy to customize the piece to a prospective client's needs.

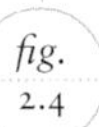

Matching business cards, printed in-house on an inkjet printer, help to continue the travel theme.

Creative Wordplay

Firm Plainspoke
Creative Direction Matt Ralph
Design Matt Ralph and Steve Richard
Website Programming Steve Richard
Production Manager Connie DiSanto
Photography Brian Wilder
Printing/Bindery Printers Square
Client Brian Wilder Photography

"I strongly believe that promotions need to connect and provoke a response. It could be as simple as making someone laugh or giving them something to think a little deeper about."

—Matt Ralph, Plainspoke

OBJECTIVE To promote his work and make his name memorable to prospective clientele, photographer Brian Wilder knew he had to come up with something really catchy, fun, and inviting. This endeavor required a complete redesign, including an identity system, promotional package, and website. Wilder sought out long-time collaborator Plainspoke to do the job.

AUDIENCE The promotional package was sent to art directors, art buyers, and designers in the editorial and advertising markets. One thousand pieces were produced.

CONCEPT To make Brian Wilder's name memorable, the design firm came up with an interesting wordplay using the photographer's first initial and last name, B Wilder. The playful combinations—B Cooler, B Leaner, and B Meaner, to name just a few—help reinforce B Wilder (Brian Wilder) and all the qualities inherent in his work. To continue this fresh, exciting theme, a series of postcards and T-shirts are in the works.

MESSAGE Brian Wilder is a photographer able to translate word into image in a fun and exciting way.

RESPONSE Since the launch of the new identity program, promotional package, and website, photographer Brian Wilder has seen a substantial increase in assignments and requests to see his portfolio. Advertising agency creative directors and editorial art directors are especially responsive to the promotion's strong use of word and image.

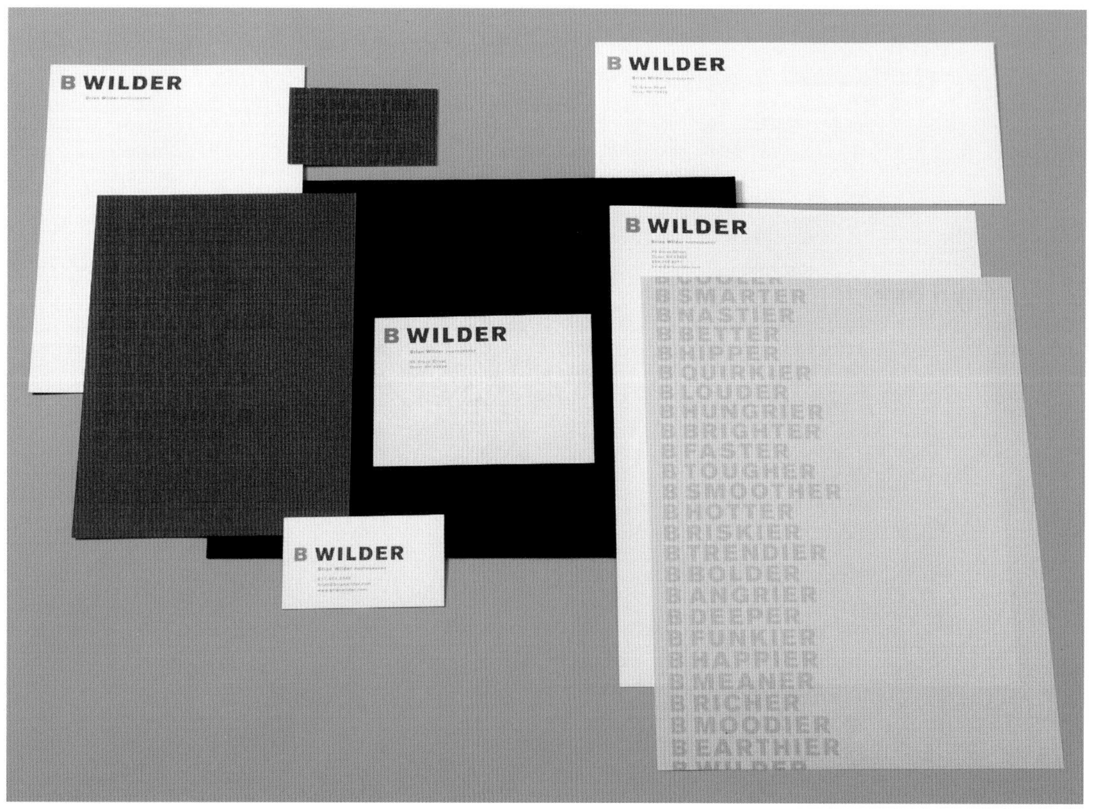

To accent the promotional package, the stationery system uses two primary colors, PMS 032 red and 7528 gray printed on Mohawk Superfine Ultrawhite smooth finish 70 lb. text and 120 lb. cover.

The font, Akzidenz Grotesk, is used throughout for its bold, assertive quality.

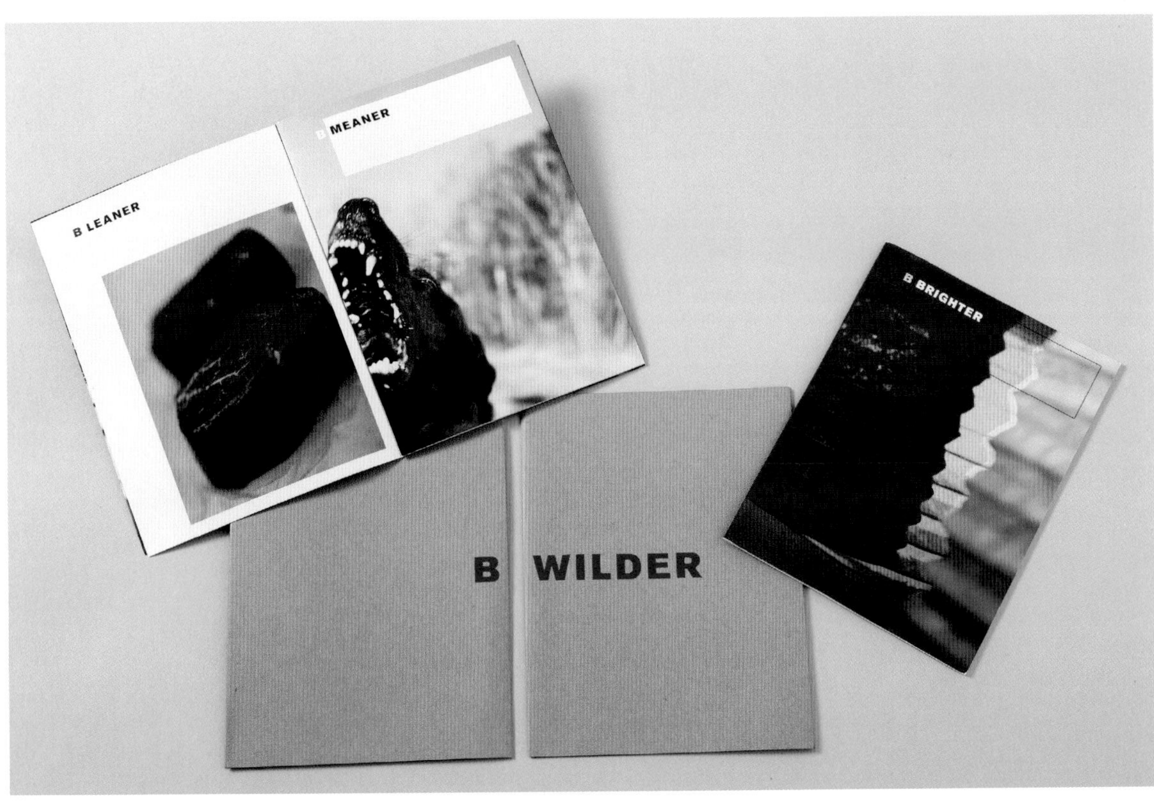

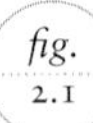

The 5" x 6 3/4" (13 x 17 cm), saddle-stitched booklet gives the piece an intimate appeal.

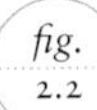

Inside the booklet, cleverly titled *B Brighter*, word and image work together in a fun, entertaining way. Gloss and matte varnishes are applied onto Scheufelen Job Parilux dull 74 lb. cover in contrasting ways to further enhance the message.

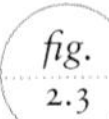

The brightly colored booklet fits in a neutral-toned, French Durotone packing brown 70 lb. text sleeve imprinted with a double hit of opaque red purple (PMS 812) to match the signature color red (PMS 032). The entire package is mailed in a clear envelope with a translucent label.

The graphic and geometric framework of Brian's website, www.brianwilder.com, continues the exciting play between word and image.

Impressive Package

OBJECTIVE Ico Design Consultancy Limited wanted to attract high-end clientele with projects that would challenge the firm to reach for new heights.

AUDIENCE The custom-built promotion was targeted toward thirty key prospects.

CONCEPT To call attention to their brand, the design team decided to create a promotion that would be of value, something a client would want to hold onto: a custom-made wooden box. Inside, several cards pose thought-provoking questions. Once opened, each card is adorned with impressive projects successfully undertaken by the design consultancy.

MESSAGE Think about how your brand is being managed.

RESPONSE Out of the thirty firms targeted, eight prospects responded right away with active projects; another nine were seriously considering working with the firm in the near future. Because of the success of the initial launch, Ico Design Consultancy Limited plans on continuing with this promotional endeavor.

Firm Ico Design Consultancy Limited

Creative Direction Steve Lloyd

Design/Photography Vivek Bhatia and Adam Thomas

Printing Identity (lithography) and Harvey Lloyd Screens (silkscreen printing)

Manufacturers Richard Poynter (wooden box) and Alan Bancroft (cardboard box)

"Speculate to accumulate. If you are serious about working for a potential client, demonstrate it."

—Niall Henry, Ico Design Consultancy Limited

fig. 1.1

The promotional package is distributed in a custom, hand-trimmed, white corrugated cardboard box with a simple white label.

fig. 1.2

The brand-building promotion comes in a handcrafted wooden box made of fiddleback sycamore veneer adhered to a birch-face plywood.

fig. 1.3

The custom box is silkscreen-printed with the company's name on the front and spine in PMS 368 orange. A water-based varnish is applied as a protective coating.

fig. 2.1

Inside the wooden box is a stack of 13" x 5" (33 x 13 cm) cards. Each is printed on Parliux 300 gsm matte coated coverstock, folded in half horizontally, and adhered to 1/10" (2 mm) white-centered display board that has been silkscreen-printed with PMS 2975 light blue on the back.

fig. 2.2

Each card is printed in four-color process with various spot colors—process magenta, process yellow, PMS 254 purple, and PMS 2975 light blue—silkscreen-printed on top.

fig. 2.3

Bertold Akidenz, the firm's corporate typeface, and Grotesque are the primary fonts used throughout.

fig. 1.1

The highly graphic front and back covers are printed with a double hit of fluorescent Fasson yellow, a special mix, on Saxton 150 gsm paper.

fig. 1.2

Gridnik and Frutiger are the fonts that underpin the new identity.

fig. 1.3

The large-scale format is sized like a broadsheet newspaper and folds in half to be either hand-delivered or mailed.

Our Stuff

Firm EMERYFROST
Creative Direction GARRY EMERY AND VINCE FROST
Design ANTHONY DONOVAN
Photography VARIOUS
Printing/Bindery PENFOLD BUSCOMBE

"Trying to get the desired fluorescent quality in the ink was a challenge. Printers told us it wasn't possible and that the color would disappear within days. Our solution was to create a special-mix ink, our very own emeryfrost color."

—Vince Frost, emeryfrost

OBJECTIVE Two internationally recognized creative leaders, Garry Emery and Vince Frost, joined forces and formed emeryfrost. To announce their joint venture, the two partners wanted to produce a distinctive piece that would communicate their new identity in a bold way.

AUDIENCE The brand-building piece was mailed to prospective and existing clientele. It was also distributed to the press. For this inaugural issue, 3,000 were printed. It is the first in a series.

CONCEPT Excited about their new venture, the firm really wanted to make a statement. To get noticed, the team developed a large-format, editorial-style piece. The bold graphics, fluorescent color, and strong vertical orientation command attention.

MESSAGE emeryfrost announces their new joint venture. Take a look at what they are doing.

RESPONSE The newly formed studio has taken on a number of new clients since *Stuff* was initially launched. The piece's bold, eye-catching presentation makes anyone stop, look, and listen.

fig. 2.1

Inside the editorial-style promotion are full-spread project features printed in four-color process. The projects cover a wide range of disciplines and are positioned in a dynamic, high-impact fashion.

Return to Sender

Firm Modern Dog Design Co.

Creative Direction Robynne Raye and Michael Strassburger

Design Clara Anders

Illustration Robynne Raye, Michael Strassburger, Junichi Tsuneoka, and Vittorio Costarella

Printing The Copy Co. (stamps) and Day Moon Press (stationery)

"Posters are our most requested item. Because we don't make enough to send out and aren't interested in selling them, we wanted to document eighteen years of poster making onto something little and portable, like stamps. Second, we've had dozens of Modern Dog identities since our inception. We find ourselves quickly bored and wanting to do something different. This is the first time all four of us are using the same company design. Part of the reason it works is that we can customize each card with a different poster design."

—Robynne Raye, Modern Dog Design Co.

OBJECTIVE Modern Dog Design Co., known for their cutting-edge poster work, wanted to document their efforts in a simple, fun, and easy-to-distribute way.

AUDIENCE The target audience was past, current, and prospective clientele. Two separate sheets were designed with 1,500 printed of each.

CONCEPT With lots of requests for posters, the design firm decided to make the designs into stamps: a convenient way to highlight and distribute their extensive body of work. To showcase the stamps, the firm developed a new stationery system. Each piece of the identity system can be customized with any one of the 132 stamps in the two-sheet collection.

MESSAGE Modern Dog Design's poster work is diverse and broad with an exciting range of illustration.

RESPONSE The stamps were a huge success. The firm still receives requests for the printed sheets. They were also a big hit internally: Each partner is now able to customize his or her own business cards and stationery.

fig. 1.1

Each 9 1/2" x 12 1/2" (24 x 32 cm) fully perforated sheet is printed in four-color process on Tromark gum label #812.

fig. 1.2

One hundred and thirty poster designs are featured, including full contact information for recipients interested in collecting the series.

fig. 2.1

The letterpress-printed business cards are produced in three passes—two for the black and one for the red—on Neenah Classic Crest 130 lb. cover in classic cream. They, too, can be customized.

fig. 2.2

The custom letterhead and envelope, printed in black and PMS 032 red on Neenah Classic Crest 24 lb. writing paper in classic cream, can be customized with any of the various sizes and styles of stamps in the collection.

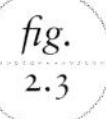

fig. 2.3

DIN Schriften is the font employed throughout the identity package.

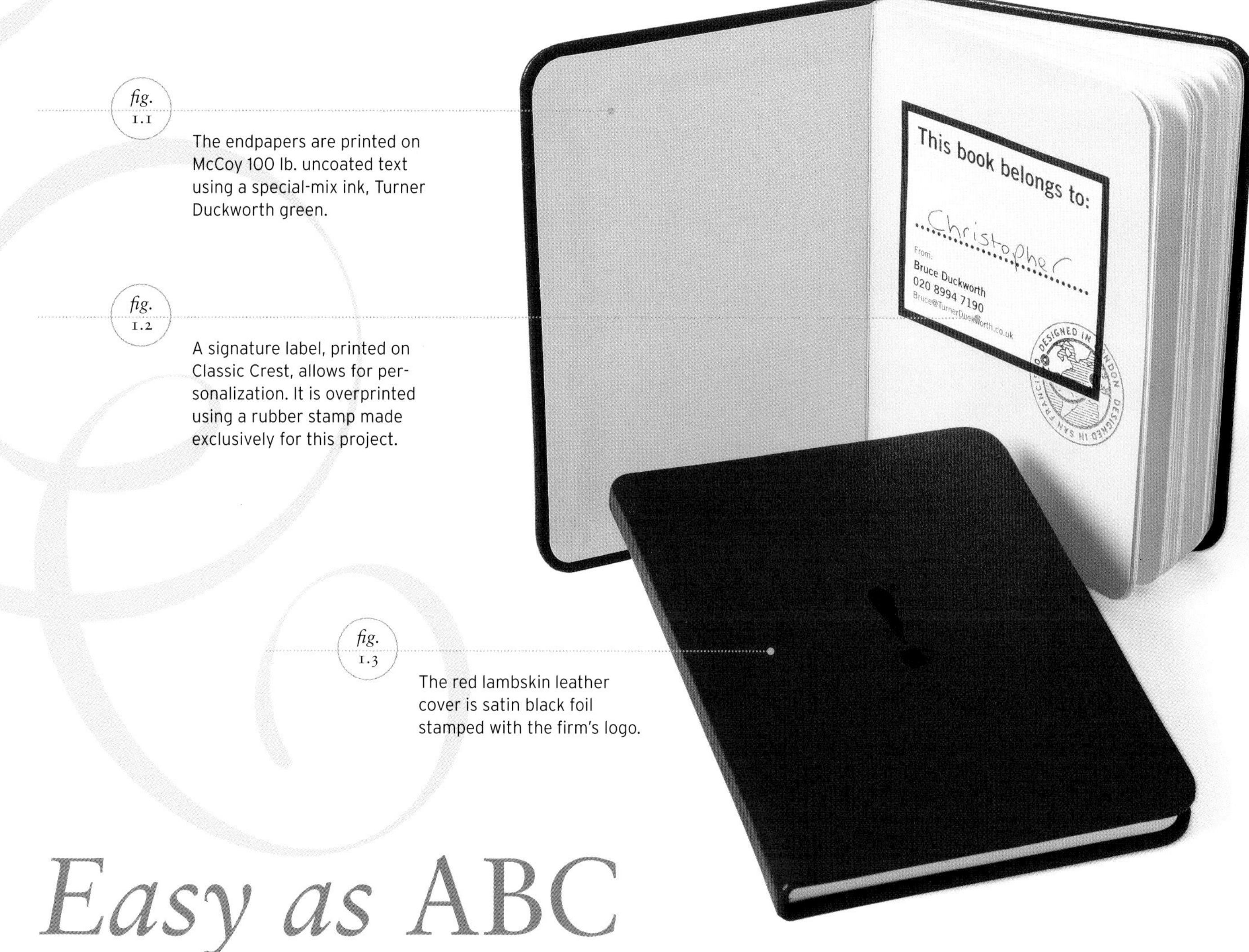

fig. 1.1 The endpapers are printed on McCoy 100 lb. uncoated text using a special-mix ink, Turner Duckworth green.

fig. 1.2 A signature label, printed on Classic Crest, allows for personalization. It is overprinted using a rubber stamp made exclusively for this project.

fig. 1.3 The red lambskin leather cover is satin black foil stamped with the firm's logo.

Easy as ABC

Firm Turner Duckworth
Creative Direction David Turner and Bruce Duckworth
Design David Turner, Bruce Duckworth, Anthony Biles, and Christian Eager
Production Artist Jaleen Francois
Account Manager Elise Thompson
Printing Paper N' Inc.
Bindery Arnold's Bookbinding

OBJECTIVE Turner Duckworth, a design consultancy with collaborating studios in London and San Francisco, wanted to create a promotion that provided insight into the firm's core principles of design.

AUDIENCE The target was prospective, current, and past clients who had lapsed. Five hundred pieces were produced.

CONCEPT The design team chose a children's alphabet book format to showcase their design principles from A to Z. Throughout the little red leather school book, key words are accented by strong graphic symbols to provoke in-depth thought about the statements being presented. The practice also demonstrates the firm's keen ability to express a concept-based idea in a simple mark.

MESSAGE Turner Duckworth has a unique approach to design and problem solving.

RESPONSE The little red book has been quite successful for the design firm. The work has also attracted the attention of the trade press.

fig. 2.1

Throughout the book, each spread is printed with black and a special-mix Turner Duckworth red on McCoy 100 lb. uncoated text.

"We're in the business of making simple, emotive, and visual statements, and this book had to demonstrate that. It had to combine depth with brevity. It's not about what we do. It's about how we do it, revealing to a prospective client the quality of our thinking."

—David Turner, Turner Duckworth

David vs. Goliath

Firm StrawberryFrog
Creative Direction/Design StrawberryFrog
Production Margo Warmerdam
Illustration Bastiaan Rijkers
Printing Haverkamp Printing (book) and Amsterdam Silkscreen (T-shirts)
Bindery Haverkamp Printing (book)

"Most agency info packs look the same with everyone claiming to be different. This book proves StrawberryFrog is different by its very existence and creation. It pays to break the rules."

—Brian Elliott, StrawberryFrog

OBJECTIVE StrawberryFrog was looking for a fresh, surprising way to show how the days of the large bureaucratic agencies are over, motivating prospects to take a chance on a smaller, more user-friendly agency such as theirs.

AUDIENCE The target audience was primarily CEOs, CMOs, marketing vice presidents, and brand managers as well as the media. The work was also distributed to current and potential staff.

CONCEPT The design team decided to use illustrative storytelling as an effective and engaging way to communicate their David vs. Goliath message. Using a children's book format, the promotion demonstrates how the large, overstaffed agencies really can't meet client needs as efficiently and effectively as a smaller firm can. The book, titled *Viva la Revolución: A StrawberryFrog Manifesto*, drives home its point through the introduction of characters such as the Bureaucratosaurus, (known for long meetings and paperwork), the Egosaurus, (concerned more about billing than your needs), and the Networkosaurus (who stomps all over really creative ideas). The frog is presented as the eager, more versatile, and creative alternative. The days of the old dinosaur ways of working are over. A frog T-shirt, also known as a tease shirt, acts as a wearable add-on to the book.

MESSAGE Why would any company want to work with a dinosaur when it can choose a frog—a StrawberryFrog that is. They may be small, but they think big.

RESPONSE The promotional storybook has been a key element in differentiating StrawberryFrog from the competition in a memorable and relevant way. The piece has been a great door opener for the firm and is welcomed by key decision makers in major global corporations. The accompanying StrawberryFrog T-shirts have become collectors items with requests coming in from around the world.

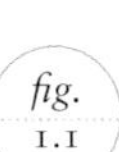
fig. 1.1

The StrawberryFrog "tease shirt," silkscreen-printed on a variety of colors, is sent along with the storybook as an add-on.

fig. 2.1

The cover is printed on 170 gsm satin stock glued onto 1/8" (3 mm) carton board and laminated for durability.

fig. 3.1

The 7 3/4" x 9 3/4" (19.5 x 25 cm) book is structured much like a traditional perfect-bound, thirty-two-page children's book.

fig. 3.2

Inside the story-driven book, printed in four-color process throughout, are two foldout spreads, each boasting a three-paneled image.

No *Bones* about It

OBJECTIVE Illustrator Denise Bosler wanted a fun, eye-catching promotional piece that would not only introduce her signature work to the children's book publishing market but also showcase her ability to think and work three-dimensionally.

AUDIENCE The target audience consisted of editors and art directors of children's books. Twenty promotions were created.

CONCEPT In the illustration business today, it is important that artists bring more to the table than just an image. To draw attention to her work, Bosler chose to translate one of her dog characters into a three-dimensional form, allowing the whimsical character to come to life. Inside the character-based packaging is a book of illustrations called *Hot Diggity Dogs*. Through familiar dog idioms like *dog days of summer, raining cats and dogs*, and *dog-eat-dog world*, the small-format storybook provides a showcase for the illustrator's signature style. The promotional package was followed by postcards, one each month. Each card introduces a new illustrated dog idiom, keeping the work and the illustrator fresh in the minds of buyers.

MESSAGE Illustrator Denise Bosler is able to create well beyond the two-dimensional surface, an asset for any children's book publisher—especially when it comes to later animating and merchandising popular characters.

RESPONSE With the success of this promotion, the illustrator is considering doing a series on cats.

Firm DENISE BOSLER, ILLUSTRATOR
Creative Direction DENISE BOSLER
Design/Illustration DENISE BOSLER
Printing PRINTINGFORLESS.COM (BUSINESS CARDS), EPSON STYLUS PHOTO 820 (BOOK AND LABELS), AND EPSON STYLUS PHOTO 1280 (DOG BOX)
Bindery DENISE BOSLER
Manufacturers JESSE JAMES AND COMPANY, INC. (DOG BONE BUTTONS), ULINE (CORRUGATED CARDBOARD BOX), TARGET (OUTER WRAPPING PAPER), AND DMC (THREAD)

"Every day editors and art directors are overwhelmed with tearsheets and samples from illustrators. What better way to make potential clients take notice than to give them a happy little three-dimensional dog to keep them company at the office. The silly grin and floppy head and tail will make anyone smile with sheer curiosity as to what's inside."

—Denise Bosler, illustrator

Cleverly titled *Hot Diggity Dogs*, the 4 1/4" x 4 1/2" (11 x 11.5 cm) book features seven well-known dog idioms, vividly illustrated in Denise Bosler's signature style.

The mini booklet boasts French-folded pages throughout, each digitally printed with a full bleed on the same stock as the container in which it sits.

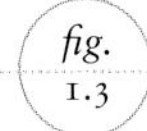

The whimsical book's hand-stitched bindery is accented with three miniature dog bones, a clever addition to the overall dog theme.

fig. 1.4 The font Naughties, created by Chank Fonts, is employed for the front cover; Optima Regular is used for the interior pages.

fig. 2.1

The highly creative package is distributed in a 200 lb. corrugated cardboard box that is wrapped with mint green paper and accented all around with custom labels.

fig. 2.2

The floral base of the box functions as a housing unit for the miniature book inside, while the blue-spotted-dog box top closes the package shut, adding movement to the character through the head and tail add-ons.

fig. 2.3

The character-based box, digitally printed on Epson 44 lb. heavyweight matte paper and adhered to 100 lb. cover cardstock, sets the stage for the illustrated work inside.

fig. 2.4

A business card, printed in four-color process on Cougar Opaque 100 lb. white uncoated cover on two sides, is inserted into the inside back cover of the book for interested recipients.

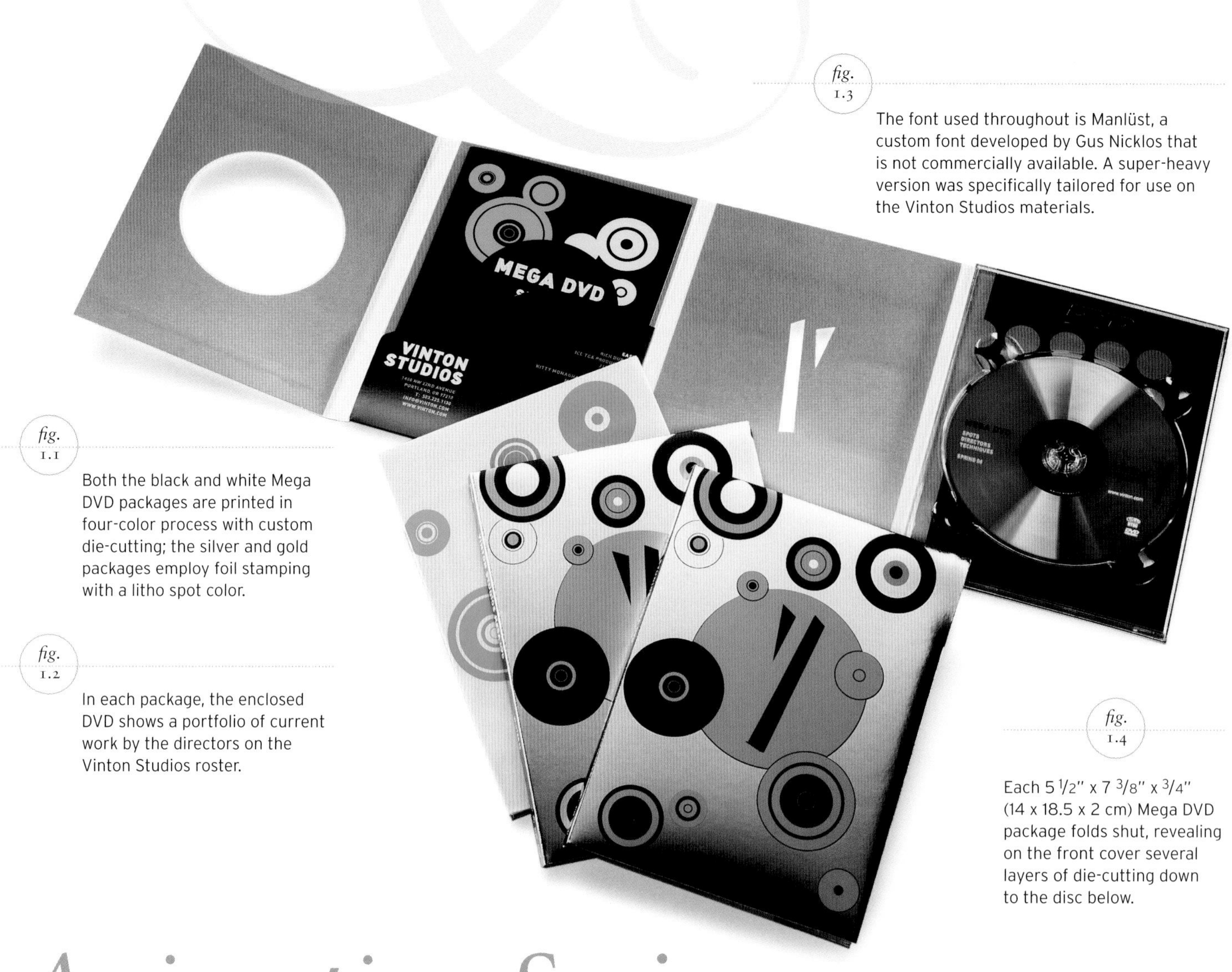

fig. 1.1

Both the black and white Mega DVD packages are printed in four-color process with custom die-cutting; the silver and gold packages employ foil stamping with a litho spot color.

fig. 1.2

In each package, the enclosed DVD shows a portfolio of current work by the directors on the Vinton Studios roster.

fig. 1.3

The font used throughout is Manlüst, a custom font developed by Gus Nicklos that is not commercially available. A super-heavy version was specifically tailored for use on the Vinton Studios materials.

fig. 1.4

Each 5 1/2" x 7 3/8" x 3/4" (14 x 18.5 x 2 cm) Mega DVD package folds shut, revealing on the front cover several layers of die-cutting down to the disc below.

Animation Series

OBJECTIVE Vinton Studios, often associated with stop-motion animation and their popular Claymation® technique, wanted to show that they had a more diverse range of capabilities. They looked to Plazm to bring them through a rebranding that would better highlight their studio's depth and diversity.

AUDIENCE The primary audience was art directors, creative directors, and art buyers as well as the industry media and executives in the areas of advertising, Hollywood film, and animation. Two thousand of each Mega DVD package were produced.

CONCEPT As part of an ongoing rebranding effort, a series of custom show-reel packages were created with the look and feel of old posters from the 1950s. The size and interesting die-cut shapes draw attention to what is inside. The Mega DVD promotional series is supported by a website (www.vinton.com) and print advertising.

MESSAGE Get excited about the diverse capabilities of this highly respected animation studio.

RESPONSE The Mega DVD concept was quite successful in drawing attention to the animation company's diverse capabilities. To continue the good fortune, yet another package is being added to the series.

Firm Plazm

Art Direction Joshua Berger

Design Eric Mast and Joshua Berger

Printing Bullseye Disc (printing of DVD 1 white and DVD 2 black) and Golden Impressions (printing and foil stamping of DVD 3 silver and DVD 4 gold)

Special Techniques Bullseye Disc (fabrication and duplication)

Client Vinton Studios

"Plazm's packaging made our Mega disc stand out from the bunch. It felt deluxe; something of value. The combination of the lovely Digipak printing and the die-cuts on the cover gave the right impression—that Vinton cares about every creative aspect of a job."

—Paul Golden, Vinton Studios

Double Take

OBJECTIVE Photographer Claudia Goetzelmann wanted to create a self-promotional piece that was distinctive, calling attention to her unique style and sense of humor.

AUDIENCE The book was primarily distributed to art buyers and photo editors. The photographer continues to hand out the book when she presents her portfolio. Fifty books were produced for the initial launch.

CONCEPT A custom, handcrafted book features the work of photographer Claudia Goetzelmann in a conceptual, story-driven context. Each spread presents a model wearing a handbag as a costume of sorts. Throughout the signature book, copy sets the stage while the images complete the story. The work is packaged in a nondescript covering, creating curiosity as to what is inside. Stitching on the binding and title page adds a tactile element to the fashion-oriented book.

MESSAGE Claudia Goetzelmann can take an ordinary, everyday object and make it extraordinary.

RESPONSE The photographer has gotten tremendous response from this self-initiated endeavor. The project has won several awards, receiving recognition from both *Photo District News* and *HOW* magazine for outstanding achievement.

Firm CLAUDIA GOETZELMANN, PHOTOGRAPHER
Creative Direction CLAUDIA GOETZELMANN
Design/Photography CLAUDIA GOETZELMANN
Printing EPSON 2200
Bindery TAURUS BOOKBINDERY

"Many love the concept, design, and feel of the book, and they remember me when I go back for meetings. It is still so much fun to observe people's reaction when they look through the book. This project really reinforced my belief in the value of executing personal projects."

—Claudia Goetzelmann, photographer

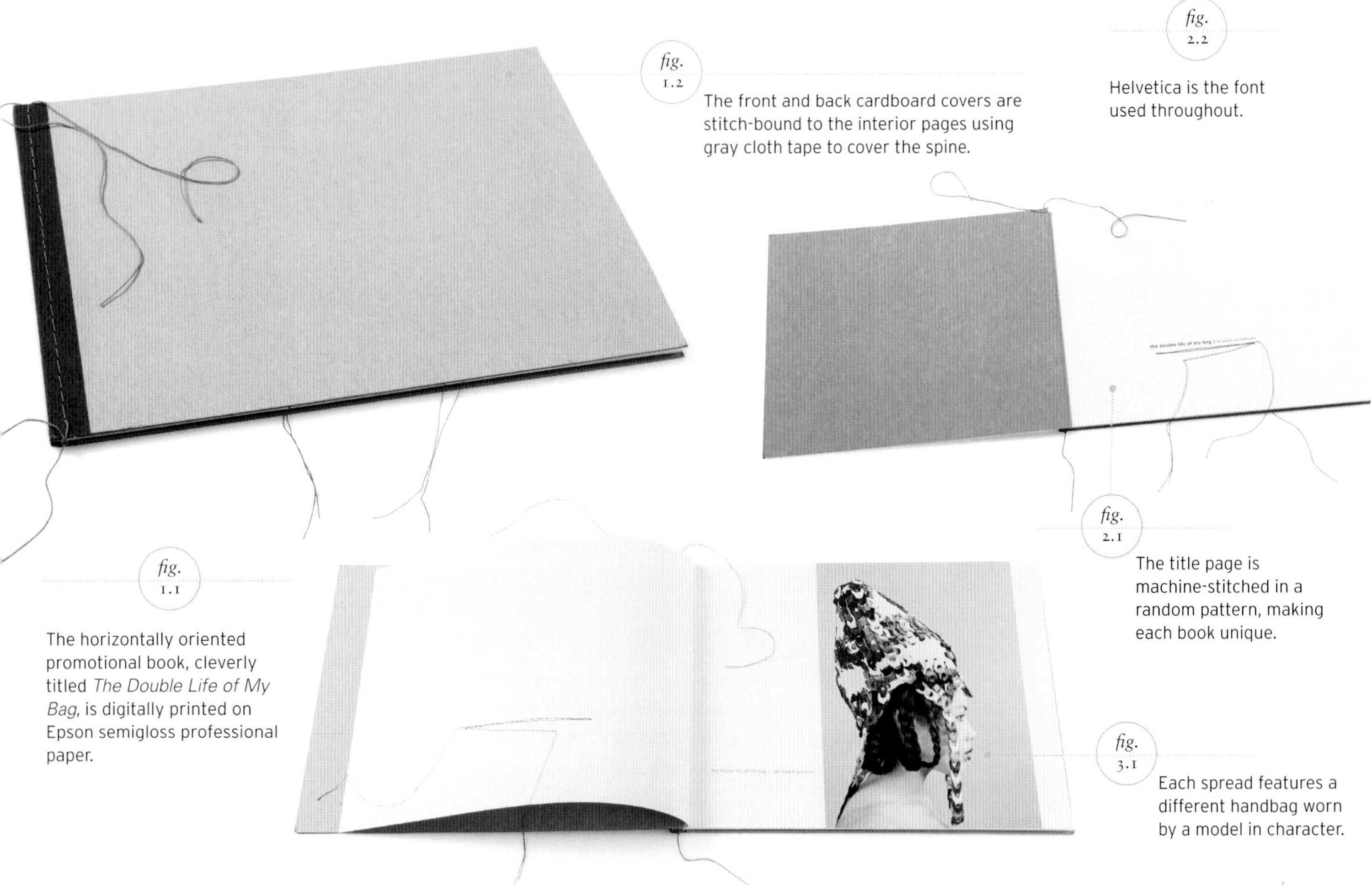

fig. 1.2 The front and back cardboard covers are stitch-bound to the interior pages using gray cloth tape to cover the spine.

fig. 2.2 Helvetica is the font used throughout.

fig. 2.1 The title page is machine-stitched in a random pattern, making each book unique.

fig. 1.1 The horizontally oriented promotional book, cleverly titled *The Double Life of My Bag*, is digitally printed on Epson semigloss professional paper.

fig. 3.1 Each spread features a different handbag worn by a model in character.

Go Mobile!

OBJECTIVE To enable their business to expand beyond the local area while still maintaining their door-to-door, personalized service, Refinery Design Company decided to transform a vintage 1967 Winnebago into a mobile design studio.

AUDIENCE The primary target was both existing and prospective clientele.

CONCEPT The firm chose a vintage Winnebago as their vehicle of choice because it is such a highly recognized part of American culture. The mobile studio was decorated with travel references—specifically maps—on the exterior. Every time the firm commutes to a new locale, they put a red dot on the side of the vehicle to map their path. Inside the Winnebago is a fully functioning design studio, equipped with a wraparound computer workstation with filing cabinets and storage, a 1950s-style dining booth conference table, a television with a VCR and a DVD player, a stereo system, air-conditioning, a fridge, a stove, a microwave, a built-in trash can, and a retractable full-size bed. The vehicle also has adjustable air-ride suspension so that it can be leveled in any condition. The firm conducts meetings and presentations right inside the vehicle—a unique door-to-door service almost unheard of today.

MESSAGE If we can make a 1967 Winnebago look like this, imagine what we can do for your company.

RESPONSE The mobile studio project is a large-scale representation of how the firm is able to think outside the box. Accessibility to clients allows for the development of more personal, one-on-one relationships. The studio on wheels is also an eye-catcher for passersby in every town the firm visits.

Firm Refinery Design Company
Creative Direction/Design Michael Schmalz
Printing Union-Hoermann Press
Manufacturers Ainley Fabrication and 3M (high performance vinyl)

"When selling design to a client, you are selling yourself and your ideas. If you have a way to make your clients feel comfortable, you are miles ahead."

—Michael Schmalz, Refinery Design Company

fig. 2.1

The studio door carries the metallic look inside with its anodized aluminum lining and grid pattern of oversized stainless-steel bolts.

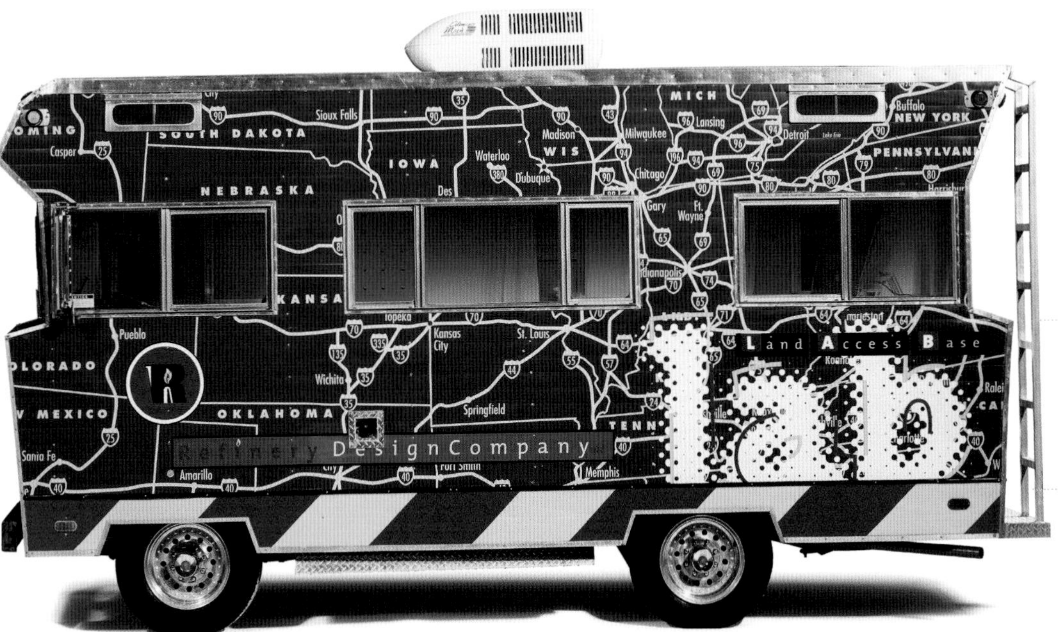

fig. 1.1

The vintage exterior is decorated with a huge map of the United States that was created in Adobe Freehand.

fig. 1.2

Custom graphics are applied to the Winnebago's metal skin using 100 yards (91.5 m) of 3M high-performance vinyl.

fig. 2.2

Inside the renovated 1967 Winnebago, an industrial rubber-tile floor and cabinetry reinforce the firm's red, yellow, and white corporate color scheme in a graphic and clean way.

fig. 3.1

The firm's portfolio case is as portable and unique as the studio. The trays that make up the top and bottom are vacuum-formed clear plastic in an industrial diamond plate pattern.

fig. 3.2

The sides of the case are made of marine-grade plywood that is painted in the firm's signature striped pattern. Aluminum inlaid corners add stability and enhance the overall industrial look and feel.

fig. 3.3

The case is expandable with various sides made in different widths to accommodate different sized portfolio boards.

fig. 3.4

A metal cover, silkscreen-printed with the Refinery Design Company logo, sets the tone of the presentation.

fig. 3.5

Inside the portfolio, black boards provide a standard format on which to showcase the firm's creative work.

fig. 3.6

The portfolio is held together by heavy-duty backpack straps.

fig. 4.1

The letterhead, business card, and side-loading envelope with a half-circle flap, each printed in black, PMS 032 red, and PMS 130 yellow-orange on 100 lb. Classic Crest super smooth solar white text, boasts high-impact, industrial graphics on both the front and back sides.

fig. 4.2

Throughout the stationery system, dull vanish is applied to areas of large coverage to seal the ink.

Be Inspired

No.
01

FINDING YOUR SOURCE

The constant pressure to meet higher expetations with increasingly tighter deadlines presents a tremendous amount of stress, a depleting of energy and resources. Continuously taking without replenishing can be very destructive and hard to repair as time goes on. Creatives need to find ways to refuel their source on a daily basis in order to move forward from a position of strength and vitality.

Creative firms as well as freelancers are beginning to realize that the success of their brand begins with self-awareness. Being honest about one's abilities and offerings, interests and aspirations, and core values and beliefs allows one to build a foundation from a place of authenticity. "Knowing where the passion reigns requires some conscious effort to recognize the feeling, the atmosphere that exists when doing the right work with the right clients," acknowledges Deb Koch of Red Canoe. "Staying true to the soul or center of our work, our mission, is an ongoing challenge." Being authentic means having the courage to venture out on your own creative path, attracting clients who share in your vision. When in tune with the spirit within, happiness and creative fulfillment are abundant. Work flows in a free and almost effortless way. Untouched by the distractions, demands, and complexities of the outside world, the creative spirit is the only true marker for navigation. Building an intimate relationship with one's inner voice generates a pathway for creative aspirations to come to fruition.

Knowing what motivates, feeds, and nurtures the creative spirit is essential for growth and stamina over the long term. It is most important to stimulate both the mind and the body, because they work in tandem. "I nourish my creativity by a continuum of learning experiences, including literary, poetic, and philosophical readings as well as listening to classical music," shares Nelida Nassar of Nassar Design. "I also go to spas and immerse my being in stillness and meditative silence." Health and wellness nourish and replenish from the inside out. This is important for team cultures as well as sole proprietors. "At Spiral Design Studio, staff members are encouraged to expand their professional education and personal wellness through company-financed seminars, workshops, and classes," notes agency principal Robert Clancy. "They are likewise encouraged to embrace their personal lives with equal vigor." The constant pressure to meet higher expectations with increasingly tighter deadlines presents a tremendous amount of stress, a depleting of energy and resources. Continuously taking without replenishing can be very destructive and hard to repair as time goes on. Creatives need to find ways to refuel their source on a daily basis in order to move forward from a position of strength and vitality.

No.
02

CHANGING YOUR ENVIRONMENT

One way to make an impact on creative energy is to restructure the environment in which one works. A studio that has an open, collaborative philosophy along with an ongoing means for stimulating thought is much more conducive for creativity. "Our open-communication office and team culture allow for new and innovative ideas to be heard and explored, flowing freely and efficiently to everyone," details Marcie Carson of IE Design. "Our team is encouraged to bring in and share what inspires them in their daily lives, producing creative momentum. We also have an inspiration board where we write quotes and sayings. It has become a common place to visit for a quick fix. These ideas promote team building as well as fill the cup of creativity." An environment that allows for the sharing of ideas, opinions, and resources will unleash a continuous flow of energy.

To evoke the senses, many creatives are surrounding their studios with sources of inspiration from music and scented candles to rare books and nostalgic objects that speak to them, regardless of any direct purpose. The stimulation sparks ideas and provokes thought. "Our entire team regularly brings in old and new items of design, ranging from an old chuck wagon metal lunch box to a gas station refrigerator magnet," says Robert Goldie of Rome & Gold Creative. "Also, our extensive library encourages everyone to check out books for as long as they like." By immersing oneself with elements that inspire and engage the senses, assimilation into the creative process becomes ongoing. "If you surround yourself with the things that interested you, those things will seep their way into your work somehow," adds Ucef Hanjani of ceft & company. The working environment needs to be an external expression of a firm or freelancer's personality, allowing the brand to live both inside and out.

No.
03

JOINING FORCES

To jump-start creativity, consider self-initiating a group-inspired project for the sheer purpose of aesthetic exploration. The Seattle-based design firm Belyea was up for the challenge when they started their own internal art club. For one year, the design team developed experimental artwork, exploring materials and techniques outside their creative repertoire. At the first meeting of every month, each staff member presented a finished piece of art to the group. Excited about what they had accomplished, Belyea held a gallery-like exhibition in their offices, inviting clients and colleagues to share in their vision. A series of notecards based on the experimental project was produced as a keepsake. By focusing on nurturing their source, the team at Belyea was able to reach new heights creatively. The fact that the initiative also sparked a successful promotional endeavor (see page 164) was just icing on the cake.

Building relationships with artists outside your discipline is another great way to infuse creativity. "Look at fashion, textiles, film, music, sculpture, painting, and architecture. It will feed and enhance your work," advises Hanjani. "If we look at our own industry for inspiration, the work becomes stale. Be open to new ideas and different ways of seeing." Collaborating with creatives in other arenas allows for a different perspective, deepening one's frame of reference and expanding what is possible. "We try to collaborate with people who challenge us to be better at what we do," explains Jason C. Otero of Art & Anthropology. "They help us look at the periphery of a solution to find new ways of visualizing." The dynamics of a multidisciplinary group endeavor create an environment that is conducive for the pursuit of ideas that are more innovative in approach. Creatives choosing to join forces are establishing alternative ways to reignite their creative process by continuing to learn and grow as artists.

Chapter Two

"Instead of spending your budget on a mass mailing, identify your best targets and surprise them in a real creative way. Use interesting textures and unexpected materials for them to touch and discover."

—Orlando Facioli, Orlando Facioli Design

INVITATIONS, ANNOUNCEMENTS, AND CARDS

ALMOST ANY NOTABLE OCCASION OR ENDEAVOR is worthy of a promotional message when it comes to maintaining that vital connection with clientele. The announcement of a new website, the celebration of an anniversary, the addition of new staff members, or the achievement of awards all open the opportunity to engage in communications.

To make a memorable impact, it is important to start with a strong overall concept. Allow the message to drive the design, not vice versa. Keep your audience small and personalize promotions as much as possible. "Instead of spending your budget on a mass mailing, identify your best targets and surprise them in a real creative way," suggests Orlando Facioli of Orlando Facioli Design. "Use interesting textures and unexpected materials for them to touch and discover." Tactile surfaces, three-dimensional formats, and tangible bindery encourage interaction, while scented add-ons, tasteful treats, and an element of sound enhance the overall sensual experience. Being a bit more innovative from either a presentation or production standpoint can pique interest.

Most important, make your promotion relevant and interesting for the audience. "We look at each promotion from the recipient's perspective by asking ourselves 'what do they normally see, in what environment, and how is it delivered?'" says Justin Ahrens of Rule29. "Then we try to be unique by taking a different approach, whether it is size, format, image, vocabulary, or materials." Pamela Zuccker of Principle agrees, "Always design with the end experience in mind. Consider where the promotion will be opened, in what state of mind the recipient will be, and what they will be pleasantly surprised to receive." Promotions that are purely self-serving will never make that ever-so-valuable connection with a target audience, ultimately leaving your efforts in the circular file, unopened and never read.

Each promotional initiative is also an opportunity to explore outside the limitations of client-driven work to showcase new skills. For Fusionary Media, this meant really pushing the envelope. The design team decided to invite clients and colleagues to a virtual New Year's Eve party held in cyberspace. By creating an animated adventure game, the firm was able to highlight recent offerings in a fun, imaginative, and engaging way. (See page 80.) "We always try to seek out new avenues in order to keep things interesting for ourselves and our audience," says creative director T.M. Camp. "We've found that clients hang onto the game and play it throughout the year, creating a far longer and more profound impact."

Whether you are hosting a real or virtual event, first plan everything out by crafting a detailed creative brief supported by a comprehensive timeline and budget. This will not only ensure that you consider the initiative as a whole before you begin designing but also that you stay on track and don't break the bank in the process. Every promotional endeavor is an investment. Each initiative strengthens client relations, building brand equity over the long term.

fig. 1.1

The mask, made of solid steel, mesh, and aluminum rivets, reinforces the overall message of protection. Each mask is treated with a clear coating to cover up any odor or residue from the welding process.

Your Game Face

Firm ceft & company
Creative Direction Ucef Hanjani
Design Ucef Hanjani and Christo Holloway
Printing The Ace Group
Special Techniques Precision Laser (laser-cutting)
Manufacturers Clockwork Apple, NYC and Shadi + Company
Client Nike

"Think about what makes you pick up something and open it. The draw is obscurity and mystery, where you become curious and want to discover what's inside."

—Ucef Hanjani, ceft & company

OBJECTIVE ceft & company was asked to develop an eye-catching press kit for a new line of apparel called Nike Pro Performance, gear that professional athletes wear under their suits to keep cool and dry. The kit had to work in tandem with the warrior theme developed for the campaign's broadcast communications.

AUDIENCE The press kit was hand-delivered to the general media to create awareness of the new line of apparel. A total of 100 kits were created, each individually numbered.

CONCEPT The design was based on the premise that athletes, like warriors, prepare for battle by putting on their game face and suiting up to win. Wanting to create something powerful and timeless, ceft & company looked toward historical references for inspiration. The mask, with its ability to protect and ward off enemies, became the primary element of communication in this promotional ensemble. With a slightly modern twist, the final look was based on warrior masks from Asia and Africa.

MESSAGE The fiercest competitors put their game face on and suit up with Nike Pro.

RESPONSE The press kit was quite successful, obtaining valuable air time from major broadcast stations such as ESPN, Fox News, and CNBC. The striking kit also captured the attention of prominent print media; the *New York Times* and the *Chicago Tribute* both ran pieces.

fig. 2.1

The press kit comes in an impressive, custom-designed, silkscreen-printed metal case that clamps shut, providing a very bold first impression.

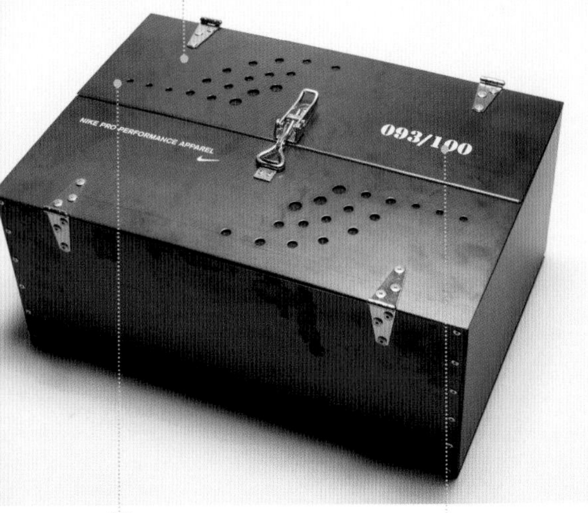

fig. 2.2

The laser-cut circular pattern on the top of the case not only provides an interesting overall design but also ignites the viewer's curiosity and anticipation about what is inside.

fig. 2.3

Each kit is individually numbered using the font Stencil, simulating the lettering printed on military trunks.

fig. 3.1

Once open, the heavy metal mask and a Nike Pro Performance shirt are revealed inside the velvet-inlaid box, furthering the warrior-like theme.

fig. 4.1

The attached hangtag reinforces the overall message and tagline. Its clean, simple design allows the other elements in the package to shine.

fig. 4.2

The mesh wrap that packages the shirt helps to convey the impression that this is no ordinary fashion apparel but the genuine armor that true athletes wear.

Experience the Sensation

Firm Hand Made Group
Creative Direction Alessandro Esteri
Design Alessandro Esteri and Davide Premuni
Client Aigner

"The entire project is based on sensations. We could never communicate the precise feeling of the project using just plans and renderings. We needed to give a piece of the whole experience."

—Alessandro Esteri, Hand Made Group

OBJECTIVE When invited to design a new interior for Aigner's shops worldwide, Hand Made Group wanted to present their proposal in a nontraditional, highly memorable fashion.

AUDIENCE The audience was specifically Aigner's international board of directors.

CONCEPT The design firm decided to create an environment surrounded and inspired by water—a pure and universal element. The interior design included water falling down the walls onto which images could be projected through slides or film. The concept also featured a water bar inside each shop. Because the overall design was based on water and fluidity, the proposal needed to convey a tangible and visible feeling of the idea.

MESSAGE Experience the fluid sensation.

RESPONSE The design as well as the proposal really pushed the boundaries for Aigner, who has been typically conservative in their approach.

The proposal is housed inside two clear 13" x 17 1/2" x 6 1/2" (33 x 45 x 16 cm) boxes made of 1/5" (4 mm) polycarbonate thermoplastic.

The Aigner logo, made of reprographic film, floats inside water, which is dyed with blue aniline.

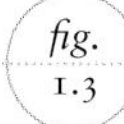

Inside the transparent boxes is a DVD containing a digital 3-D presentation, select material samples and renderings for the interior redesign, and a prototype of an Aigner water bottle for the proposed water bar.

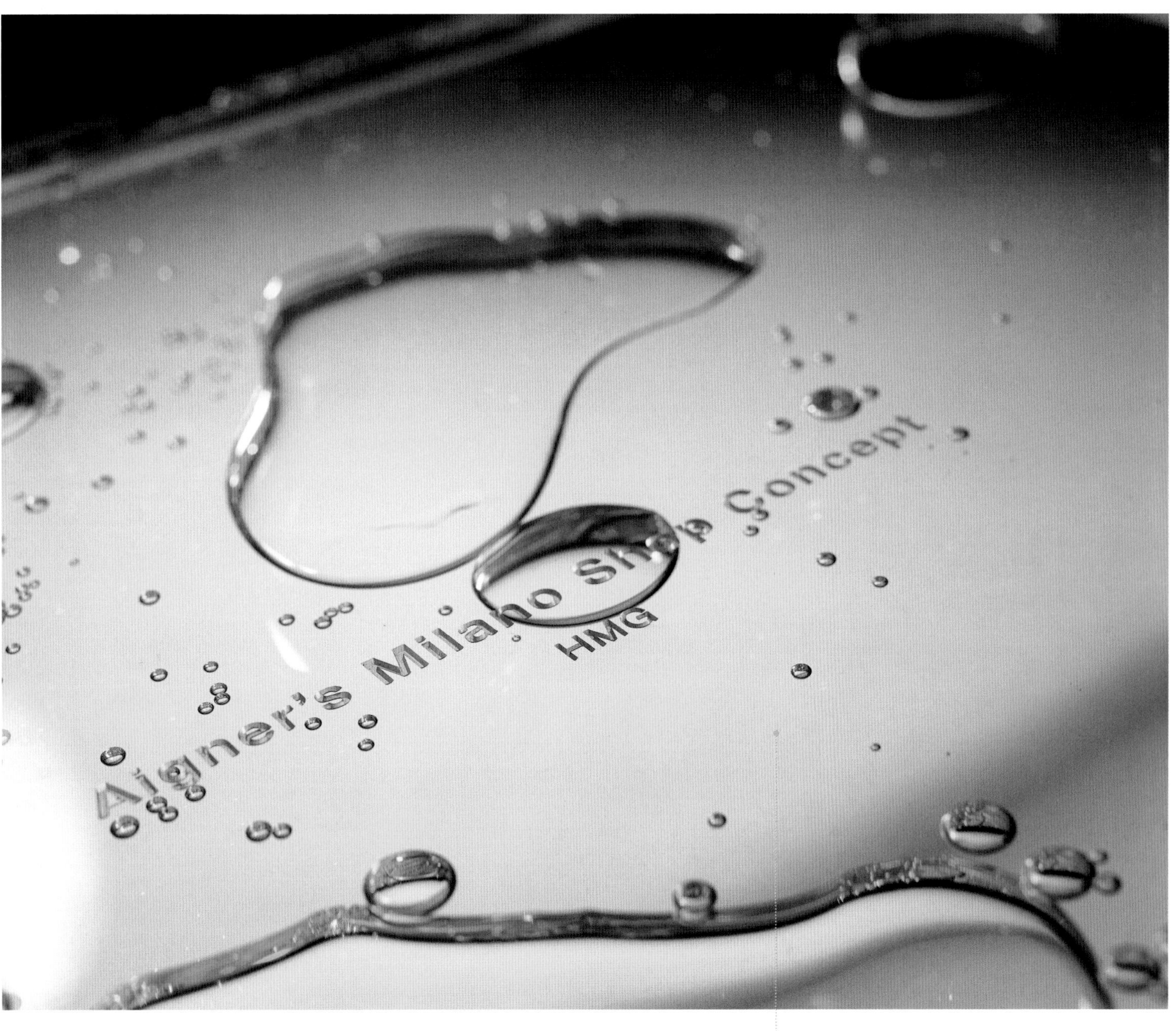

fig. 2.1

Each boxed is imprinted using an electronically controlled milling machine.

fig. 2.2

Inside the top cover of each box, liquid is inserted using a syringe. The box is then sealed shut with silicone.

Innovative Invites

OBJECTIVE To position his company as a major player in the minds of object design buyers and to attract attendees to a major biannual event, Orlando Facioli worked with the Marco 500 to design extraordinary invitations.

AUDIENCE The highly graphic invites are distributed to leading object design buyers and retailers who come to the Marco 500 to see what's new in object design. Three thousand are produced for each event.

CONCEPT The invitation for the Marco 500 cannot be conventional if it is to stand out and be memorable. For three years, the Brazilian design firm has chosen to use polypropylene as the substrate and serigraphy as the imprint of choice, playing with shape, graphics, and color each time.

MESSAGE Come see the best in Brazilian object design.

RESPONSE Over the three years that Orlando Facioli Design has designed the innovative invitations, the rate of response has been consistently high. More than 90 percent of the audience responds by attending the Marco 500, a design show that features the best work of Brazilian object designers. The event is held twice a year.

Firm ORLANDO FACIOLI DESIGN
Creative Direction ORLANDO FACIOLI
Design/Illustration ORLANDO FACIOLI
Printing CONFETTI (SERIGRAPHY)
Manufacturers CONFETTI (POLYPROPYLENE)

"For seduction, I focused on the illustrations and the use of different material effects. I kept the fonts simple and rational so that the information is very clear."

—Orlando Facioli, Orlando Facioli Design

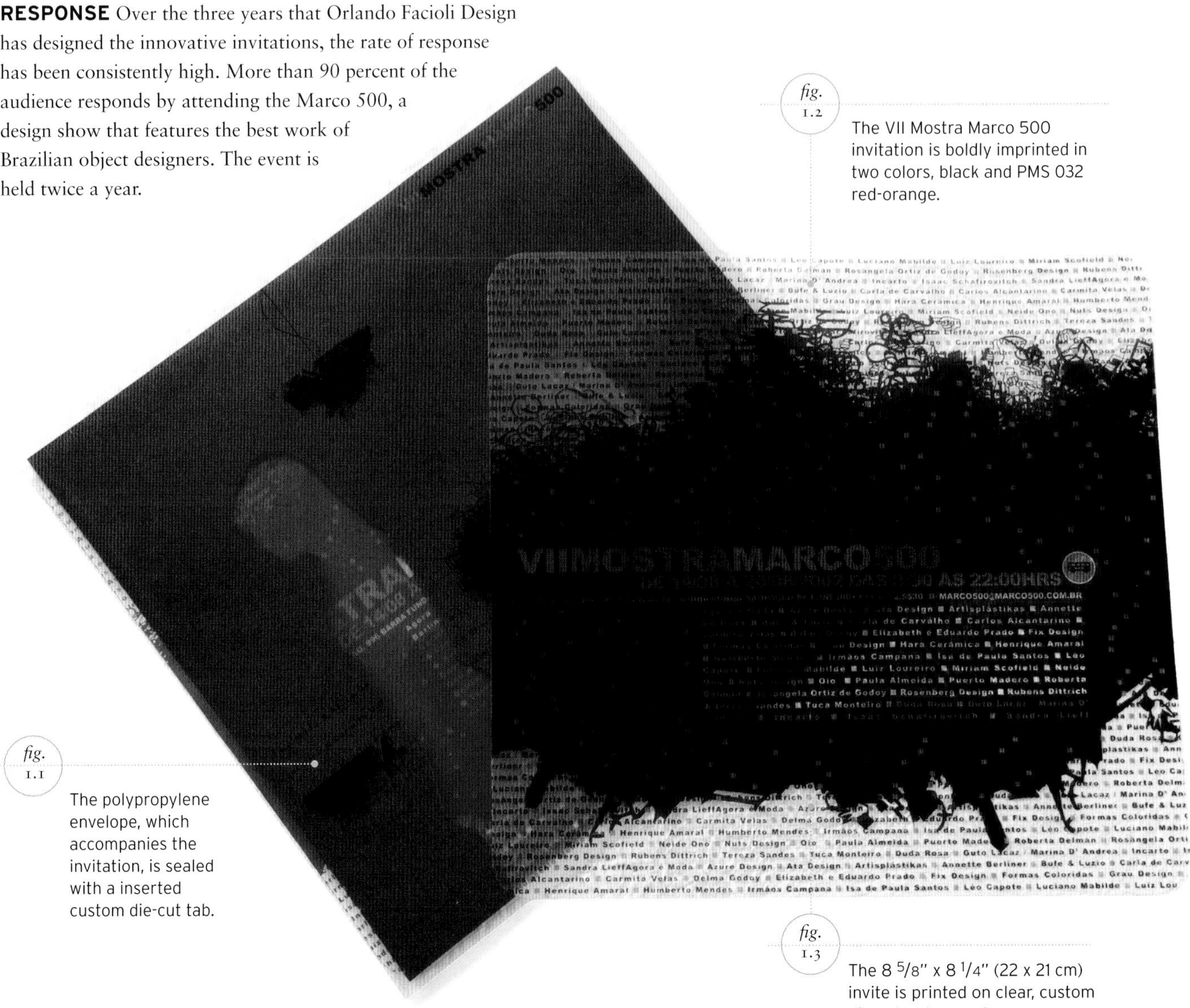

fig. 1.1 The polypropylene envelope, which accompanies the invitation, is sealed with a inserted custom die-cut tab.

fig. 1.2 The VII Mostra Marco 500 invitation is boldly imprinted in two colors, black and PMS 032 red-orange.

fig. 1.3 The 8 5/8" x 8 1/4" (22 x 21 cm) invite is printed on clear, custom die-cut polypropylene.

fig. 2.1

The VIII Mostra Marco 500 invitation is vividly detailed in a complementary color scheme of blue, orange, yellow, magenta, and black.

fig. 2.3

The matching polypropylene envelope continues the same color scheme as the invite but with the addition of green, all of which is reproduced in four-color process.

fig. 2.2

The invite is not only eye-catching and fun, it is also functional. The overall rounded shape is wide at the top and narrow at the bottom, doubling as a personal fan for attendees to use at the summertime event.

fig. 3.1

The 11" x 16" (28 x 40.5 cm) invite comes with a handle, encouraging attendees to bring the boldly colored object along to the event. The invitation is functional as well as informative.

fig. 3.2

The XI Mostra Marco 500 invitation also uses polypropylene as the substrate of choice.

fig. 3.3

Red, blue, white, and black are applied to the plastic surface using serigraphy.

fig. 1.1 The promotion is distributed in an orange translucent polyethylene envelope and sealed shut with a black elastic cord.

fig. 1.2 The enclosed CD-ROM is custom labeled using matte white label stock. It is placed in a plastic translucent clamshell-style CD holder, allowing the orange-printed label to show through.

fig. 1.3 The chosen typeface is Filosofia by Émigré, a nice accent to the illustrator's whimsical work.

Web Unfolding

OBJECTIVE Traditional illustrator Diana Marye Huff needed to have a presence on the World Wide Web. To create a distinctive mark in the digital arena, she contacted the design team at Red Canoe.

AUDIENCE The target audience was creative directors and art directors.

CONCEPT After developing a portfolio-based website for the illustrator, Red Canoe needed to create an announcement to draw clients and prospects to the site. Fashioned after a handmade artist book, the Web announcement uses a fabric-wrapped cover and an accordion-folded interior made of fine art drawing paper. To make a connection to the digital portfolio, the interior spreads mimic the simple navigation of the website design in both look and function. The book, much like the site, operates in two ways. If opened from one end, the illustrator's gestural work, eloquently titled *just fine line*, is featured. Once flipped around, the book highlights more realized work in both two and three dimensions, entitled *finesse and finishings*. To ensure recipients experienced the digital portfolio, an offline viewable CD-ROM was also included in the package.

MESSAGE Visit the new website of illustrator Diana Marye Huff.

RESPONSE The promotion was quite successful for the illustrator, attracting prospects to bookmark the site. Huff also acquired several new clients as a result of the initiative. In addition, the Web announcement has received several awards for excellence in design.

Firm Red Canoe
Creative Direction Deb Koch
Design Caroline Kavanagh
Illustration Diana Marye Huff
Printing Epson 2200 inkjet
Manufacturers Dick Blick Art Materials (accordion-fold book), Associated Bag (polyethylene routing envelope), Uline (CD clamshell), Staples (epson paper and elastic cord)
Client Diana Marye Huff

"In illustrator Diana Marye Huff's perfect world, there would be no Internet or email. Positioning her within the World Wide Web was Red Canoe's focus for her website and promotional announcement, bridging the two-world gap."

—Deb Koch, Red Canoe

fig. 2.1

A muted orange wrap, printed on Epson heavyweight matte text stock, encompasses the entire 6 1/2" x 4 1/2" (16.5 x 10 x 0.5 cm) book.

fig. 2.2

The handcrafted book is illustrated with tipped-on images, each printed on Epson heavyweight matte paper, on both the back and front.

fig. 2.3

The accordion-folded book is made of a Khaki linen cover with fine art drawing paper used for the interior, maintaining the illustrator's signature fine art appeal.

fig. 3.1

Much like the print announcement, the easy-to-navigate website design has only two main areas of navigation, titled *just fine line* and *finesse and finishing.*

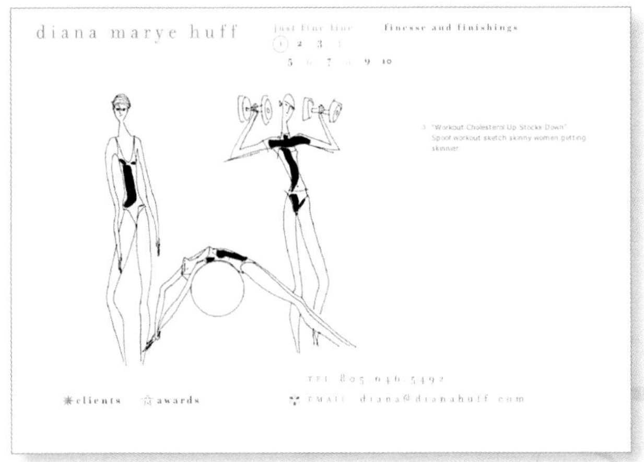

Active Participation

Firm Hand Made Group
Creative Direction Alessandro Esteri
Design Alessandro Esteri and Dave Premuni
Illustration Ria Dunn
Printing Xerox DocuColor (insert sheet)
Special Techniques Craftsmen from Turcany (wooden stamp, steel ink holder, and box)
Client Zenobia

"I want people to work hard to be able to read the invitation. In this way, I can stimulate their curiosity."

—Alessandro Esteri, Hand Made Group

OBJECTIVE Zenobia, a haut couture firm in Canada, approached Hand Made Group to create a fashion show invitation that would create curiosity, attracting buyers to the event.

AUDIENCE The target audience was primarily North American buyers. Two hundred invitations were produced.

CONCEPT Because buyers receive thousands of invitations every season, Hand Made Group needed to make this one stand out from the rest to generate interest. The design team decided to create an invitation that would bring the recipient into the creative process. A personalized wooden stamp encouraged buyers to print their own invitation. Black, the corporate color of Zenobia, was used throughout.

MESSAGE Be curious, open the package, and print your own invitation.

RESPONSE Everyone was enamored by the signature piece. It drew an amazing 80 percent response from invitees eager to attend the fashion event.

fig. 1.1

The unconventional invitation comes in a handmade box, made out of Gruppo Cordenons 300 gsm, and is held together by iron rivets.

fig. 1.2

Inside the custom box, Fedrigoni GSK gold paper is used as a wrap.

fig. 2.1

The intriguing package is tied shut with black hemp yarn.

fig. 3.1

A steel ink holder and wooden stamp, painted black and silkscreen-printed with transparent ink, can be used to print a personalized, one-of-a-kind invitation.

fig. 3.2

The ink contained in the custom holder is a special-mix black and is employed when the recipient prints his or her own invitation.

fig. 3.3

An insert sheet, printed in black on Saville 200 gsm raw white paper, contains instructions on how to operate the custom stamp.

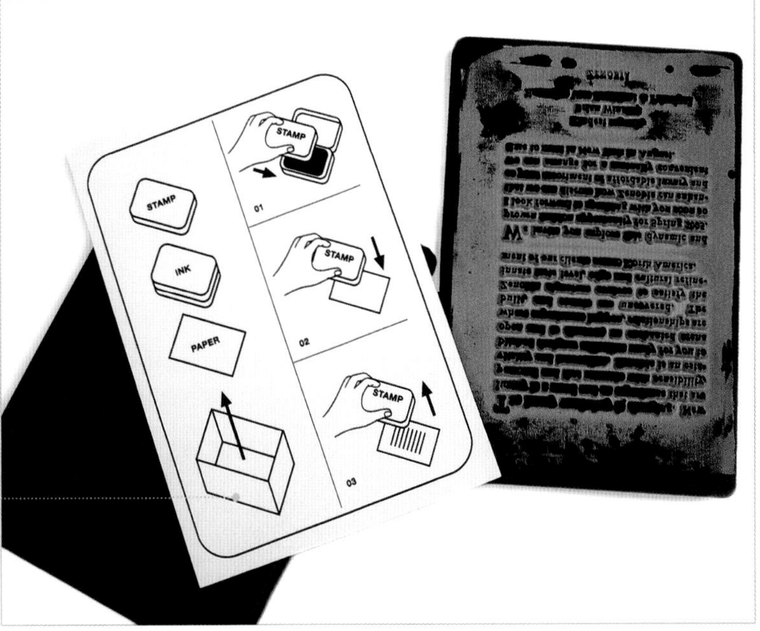

Sampling Our Work

Firm Spiral Design Studio, LLC

Creative Direction/Design Maureen Mooney and Anne Hobday

Illustration Robert Clancy, Neil Wright, Anne Hobday, Maureen Mooney, Jeanie Guity, and Lynne Allard

Printing Digital Imaging Technologies (flipbook) and Xerox Phaser 7700 (bellyband, box insert, and vellum sheet)

Manufacturers Ball Chain Manufacturing Co., Inc. (chain), Siska Inc. (grommets), Specialty Box & Packaging Co., Inc. (boxes), and Cambridge Silversmiths, Ltd. (forks)

"People respond to humor, fun, and originality. Food, a unifying force, can be a very effective incentive."

—Robert Clancy, Spiral Design Studio

OBJECTIVE Spiral Design Studio sought to create a promotion that would entice prospective clientele to take time out of their busy schedules for an introductory meeting and portfolio presentation.

AUDIENCE The delectable promotion was sent to prospective clientele in various industries. About seventy-five promotions were distributed.

CONCEPT The design team knew that to capture the audience's attention, the promotion needed to be packaged in an eye-catching fashion and the hook had to be strong enough to motivate. An elegant spiral-accented fork, interactive flip cards, and entertaining copy all packaged in a jewelry-style box made the promotion stand out. An offer for a free lunch at a restaurant of the recipient's choosing made the offer hard to refuse. "You are what you eat. With an appetite for creativity, we have what you hunger for" was the tagline used throughout. Each promotion was followed up with a phone call one week after the initial mailing.

MESSAGE Get a taste of Spiral Design Studio's delectable marketing expertise and receive a gift certificate to one of the area's top eateries.

RESPONSE The promotion opened doors to opportunities previously unavailable to the firm. While the team was following up with a phone call to each recipient, many prospective clients beat them to the punch and called first.

fig. 1.1

The promotion comes in an 8 1/2" x 2 1/4" x 1" (21 x 5.5 x 2.5 cm) burgundy box that is closed shut with a custom-designed bellyband printed on Fraser 80 lb. Synergy refined orange cover with a smooth finish. The overall palette is reflective of the Spiral Design Studio corporate color scheme.

fig. 1.2

Inside the box, two inserts are fitted into both the cover and base, allowing a place for the fork to be inserted and contact information to be applied. The inserts utilize the same coverstock as the bellyband to tie the inside to the outside.

fig. 1.4

A personalized invitation to sample the firm's portfolio is printed in black on vellum (Chartham translucent 30 lb. in leaf green) and accented with a grommet.

fig. 1.5

The flip cards, printed on Mohawk Superfine 80 lb. Ultrawhite smooth uncoated cover and held together by a silver chain, demonstrate a variety of styles—"simple, classic, organic, contempo-rary, refreshing, eclectic, avant-garde, and raw"—and are uniquely illustrated under one unified design.

fig. 1.3

The spiral-accented fork add-on is held in place by two white bands that wrap around the handle through grommets.

fig. 1.1 The seedling and invite are wrapped with silver tissue paper that has been crinkled for a highly reflective effect.

fig. 1.2 To accent the invitation, a Christmas tree seedling is used as an add-on. It is placed inside of a glass tube with water to keep it hydrated. To further the Christmas theme, the seedling is adorned with a small bell.

fig. 1.3 The package is sent in a white corrugated cardboard box with a custom die-cut label that is printed in-house on Avery label stock.

Celebrate Growth

OBJECTIVE Curb-Crowser wanted to have a holiday open house to celebrate their expanded studio space. They needed an invitation that would not only stand out in a sea of holiday mailers but also speak to the firm's recent growth.

AUDIENCE The invitation was sent to existing clients, friends, and family. One hundred invitations were distributed.

CONCEPT The promotion was built around the concept of celebrating growth. The firm used a Christmas tree seedling as the perfect add-on to accent their open house invitation. For all attendees, a holiday music CD was handed out as a thank-you gift.

MESSAGE Celebrate the recent growth of Curb-Croswer.

RESPONSE The firm received phone calls from more than half of the invite list, many commenting on how well their seedling was growing. Roughly eighty people attended, and several projects were cultivated from the endeavor.

Firm Curb-Crowser
Creative Direction Tracie Curb-Crowser
Design Caitlin Nugent and Chris Van Ert
Photography Joe St. Onge
Printing Xerox Phaser 7750
Manufacturers Rimage Corporation (CD)

fig. 1.4

The type, Rotis Semi Serif and Trade Gothic Condensed, is knocked out of the full-bleed image to show the white of the paper.

fig. 1.5

The 3 1/2" x 13 1/2" (9 x 34.5 cm) invitation, digitally printed in-house on a Xerox Phaser 7750 using Epson premium bright white 24 lb. paper, features a soft-focus image of a pinecone.

A music CD, given out to attendees as a gift, is labeled with a digitally printed insert and comes in a standard jewel case. The graphics and color scheme are reminiscent of the invitation.

fig. 2.1

fig. 2.2

Inside the jewel case, a music sampler CD is presented with a custom label printed in-house on a Xerox Phaser 7750. Sixteen favorite holiday tunes are featured.

"Our biggest challenge was planning the kitting in-house as soon as the seedlings arrived. We did not want the small trees to be overhandled or dried out."

—Tracie Curb-Crowser, Curb-Crowser

A Grand Slam

Firm Rome & Gold Creative
Creative Direction Robert Goldie
Design Lorenzo Romero, Donna Romero, and Zeke Sikelianos
Photography Robert Goldie
Illustration Lorenzo Romero
Printing JB Graphics (screen printing)
Manufacturers Paper Mart (brown window bag and canvas bag), Staton Wholesale (shirt), Hobby Lobby (pennant), and Sam's Club (peanuts)

"You need to make it a goal to have fun and make sure that your promotion is going to be unique enough to warrant a response. You can't send out a mediocre promotion and expect a positive result. These types of projects also give our staff an opportunity to create without any barriers."

—Robert Goldie, Rome & Gold Creative

OBJECTIVE Rome & Gold Creative was eager to produce a fun and memorable promotional initiative to announce their new studio location and website.

AUDIENCE The target audience consisted of the firm's core clientele as well as potential prospects. Approximately forty invitational packages were produced and hand-delivered.

CONCEPT The creative firm decided to use baseball as a way to captivate their audience. An invitation to see the Albuquerque Isotopes—a local, semipro team—came packaged in a canvas bag along with a custom T-shirt and pennant, peanuts, and a scorecard.

MESSAGE Spend some time with Rome & Gold Creative, an all-star creative team, and come visit their new "clubhouse."

RESPONSE The promotional endeavor helped to solidify relationships with Rome & Gold Creative's existing client base, resulting in more ongoing work. In terms of winning over prospects, the firm was able to expand into new industries, broadening their reach.

A three-panel, letter-fold invitation, which also functions as a scorecard and ticket holder, is printed in PMS 2757 navy blue, PMS 138 burnt orange, and PMS 614 cream on French Paper 100 lb. whitewash cover.

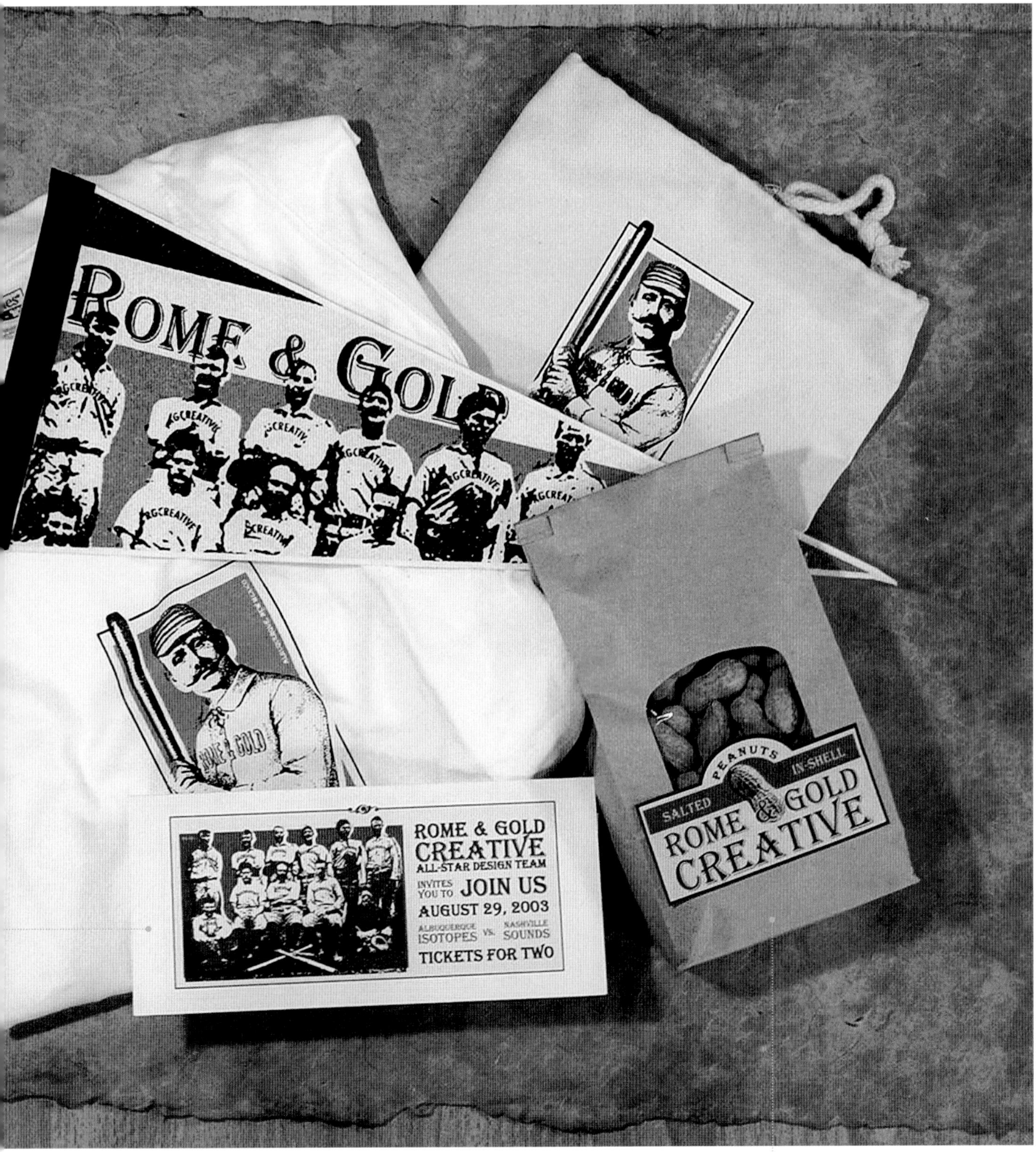

fig. 1.2

The invitational package includes a short sleeve, 100 percent cotton T-shirt and a custom-stitched felt pennant, each silkscreen-printed in three custom-mixed colors.

fig. 1.3

The vintage, baseball-inspired promotional ensemble comes in a silkscreen-printed canvas bag that employs the same custom color scheme as the shirt and pennant.

fig. 1.4

Brown window bags, custom labeled and filled with peanuts, complete the ballpark experience.

Client Appreciation

Firm Motive Design Research
Creative Direction Michael Connors and Kari Strand
Design/Illustration Peter Anderson and Michael Connors
Printing Cenveo Seattle (posters) and Epson Stylus Photo 2200 (beer labels and name tags)

"Many clients are familiar only with the work we have produced specifically for them. It helps tremendously for clients to see what we have done in other media and markets."

—Michael Connors, Motive Design Research

OBJECTIVE Motive Design Research wanted to thank long-term clients and vendors for their support in making their design firm a success. They decided to host an annual client appreciation party on St. Patrick's Day, a time of year that is not overly celebrated by the industry with promotional endeavors.

AUDIENCE Every year a poster invitation is sent to past, current, and prospective clients as well as suppliers. More than 750 invitations are produced each year. About seventy five to one hundred people attended the annual event.

CONCEPT The design team creates various promotional materials for the annual St. Patrick's Day event, showcasing the firm's expertise in both print and interactive media. Name tags, invitational posters, animated save-the-date emails, and homemade beer with custom labels are all created. A signature icon, a shamrock made of hearts, is used throughout. It symbolizes the affection that the firm has for the people who have supported the business through the years. At the party, the firm runs a continuous, on-screen show of their work. As a follow-up, they send out an April Fool's Day email, including links to their website to see an illustrated party recap.

MESSAGE Motive Design Research values and appreciates their clients and vendors.

RESPONSE The annual party generates a great deal of attention. Many clients and vendors are now making plans to attend the firm's next St. Patrick's Day event. In addition, several new and exciting projects are commissioned each year.

The annual invitational poster is mailed in a tube with a custom label. A rubber stamp of a red-orange flame, the Motive Design Research logo, serves as a dynamic accent.

fig. 1.1

fig. 1.2

The 2005 poster invitation, printed in PMS 179 red, PMS 383 green, and a special-mix blue on Cougar Natural Opaque 80 lb. cover, features the names of clients being poured into the heart of the signature shamrock. It is symbolic of how much the firm has grown through the support and trust of clients.

fig. 1.3

The 2004 poster, featuring the signature icon floating above grass in the form of a client list, is printed in PMS 179 red, PMS 383 green, and PMS 604 yellow on Cougar Natural Opaque 80 lb. cover. The overall graphics are symbolic of how much the support of clients elevates the firm's work to new heights.

fig. 2.1

Home brew—Clover Honey Wheat Ale and Good Dog Irish Stout for 2004, and Jake's Awesome Aussie Honey Wheat Ale and Ellie's Luscious Labrador Porter for 2005—is given out at the St. Patrick's Day bash each year. The custom beer always boasts signature labels, created and printed in-house on Epson label stock.

fig. 2.2

Name tags, printed in-house on Epson label stock, continue the heart-filled clover theme.

fig. 3.1

An animated email, sent out on Valentine's Day, serves as a reminder to save the date. The signature icon is animated in HTML using Adobe Photoshop GIF files.

Reaching New Heights

Firm Rome & Gold Creative

Creative Direction Robert Goldie

Design Lorenzo Romero, Donna Romero, Zeke Sikelianos, and Merilly Duncan

Photography Robert Goldie

Illustration Lorenzo Romero

Printing Covenant Printing (offset), JB Graphics (screen printing), and Branders (pad printing)

Manufacturers Uline (boxes and corrugated wrap), Al-style Apparel (T-shirts), Branders (thermos), and Staton Wholesale (fleece blanket)

"It is great to have a mix of both core and potential clients at events because it allows core clients an opportunity to rave about the work you do. It's always better to have someone else say something great about you than to say it yourself."

—Robert Goldie, Rome & Gold Creative

fig. 1.1 The promotional package comes in a rectangular cargo-inspired cardboard box. A central label, printed on Fasson Crack-N-Peel 60 lb. uncoated stock in three colors—PMS 614 cream, PMS 2985 blue, and black—is accent by two square labels that are printed in black ink only.

OBJECTIVE Rome & Gold Creative was looking for a unique way to thank clients for giving them the opportunity to reach for new heights.

AUDIENCE The package was distributed to core clients and prospects. Approximately sixty were each hand delivered.

CONCEPT In New Mexico, the International Balloon Fiesta is an exciting annual event. To share in the uplifting experience, Rome & Gold Creative invited clients to mingle and socialize over dinner and drinks under their corporate tent. An eye-catching, post World War II–inspired promotion was sent to entice clients to the upcoming event. The invitational package included tickets, a fleece blanket, a custom T-shirt, an imprinted thermos—everything one would need for a night at the balloon fiesta. The overall theme positioned the firm as design aces.

MESSAGE For the firm's existing client base, the primary message was one of thanks. For prospects, it was certainly a first-class introduction.

RESPONSE The promotional endeavor was successful at continuing to grow existing client relationships. The firm also developed three new clients in areas in which they wanted to grow. Both the invitational package and festive event were a complete success.

fig. 1.6

Marcel and Futura are the fonts used throughout.

fig. 1.5

The stainless-steel thermos is imprinted with black ink using pad printing, a transfer process that allows printing onto unusual shapes or materials.

fig. 1.4

A long-sleeve, chocolate brown T-shirt is silkscreen-printed with a special-mix cream ink made to match the Classic Crest paper stock.

fig. 1.2

The balloon event invitations are printed on Classic Crest 100 lb. uncoated cover in natural white. It comes in a black envelope topped with a custom label.

fig. 1.3

The embroidered fleece blanket is wrapped with a corrugated cardboard bellyband that is custom labeled.

Artistic Endeavor

OBJECTIVE In an ongoing effort to create promotions that involve the artistic community, Blue River and its team developed *Nimbus Concertina*, a temporary site-specific public art installation in an underdeveloped inner city area of Newcastle upon Tyne, United Kingdom.

AUDIENCE The site of the installation was highly visible, encompassing a wide-range demographic. Invitations to the unveiling were sent to arts organizations, artists, public sector arts supporters, and public art aficionados. The posters were distributed around the center of the city in all the cafes, bars, restaurants, clothing shops, and university campuses. Four hundred invitations and 2,000 posters, in two variations, were produced.

CONCEPT The contemporary art installation was made from more than 1,000 plumbing pieces twisted and intertwined with an old concertina-style gate to form an unexpected cloudlike structure. To create interest in visiting the work, the design team developed promotional invitations and posters. To play up the unique shape of the structure, the posters' were die-cut into two distinct, pipelike shapes with the type repeating itself in various directions. They were placed on walls in an interlocking, puzzlelike manner. The posters' various folds allowed the work to go around corners when necessary, adapting to any environment. The invitations also adopted the pipelike structure, folding down to an interesting package. Both the posters and invitations helped to create interest in the contemporary art installation. *Nimbus Concertina* is the third in a series of on-site commissions by Blue River.

MESSAGE Come visit this extraordinary artistic endeavor.

RESPONSE The invitations and posters were very effective, attracting many visitors to see the intriguing site-specific sculpture. About 350 people attended the inaugural launch.

Firm Blue River
Creative Direction/Design James Askham and Lisa Thundercliffe
Installation Art Jennifer Douglas
Printing Field Print

"We always try to promote ourselves by supporting the arts rather than just doing a straightforward promotional brochure that talks just about Blue River and its team. This approach is a bit unconventional, but it works for us."

—Jane Longrigg, Blue River

fig. 1.1 The custom die-cut invitations are printed using two colors, black and PMS 361 green, on Edixion 140 gsm white stock and folded shut in an engaging way.

fig. 1.2 The fonts Bookman bold and Avenir (light/roman/black) are used throughout.

fig. 1.3 The invitations are sent in crisp white envelopes with a standard label.

fig. 1.4 Matching flyers are used as drop-offs at all the local hot spots to attract people to the installation.

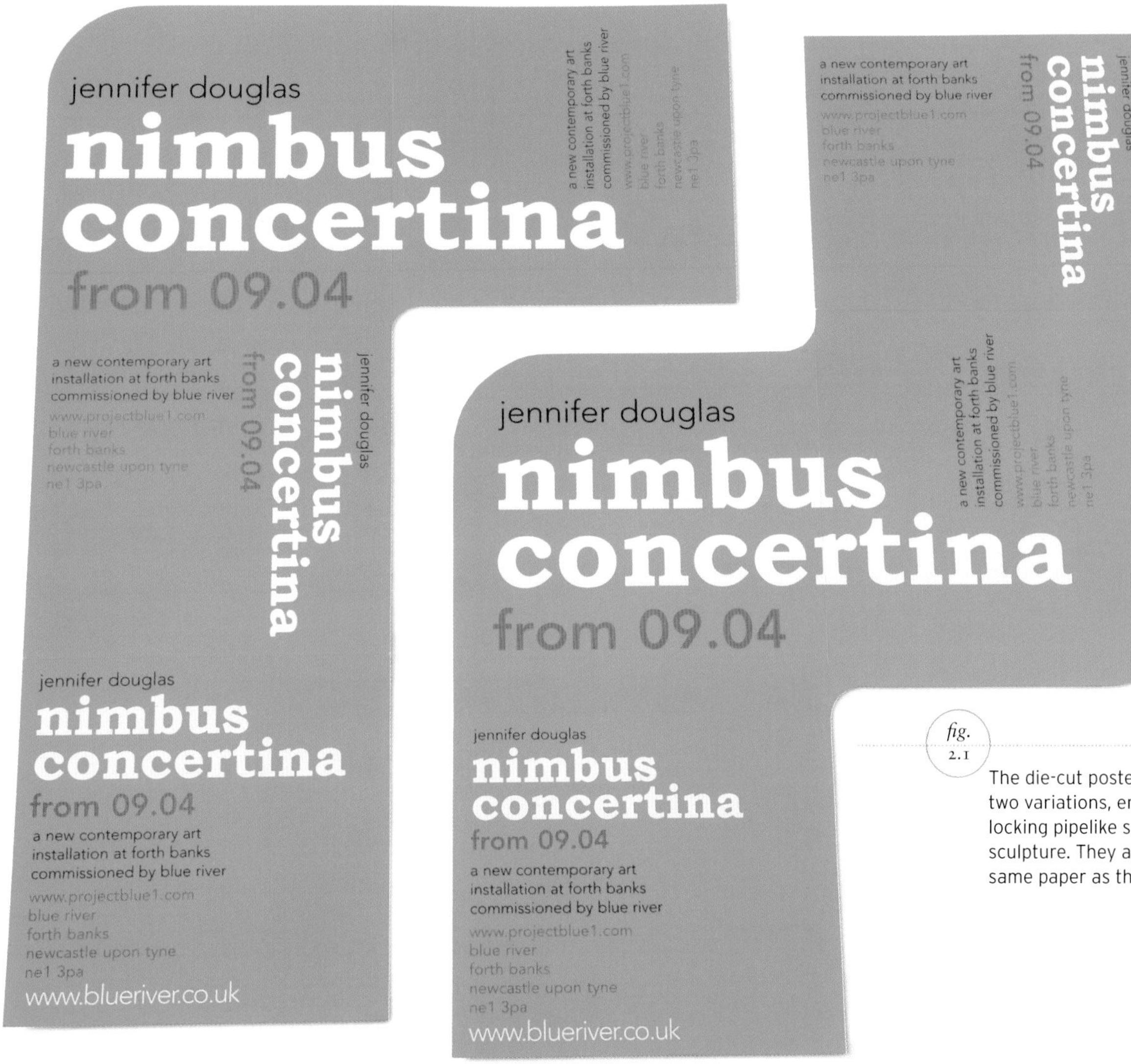

jennifer douglas
nimbus
concertina
from 09.04

a new contemporary art
installation at forth banks
commissioned by blue river
www.projectblue1.com
blue river
forth banks
newcastle upon tyne
ne1 3pa

jennifer douglas
nimbus
concertina
from 09.04
a new contemporary art
installation at forth banks
commissioned by blue river
www.projectblue1.com
blue river
forth banks
newcastle upon tyne
ne1 3pa
www.blueriver.co.uk

a new contemporary art
installation at forth banks
commissioned by blue river
www.projectblue1.com
blue river
forth banks
newcastle upon tyne
ne1 3pa

jennifer douglas
nimbus
concertina
from 09.04

jennifer douglas
nimbus
concertina
from 09.04
a new contemporary art
installation at forth banks
commissioned by blue river
www.projectblue1.com
blue river
forth banks
newcastle upon tyne
ne1 3pa
www.blueriver.co.uk

fig. 2.1

The die-cut posters are created in two variations, emulating the interlocking pipelike shapes used in the sculpture. They are printed on the same paper as the invitations.

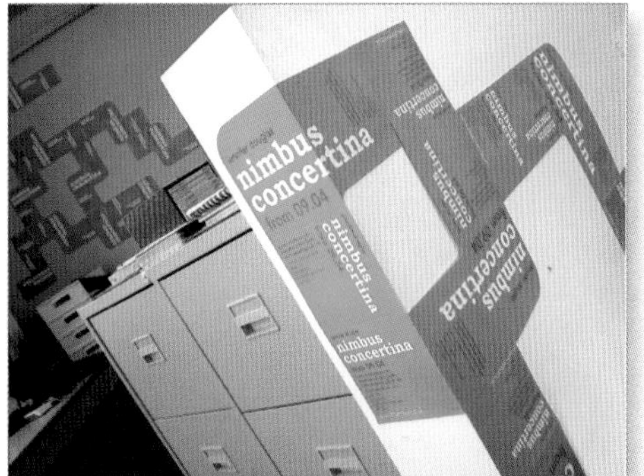

fig. 3.1

The almost organic-looking structure is made from plumbing pipes twisted and intertwined with an old concertina-style gate.

Photo Credit: Critical Tortoise

It's a Wrap!

Firm Blu Concept

Creative Direction Richard Klingle-Watt

Design Richard Klingle-Watt and Lindsay Rankin

Photography John Sinal

Printing Glenmore Printing (mailer) and Everett Graphics (poster)

Client John Sinal Photography

"Never propose an idea that you aren't prepared to go all the way with. As creatives, we have to consider that a client trusts in our counsel and advice. So, we must be willing to walk a mile in their shoes, or in this case, about 45 feet of bubble wrap!"

—Richard Klingle-Watt, Blu Concept

OBJECTIVE John Sinal, a commercial photographer, was moving his studio and needed a creative way to inform clients of the new locale. Blu Concept was chosen to develop an interesting mailer that would portray Sinal's quirky sense of humor and unique approach to storytelling.

AUDIENCE The announcement was sent to existing clientele, primarily art directors, designers, and magazine editors. A total of 500 were sent; roughly fifty were produced as posters.

CONCEPT The main concept was to visually tell the story that John Sinal is moving, in an entertaining and captivating way. The design firm chose to focus on a single image delivered in two formats. Because most art directors don't have a lot of space, the design team created a small mailer, conveniently sized to fit on a desk or corkboard, in addition to a larger-format poster. The lead image portrays the photographer packaged up and ready to be hauled off to his new location.

MESSAGE Photographer John Sinal is moving.

RESPONSE The overall reaction to the highly imaginative announcement has been very positive. Although most were entertained by what they saw, there were a few good-natured clients who just didn't get Sinal's sense of humor. Many inquiries came in wanting to know if it was really Sinal under all that tape and bubble wrap. No go—Sinal was smart and took the picture instead of modeling for it. Blu Concept art director Richard Klingle-Watt, who is the same weight and height as Sinal, filled in for the "highly coveted" role.

fig. 1.1

The digitally printed 16" x 21 1/2" (40.5 x 54.5 cm) poster announcement boasts an almost theatrical mood with its overall cool setting. Red-orange accents were subtly worked in to contrast with the overall blue tone, drawing attention to key points.

The mailer was sent in a translucent envelope, creating curiosity as to what was inside.

fig. 2.1

fig. 2.2

The 6 1/4" x 6 1/4" (16 x 16 cm) small-format moving announcement is offset-printed in four-color process on Domtar Luna Silk white 100 lb. cover.

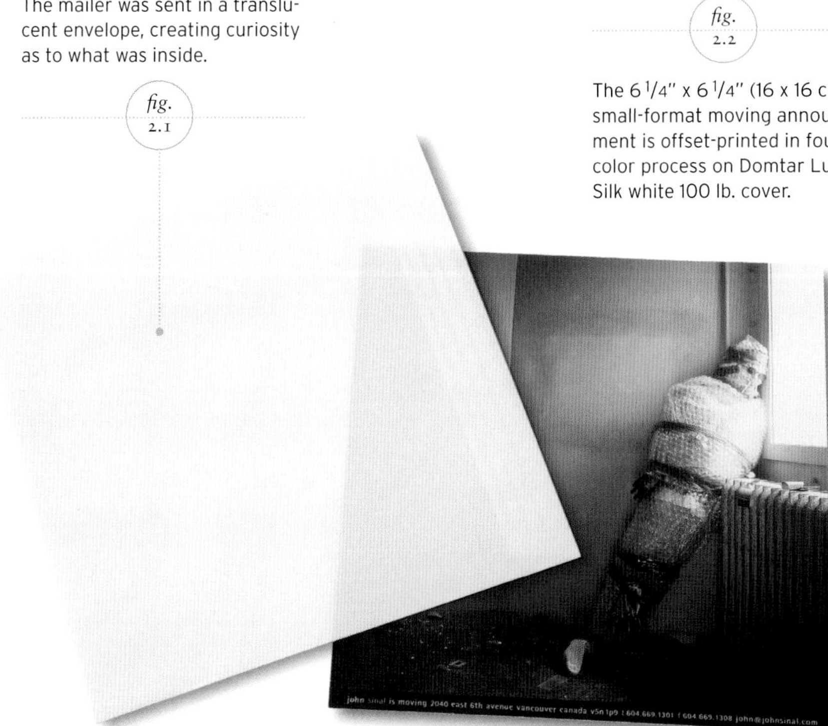

With a Bang

Firm GJP Advertising + Design
Creative Direction Lisa Greenberg
Design Lisa Greenberg and Sharon Gittens
Printing Rush Simpson
Manufacturers Rush Simpson (bubble wrap, cardboard, and green staples)

"I love bubble wrap and always knew that I would find a way to use it. This was a perfect opportunity. Each day is punctuated with a little pop, making the card fun for more than just a day."

—Lisa Greenberg, GJP Advertising + Design

OBJECTIVE Gee Jeffery & Partners was interested in creating an unexpected yet playful holiday card that would be truly unique among the plethora of holiday greetings sent at the end of the year.

AUDIENCE The target audience included existing clients, suppliers, and friends. Eight hundred cards were produced.

CONCEPT The design team chose to produce a card that recipients could enjoy and interact with as they count down the days until the end of the year. Each day offers fun and witty suggestions of things to do to prepare for the upcoming New Year.

MESSAGE Have fun, enjoy the holidays, and go out with a bang.

RESPONSE Everyone enjoyed the clever wit and innovation. Many called in for extras, wanting to share the feeling of popping a new bubble each day. The eccentric card has also won several accolades, including *HOW* magazine's International Design Awards and best in show in *Coupe* magazine.

fig. 1.1 The small numbers that appear on the corrugated cardboard packaging are a knock-out to the natural kraft color.

fig. 1.2 The unusual card utilizes bubble wrap stapled with green staples to kraft packaging board, imprinted with a hit of opaque white and then fluorescent PMS 802 green, that wraps over the top.

fig. 1.3 Helvetica Neue, the firm's corporate font, is used throughout.

fig. 1.4 The countdown numbers are silkscreen-printed on a clear sticker and adhered to the back of the bubble wrap.

Come View

OBJECTIVE Claudia Goetzelmann, a San Francisco–based photographer, wanted to create an attention-getting invitation to draw clients, collaborators, and friends together for a celebration to thank them for their support.

AUDIENCE The invitation was distributed to advertising agencies, design firms, editorial contacts, suppliers, and production crew. Five hundred were produced.

CONCEPT To make the invitation stand out, a bright orange viewfinder with one of the photographer's signature images inside was employed as an add-on. For more details about where and when the celebration would be held, a matching card was attached using a gold ball and chain. Vibrant orange crinkle-cut paper helped add a dynamic and festive component to the overall package. As a follow-up, an email invitation was sent, announcing the launch of the photographer's new website. The event was designed to thank existing clients, reconnect with former ones, and ultimately to make new contacts.

MESSAGE Attend the upcoming celebration.

RESPONSE The invitation worked quite well, drawing about 220 people to the fun-filled event.

Firm CLAUDIA GOETZELMANN, PHOTOGRAPHER
Creative Direction CLAUDIA GOETZELMANN
Design/Photography CLAUDIA GOETZELMANN
Printing LEEWOOD PRESS
Manufacturers RADEX INC. (VIEW FINDER) AND LOCAL PACKAGING SUPPLIER (BOX AND CRINKLE-CUT PAPER)

"I wanted to create an invitation that would be unique, fun, and memorable. The combination of the viewfinder, card, and packaging makes an attention-getting piece, carrying both my style and wit."

—Claudia Goetzelmann, photographer

fig. 1.1 The invitational card is printed in orange, red, and black, the signature colors of the Claudia Goetzelmann brand. White is incorporated in the color scheme as a knock-out color.

fig. 1.2 The orange plastic viewfinder is an intriguing add-on, because it creates curiosity and encourages interaction.

fig. 1.3 A matching invitational card is connected to the viewfinder using a gold ball and chain.

fig. 1.4 Inside the mini viewfinder is one of the photographer's signature images, reinforcing the connection between the photographer's name and her work.

fig. 1.5 The festive ensemble is sent in a brown cardboard box filled with bright orange crinkle-cut paper and sealed with orange packing tape.

fig. 1.6 A return address is applied on the top of the kraft box using a custom rubber stamp and black ink.

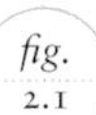

At the event, Goetzelmann's work played in the background on two large screens.

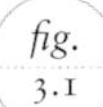

Excitement was in the air with live music, hoop artists swinging from the ceiling, and wax lips being served on trays.

Sweet Tidings

OBJECTIVE Designer Lynn Cyr wanted to create a unique, handmade holiday greeting that would really stand out from the sea of seasonal cards.

AUDIENCE The target audience was both current and prospective clients, mostly midsize to large businesses and design firms. One hundred holiday cards were produced.

CONCEPT Every holiday season, the design firm creates a new and unique card concept, and this year was no different. After a recent interest in bookmaking, the designer decided to incorporate a scroll format, using a candy cane as support. The rest of the concept, from the duplex red-and-white paper to the wishing of sweet tidings, just fell into place.

MESSAGE Wishing you a sweet holiday season.

RESPONSE The designer has received many flattering comments on the creativity of the dimensional card. The project was also recognized in the *Graphic Design: USA In-house Design Annual.*

Firm LYNN CYR DESIGN

Creative Direction/Design LYNN CYR

Printing EPSON C82 INKJET

Bindery HAND-ASSEMBLED

Manufacturers PENNSYLVANIA DUTCH CANDIES (CANDY CANES), ARNIES, INC. (RED WAXED LINEN STRING), AND A.C. MOORE (WHITE RATTAIL TIE)

"I want my cards to stand out from all the others clients would receive. They help people remember me and realize that my business is still active."

—Lynn Cyr, Lynn Cyr Design

The holiday card employs a custom matte red-and-white duplex scroll supported by a 5" (12.5 cm) stick candy cane.

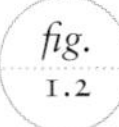

Four-ply waxed red linen string is used to attach the candy to the paper, while a white rattail ribbon ties the scroll shut.

The font, Helvetica Neue Thin Extended, is the font of choice.

The holiday greeting is delivered to the target audience in white 9" x 12" (23 x 30.5 cm) padded envelope accented by a white mailing label with a red border.

Warming a Cold Call

OBJECTIVE Eureka was looking to create a fun and lighthearted promotion that would serve as a warm introduction, a precursor to a business development cold call.

AUDIENCE The promotion was distributed to more than 300 prospective clients in various markets.

CONCEPT A cold call is a very direct approach to sales. Eureka wanted to preempt their strike with a promotional package that preheated the cold call. Red Hots candy, cleverly changed to Hot Rox, provided a simple but effective solution.

MESSAGE Eureka will give a call soon.

RESPONSE Many prospective clients remembered the witty promotion. Appointments were landed with about 35 percent of the companies targeted.

Firm Eureka
Creative Direction Jack Harris
Design Jack Harris
Copywriting Jack Harris
Printing Union Press
Special Techniques Jeremy Harris (assembly)
Manufacturers Ferrara Pan (candy) and Independent Can Company (tin)

"Sometimes a humorous approach to business development can make you stand out, leading to superior results."

—Lisa Harris, Eureka

fig. 1.1 The Hot Rox promotion comes in a metal tin with a custom-designed label.

fig. 1.2 To encourage the recipient to open the package, high energy display fonts are employed—Stiltskin Regular, Blue Moon, and Colossalis, to be exact.

fig. 1.3 The playful promotion was sent in a plain white corrugated cardboard box filled with eye-catching lime green shredded paper.

fig. 1.4 Inside, a custom die-cut insert not only highlights Eureka's services but also informs prospects that they will soon be receiving a follow-up call.

Killer Portfolio

OBJECTIVE Photographer Claudia Goetzelmann wanted to create an intriguing, off-the-wall promotional piece that would stand out from the typical printed brochure or mailer to draw prospects to her website.

AUDIENCE The target audience included art buyers, art directors, and photo editors. Roughly 200 promotional CDs were produced. The QuickTime movie can also be seen from the photographer's website, www.claudiagoetzelmann.com/evidence.

CONCEPT A series of hilarious slapstick sudden passings occur immediately after viewing Goetzelmann's breathtaking work. The short flick closes with the punch line, "Claudia's killer portfolio." The website address follows. A series of outtakes at the end add further humor to the highly memorable piece. The promotion uses actual crime scene tape and labels to set the stage.

MESSAGE Visit www.claudiagoetzelmann.com and check out Claudia's killer portfolio. It will knock you dead!

RESPONSE The response for the promotional endeavor has been outstanding, drawing quite a bit of traffic to the photographer's site.

Firm Claudia Goetzelmann, photographer

Creative Direction Claudia Goetzelmann, Ronny Knight, and Mark Day

Design/Photography Claudia Goetzelmann

Editing Claudia Goetzelmann and Ronny Knight

Music Reid Oda

Printing Epson 2200 (labels)

Special Techniques Video (digital), Final Cut Pro (editing), QuickTime (movie)

Manufacturers Evident Crime Scene Products (evidence tape and label) and local art store (cardboard envelope)

"The goal was to create a quirky and funny promotion that would highlight my creativity and sense of humor. I wanted to do something completely different from the usual mailer. I even avoided showing my work in the piece."

—Claudia Goetzelmann, photographer

fig. 1.1 The promotion comes in a clear plastic zipper bag that is accented with an evidence label.

fig. 1.2 The promotion is mailed in a 6 1/4" x 6" (16 x 15.5 cm) white cardboard envelope that is wrapped with yellow-and-black crime scene tape.

fig. 1.3 A return address is placed on the back of the envelope using a custom rubber stamp.

fig. 1.4 The CD is adorned with a label that is printed in four-color process in-house on an inkjet printer.

fig. 2.1

The short QuickTime movie, shot digitally and edited in Final Cut Pro, shows various people being shocked to death and slain by Claudia Goetzelmann's killer portfolio.

Initially Speaking

OBJECTIVE Rabih hage—an interior design company specializing in contemporary design, furniture, and art—wanted a sophisticated holiday card to send to clientele. Hat-trick design, the creator of the rabih hage identity and showroom design, was the natural choice to do the job.

AUDIENCE The target audience was primarily existing clients that frequent the showroom. Five hundred cards were produced and distributed.

CONCEPT The rabih hage corporate logo plays with the company's *r* and *h* initials. This graphic identity is prominent in all the interior design company's collateral and on their website. Wanting to be festive while still maintaining the overall brand, the design firm used the logo and made a reindeerlike character on the cover. Die-cutting helped to further delineate the *r* and *h* initials, creating curiosity as to how the letters transitioned from front to back.

MESSAGE Merry Christmas and Happy New Year from rabih hage.

RESPONSE Everyone enjoyed the eye-catching card.

Firm HAT-TRICK DESIGN
Creative Direction DAVID KIMPTON
Design LEON BAHRANI
Printing BOSS PRINT
Client RABIH HAGE

"Simple twists work well."

—David Kimpton, hat-trick design

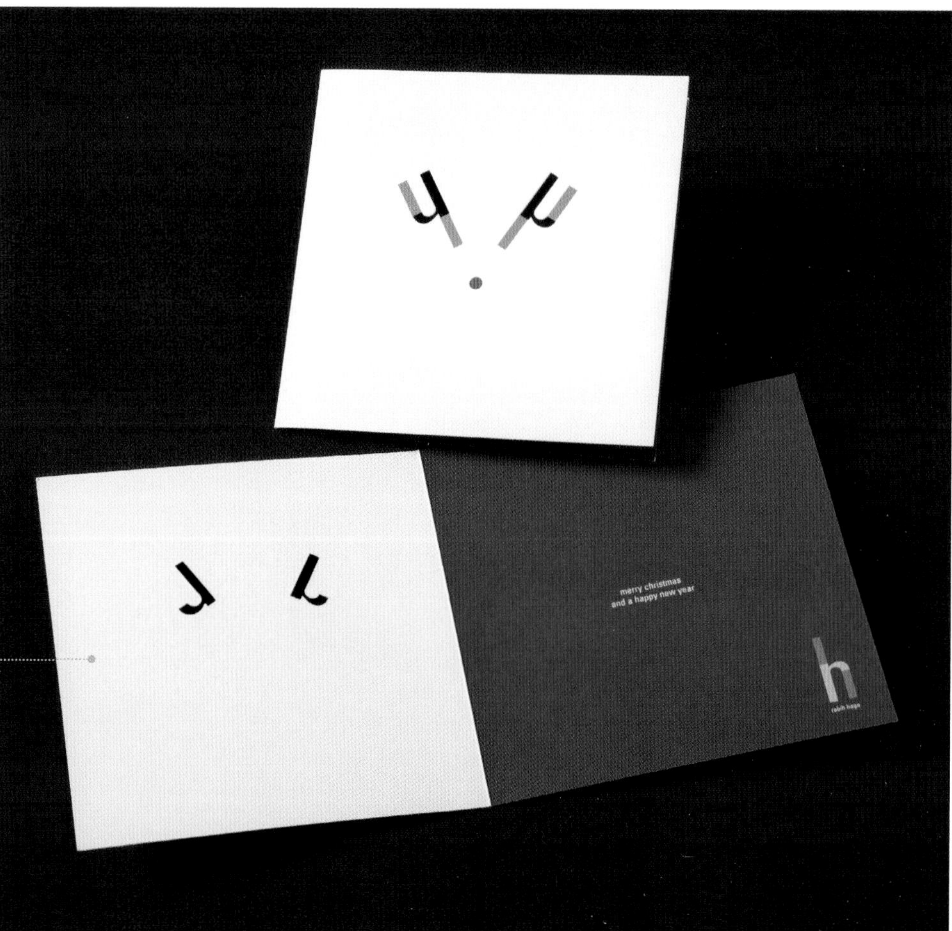

fig. 1.1 Univers 57 Condensed is the font used throughout.

fig. 1.2 The square greeting card is printed on McNaughton 400 gsm regal smooth ultra white paper using PMS 412 gray and PMS 1925 red.

fig. 1.3 The card is sent in a standard 6" x 6" (15.5 x 15.5 mm) envelope.

Sentimental Touch

OBJECTIVE To remind clients, vendors, and friends that their relationship is truly cherished, Michael Osborne Design created a precious, hand-signed miniature print to send out as a Valentine's Day greeting.

AUDIENCE This sentimental token of appreciation is sent to exiting clients, long-time vendors, and friends. Anywhere from 300 to 500 are printed each year.

CONCEPT Each year Michael Osborne Design creates a new signature-style Valentine's Day card. It not only shows off their creativity and design but also the custom letterpress services offered by One Heart Press, also owned by Michael Osborne. The precious card lets clients, vendors, and friends know that they are important and worth remembering on this special day.

MESSAGE Happy Valentine's Day!

RESPONSE Over the past fifteen years, the one-of-a-kind cards have become so popular that they have become collector's items.

Firm Michael Osborne Design
Creative Direction Michael Osborne
Design/Illustration Michael Osborne
Printing One Heart Press

"I sign the cards differently each year, depending on the design. I think it lends a real personal touch."

—Michael Osborne, Michael Osborne Design

fig. 1.1 This handsome card is letterpress-printed in black and PMS 187 cranberry red on gray Rives BFK, a well-known fine-art printmaker's paper.

fig. 1.2 All of the custom-designed graphics and lettering are personally created by designer Michael Osborne.

fig. 1.3 The limited-edition, hand-signed card is sent in a 7 1/4" x 5 1/4" (18.5 x 13.5 cm) white envelope.

fig. 2.1 The Valentine's Day greeting is letterpress-printed in PMS 485 red and PMS 643 light blue on radiant white Somerset 280 gsm with a delicate deckled edge at the bottom.

fig. 2.2 It comes in a light-gray envelope with a laid finish.

fig. 2.3 Each card is individually signed, giving it a keepsake quality.

Seductive Appeal

OBJECTIVE Contemporary fashion designer Mario Queiroz was having a show of his winter collection at Sao Paulo Fashion Week and needed to attract buyers to the event. Orlando Facioli Design was hired to create the invitations.

AUDIENCE The fashion invites were distributed to journalists and buyers. About 1,500 invitations were sent.

CONCEPT The theme of the fashion show was called *Drunk by Love*. The idea was to seduce and intoxicate the audience. It was about a boy that thinks about his lover in a very romantic yet melancholic way all day long. The symbols chosen—blood, wine, and tears—all help to support the overall concept.

MESSAGE Experience the romance and seduction.

RESPONSE More than 1,000 people attended the event. Many stood in line waiting for a seat to become available.

Firm Orlando Facioli Design
Creative Direction Orlando Facioli
Design/Illustration Orlando Facioli
Printing Lavezzo Gráfica e Editora
Special Techniques Relevo Araujo (foil stamping)
Client Mario Queiroz

"We expressed the collection through images, capturing the romantic feeling in a contemporary way."

—Orlando Facioli, Orlando Facioli Design

fig. 1.1

The illustrative invitation, printed in four-color process on Supremo 300 gsm stock, is accented by a blood red foil stamp that appears to drip down the page.

fig. 1.2

The hand-lettering is custom and created exclusively for the fashion invitation. The drawings, created traditionally, are digitally composed in a montagelike fashion.

fig. 1.3

The invitation comprises two pieces that when placed together form a cross.

fig. 1.4

An overall aqueous coating is applied for durability.

Virtual Party

Firm Fusionary Media
Creative Direction Steve Lewis
Design Ryan Masuga and Dan Tobolic
Photography Bryan Lewis and Ryan Masuga
Illustration Dan Tobolic and Ryan Masuga
Printing/Bindery The Computer Group Inc.
Manufacturers Digipak (CD-ROM packaging)

"Every year the Coaster project creates an opportunity, a chance to experiment with our process and to maximize the talents, skills, and abilities we have in-house. This year, we used animation and photography techniques, allowing us to flex some new creative muscles. We found that clients and colleagues hang onto it and play it throughout the year, creating a far longer and more profound impact."

—T.M. Camp, Fusionary Media

OBJECTIVE Fusionary Media wanted to create a promotional endeavor that would innovatively demonstrate the creative and technical capabilities of their firm. The project also needed to provide an opportunity for the design team to explore outside the limitations of client-driven projects.

AUDIENCE The interactive promotion was distributed to clients, vendors, colleagues, and friends. After the initial launch, it was also used throughout the year as a give-away at industry events. Five hundred were produced. In addition, the firm created a mini-site off their corporate website to showcase the project, providing a download-able version for visitors (www.fusionary.com/minisites/coaster2004/).

CONCEPT The interactive invitation, titled *Winteractive Coaster,* was designed to invite clients, vendors, and colleagues to a virtual New Year's Eve party in cyberspace. The adventure game begins by having a cab drop the invites off at the doorstep of Fusionary Media, located in Grand Rapids, Michigan. The invitee naturally gets out of the cab and approaches the door only to discover a password is needed to enter. The invitee, now an active player in the game, needs to explore the virtual surround-ings, gathering clues and solving puzzles, to figure out the password. The graphics and sound effects are captivating, and the desire to find the password is quite motivating.

MESSAGE Fusionary Media is a highly creative and imaginative group that will find unique ways to engage an audience.

RESPONSE For the past ten years, Fusionary Media has created a new *Winteractive Coaster* experience to share with clients. Each year, the firm pushes themselves to do something even more spectacular. The 2004 *Winteractive Coaster* was a breakthrough year. The team made great strides in their ability to entertain and engage. The response has been extremely positive as a result. The firm received numerous phone calls, many requesting the highly coveted password. After a decade, the *Winteractive Coaster* has become its own brand, and clients ask for it by name.

fig. 1.1

The interactive invitation comes in a custom die-cut case that is printed in four-color process on one side. The color palette is dark and mysterious, setting the overall tone of the game.

fig. 1.2

The CD-ROM is silk-screen-printed in three colors: black, PMS 7503, and a full coverage of white.

fig. 1.3

The package is shrink-wrapped shut and sent as a self-mailer.

fig. 2.1

Each interactive scene draws the player further into the game. The static graphics are created using Adobe Photoshop; the points of interactivity are produced using Macromedia Flash. The animated transitions are all created in Motion.

fig. 2.2

The various objects at the bottom of the screen serve as inventory items discovered and used by players to solve the password. Specifically, the scissors cut the string on a balloon, and the coins can be used in the pay phone.

The Big Idea

No.
01

EXTRAORDINARY EFFORTS

ON A GLOBAL SCALE, prospective buyers are flooded with communications messaging from print, broadcast, and electronic media. To make their target audience stop, look, and listen, creatives need to produce memorable promotions that speak to the recipient's needs in unique and innovative ways. For promotional initiatives to truly inspire and motivate, they must present something distinctive, a refreshing break from the everyday sea of mediocrity. "I think truly captivating promotions engage us on an emotional level to the degree that we no longer feel marketed to," says Mike Tuttle of Planet 10. "They shape perception through targeted, unobtrusive marketing that feels very natural and familiar. They engage, entertain, and allow the customer to fall in love with the brand." Ucef Hanjani of ceft & company agrees, "It's like filmmaking where the best ones stay with you. You think about the film, talk about it, and may even go to see it two or three times, versus a movie that almost washes through you, becoming forgettable instantly." Creatives must go beyond the norm with their initiatives to build their brand and make a lasting impression with clients.

To produce promotions that are truly extraordinary, creatives must be willing to push outside their comfort zone and not be afraid to experiment and try new things. "We're entertained by the idea of different ways of thinking and find the challenge liberating. One should never limit oneself to what is comfortable," explains Nicholas Timmons of Double Image Studio. "Excitement comes from learning, trying, and doing. Letting your senses be immersed allows for so many more variations. All you have to do is be open to the experience." Creativity in approach, presentation, format, and message will rival the mundane, putting only the best work top of mind. "With mass-production and promotional mediocrity, there is so much poverty of the imagination," remarks Ric Riordon of Riordon Design. "Only true creativity stands a greater chance of getting noticed. The current paradigm helps differentiate the real pros from those who only aspire to be." Lars Lawson from Innovative adds, "I am a big advocate of the philosophy that good is the enemy of great. Good gains quite a lot of acceptance because it's safe. But, achieving greatness is all too rare." It is important to continually find new and inventive ways to promote. The business remains vital by taking risks and exploring new avenues. Self-promotion is an opportunity to try new skills and create without client-set limitations. With every promotional endeavor, the opportunity to reach for new heights presents itself. For those who are willing to embrace the challenge, their efforts will bring about great rewards.

No.
02

DIFFERENT APPROACH

The best promotional initiatives begin with great ideas. To breathe new life into your problem-solving abilities, consider changing your process or approach. By breaking out of existing patterns or routines, you are better able to push outside preexisting barriers to explore alternative solutions. When it comes to brainstorming, many are doing imaginative and creative things to get the most from their team and themselves. Some firms are using inspirational think-toys, decorating meeting rooms in unusual ways, employing mood-setting light and sound, dressing up in costumes, or bringing in creative people from outside the communications industry as a way to engage and challenge their team to look at things in a myriad of ways. "To be truly creative, sessions need to be a wild mix of wishing, fantasizing, dreaming, and scheming," suggests Patricia Belyea of Belyea. "It is important that all ideas—the good, the bad, and the ugly—be written down and allowed to live until the last possible moment. Then, the slightly outrageous and functional ideas can be picked out of the pool of possibilities, already touched by reckless and wonderful energy."

No longer limited to an indoor experience, ideation meetings are being conducted during walks and visits to places that inspire and transcend. "I encourage my staff to get out of the studio and experience life," shares Richard Klingle-Watt of Blu Concept. "We take trips as a group to exhibits, retail outlets, restaurants, furniture stores, and galleries as a great way to discover concepts that we wouldn't normally come in contact with." Outside the confines of the workplace, intriguing ideas can be found almost anywhere. The color palette and pattern of a retro-fashioned fabric, the signature type on a graffiti wall, or the texture of a worn, tattered piece of carved vintage wood—each inspires and sparks alternative ideas and approaches. "Being creative is a way of seeing the world, not just a thing you turn on and off at work," reminds Riordon. Firms are also finding that the brainstorming process doesn't need to be limited to the creative team. "We make a point of getting the thoughts of people who aren't in our line of work. We also maintain good relationships with other studios and meet regularly to discuss marketing approaches and current projects," admits Dawn Ripple McFadin of Fan Works Design. "It keeps us from working in a fish bowl." As the marketplace becomes more and more global, it is becoming increasingly important for creatives to go beyond the confines of the studio to experience a different mindset. "My creativity is nourished by strong impressions of places, people, and objects," acknowledges Nelida Nassar of Nassar Design. "The creative output of other cultures stimulates my own." When it comes to problem solving, going outside your frame of reference helps bring in a fresh perspective. By changing your process or approach, you alter your experience and, in turn, the outcome, igniting alternative solutions and newfound possibilities.

To produce promotions that are truly extraordinary, creatives must be willing to push outside their comfort zone and not be afraid to experiment and try new things. Creativity in approach, presentation, format, and message will rival the mundane, putting only the best work top of mind.

No.
03

COMMITTED TO SUCCESS

With conference calls and meetings overbooked, emails and phone messages piling up, and deadlines beckoning, creatives oftentimes struggle to reserve time and energy from client work to focus on their own pursuits and aspirations. "Self-promotion is always a challenge. It gets pushed to the back burner when paying projects get hot, and sometimes it never happens at all," admits Sheree Clark of Sayles Graphic Design. "Yet it's the most important thing that you can do to grow your business." Creatives need to make their business a priority, allotting time away from the day-to-day madness to focus on goals and future endeavors. Promotional initiatives should be an ongoing part of a firm or freelancer's creative process, given the same attention, commitment, and follow-through as client-driven projects. Scheduling is key. "For promoting our firm, we work out a yearly plan," says Alexander Isley of Alexander Isley Inc. "It includes targeted mailings and holiday promotions as well as customized mailings for specifically targeted new business efforts." It is important to incorporate into your promotional initiatives a way to access feedback and track results. The information will provide valuable insight when it comes to future initiatives. Don't be so focused on running the ship that you lose hold of the wheel. It is important to the longevity of your business to set time apart, on a regular basis, to focus on ways in which to keep your creative business on track and moving forward. In a highly competitive marketplace where everyone is jockeying for position, creatives must stay on top of their game when it comes to promotion.

Chapter Three

"There are so many out-of-the-catalog promotional items out there that they lose impact. An effective promotion needs to inspire people, encouraging them to experience your way of thinking."

—Alexander Isley, Alexander Isley, Inc.

KEEPSAKE PROMOTIONS

Keepsake promotions serve as tokens of appreciation for a successful business year. They generate goodwill and can go a long way in solidifying client relations. Given primarily during the holidays to an existing client base, keepsake promotions can also be adopted for new business-development initiatives year-round. "Every year we produce a holiday gift that we hope will be used and remembered," says Alexander Isley of Alexander Isley, Inc. "We create these items so that they can also be implemented as new business tools throughout the year. We order a surplus of inventory and craft the messages so that they are not specific to a certain time of year. We also provide a place to personalize each gift by writing a little note."

From handmade and custom notecards and journals; photo albums and scrapbooks of all shapes and sizes; and calendars that pop up, fold out, and assemble to pocket-sized restaurant guides and handy travel planners, keepsake promotions remain with the recipient long after the initial launch. Providing clients with something they will cherish, value, and use on a daily basis greatly increases the chances that your promotion will have a longer shelf life, increasing the chance for potential work down the road. "Creating custom promotional pieces gives us the opportunity to get in the heads of a client, to dig for what hits them emotionally, and to know them intimately," shares Lauren Payne of Spiral Design Studio. "We regularly hear from clients who are the envy of their organizations because they received a Spiral holiday gift. It becomes a presence in their office, keeping us at the top of their mind all year long." When a keepsake is designed with the client in mind, the effort shows that you truly value their business and are sensitive to their needs.

Promotional keepsakes also need to speak to your sensibilities, revealing something about your personality, philosophy, or approach. "There are so many out-of-the-catalog promotional items out there that they lose impact," reminds Isley. "An effective promotion needs to inspire people, encouraging them to experience your way of thinking." Many use keepsake initiatives as a way to flex their creative muscles; a chance to work without limitations to show what they can do. "By assigning ourselves a self-promo every year, we're guaranteed that at least once a year we step outside the constraints we may have in client projects," adds Kim Baer of KBDA. "Doing a group project stimulates everyone to think about things in different ways and to invest in a team effort." When free to express ideas without constraints, creativity and originality is enhanced, bringing design back to an art form. "These types of promotions have turned out to be some of our best pieces, rewarding both personally and with the media," admits Justin Ahrens of Rule29. "They have also opened the door for our clients to take more chances, leading to more successful and rewarding work." With keepsake initiatives, creatives are challenging themselves to venture outside the norm, pushing their creative and production abilities to the next level.

Sophisticated and Fun

OBJECTIVE Rule29, O'Neil Printing, and Roswell Bookbinding joined forces to create a collaborative promotion that not only was memorable and thought-provoking but also served as a vehicle to highlight their various services.

AUDIENCE The 2005 celebratory calendar was sent to existing clients of each collaborator. Two thousand pieces were created in all.

CONCEPT To stand out from a sea of generic and uninspiring year-end promotions, the collaborative team focused tightly on concept, letting the copy drive the design. The calendar's personal approach and interactive format is engaging and uplifting. Each month encourages the recipient to participate with the overall messaging.

MESSAGE Rule29, O'Neil Printing, and Roswell Bookbinding provide high-quality work with a personal approach and a keen attention to detail.

RESPONSE The return on investment from this fun yet highly sophisticated piece far outweighed the costs incurred to create it. Each partner has seen tangible results not only in terms of new business but also in solidifying existing client relationships for the long term.

Firm Rule29
Creative Direction Justin Ahrens
Design Justin Ahrens and Kerri Herner
Illustration Cathie Bleck, Joel Nakumura, and Terry Marks
Photography Brian McDonald, Bill timmerman, and James Leland
Copywriting Terry Marks
Printing O'Neil Printing
Bindery Roswell Bookbinding

"When working collaboratively, you need to establish a working schedule with some flexibility. You also need to choose really talented people to work with, allowing each party to do their thing. Working with others has helped us with our ideas. We wish we could do collaborative projects like this all the time."

—Justin Ahrens, Rule29

fig. 1.1 Inside, each month presents a new way in which to interact with the design. The month of January, a time for new beginnings, focuses on growth. Seeds, symbolic of the potential that each new start brings, are prominently featured on a series of cards that lie in a custom die-cut slot.

fig. 1.2 The neutral-tone fabric cover draws attention to the calendar's vibrant title *Li5e*, an interesting combination of the word *life* and the year '05.

fig. 1.3 The clear foil-stamped text reads, "Calendars are roadmaps to your everyday. It will know all you value. Tell it your secrets. Plan with hopes held high. It may be true..." The title and engaging copy help create curiosity, encouraging the recipient to explore further.

fig. 2.1

Throughout the concealed wire-o bound calendar, various pieces pop up, fold out, perforate off, and assemble. The various production accents not only highlight the services of the printer and bindery company but also show how strong design, image, and copy can come together to motivate.

fig. 2.2

The promotion is printed in four-color process plus black, PMS 7518 tan, and PMS 8003 metallic on Strathmore Premium Opaque.

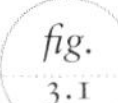

fig. 3.1

In contrast to the very sophisticated, more monochromatic spreads, vibrant and whimsical work is incorporated into the lineup, providing a dynamic rhythm and varied range of work.

fig. 3.2

The month of February plays on life's greatest emotion, love. Inside the tipped-on envelope is series of three letters of correspondence, from an "I love you" to a "Get lost please!" The witty charm sends a chuckle and warm feelings throughout the month.

fig. 3.3

October, on the other hand, invites the recipient to tear out and illuminate the perforated holiday luminary.

Signature Look

Firm Riordon Design
Creative Direction Shirley Riordon and Ric Riordon
Design/Illustration Shirley Riordon
Photography Ric Riordon
Printing/Bindery C.J. Graphics
Manufacturers Progress Packaging Ltd. (bags and gold stickers) and Creative Bag Co. Ltd. (ribbon)

"In a world of such a deluge of commodity, I think people crave small luxury signatures in their gifts, something unique and personal. Our efforts have led clients to approach us to do something similar for them."

—Ric Riordon, Riordon Design

OBJECTIVE Riordon Design wanted to create an aesthetically beautiful yet functional year-round promotion that would showcase their passion and expertise in specialty packaging. They also wanted the piece to have commercial value in the local retail market.

AUDIENCE The specialty keepsake was personally hand-delivered to existing and prospective clientele. It was also distributed to local retail shops. One thousand were produced.

CONCEPT The notecards, guest journal, and packaging each use unique custom accents, showing off the firm's packaging expertise. Its distinctive construction, clever inserts, interesting die-cut shapes, and unusual bindery encourage interaction and make the overall piece memorable. The decorative graphics, ornate details, and rich color palette reflect the ambiance and architectural heritage of the Oakville community. Marking the tenth anniversary of the studio's relocation to Oakville, Ontario, Canada, the promotion serves as a way to celebrate.

MESSAGE Revel in the custom details, seeing Riordon Design as an innovator in specialty packaging.

RESPONSE The firm received many emails expressing delight in receiving the guest book and cards. Many wanted to buy the matching set to give away as gifts. Local retail shops in Oakville are now carrying the distinctive package during the peak tourist season, and real estate agents have purchased the ensemble to give away as unique gifts to clients. There has also been interested in marketing a similar package to other communities across Canada.

fig. 1.1 The ensemble is delivered in a black matte polypropylene bag that is accented with a gold seal and tied shut with a black ribbon.

fig. 1.2 The signature guest journal and notecards come in an embossed, clear-foil-stamped, and die-cut box made using Monadnock Papers Astrolite 130 lb. smooth white cover.

Inside the custom die-cut box are two compartments. The notecards and matching envelopes are housed on the left side and sealed shut with a black tie that wraps around two rivets; the guest journal is located on the right and can be seen through a die-cut window. A vellum fly sheet insert separates the two.

fig. 2.1

A simple pastel palette of yellows, greens, and blues accented with black is reproduced in four-color process using stochastic printing. A matte aqueous coating is applied as a finishing touch.

fig. 2.2

fig. 2.3

Requiem, a serif font, and Sudestada, a script font, are used throughout.

fig. 2.4

The guest journal cover is printed on Monadnock Papers Atrolite 160 lb. smooth cover with Strathmore Grandee 100 lb. true white text used for the interior pages. It is bound by a ribbon tied on the inside.

fig. 2.5

The notecards are printed on Monadnock Papers Astrolite 100 lb. smooth cover, and the matching envelopes use Fraser Papers Synergy 70 lb. smooth text in citrus green.

Picture This

Firm Fan Works Design, LLC
Creative Direction/Design Dawn Ripple McFadin
Illustration Kevin McFadin
Copywriting Blue Ridge Communications
Printing/Bindery York Graphic Services (journal and insert card) and HP laser printer (instructional sheet)
Manufacturers Bliss Wedding Market (sage green envelopes), Paper Mart (boxes), Dick Blick (matt board), and Kolo (photo corners)

"There's a very personal touch to our promotion, and people respond to that. The usefulness and sentiment stretches way beyond just the season, which helps us and our work stay in people's minds year-round."

—Dawn Ripple McFadin, Fan Works Design, LLC

OBJECTIVE Wanting to give something to clients that would enrich their lives on a daily basis, the design team at Fan Works Design chose to produce a personal, handcrafted keepsake album.

AUDIENCE The primary audience was existing clientele. The keepsake piece has also been given out to prospective clients as a follow-up. A total of 500 albums were created; most of them were hand-delivered.

CONCEPT The self-standing album, inspired by a gallery exhibition of handmade artist books, can be personalized by the recipient with special mementos, notes, or drawings. The handwork and attention to detail make the keepsake promotion look like a handcrafted, signature piece, while the copy makes it feel sincere and heartfelt.

MESSAGE Life has many special moments. Don't forget to cherish them.

RESPONSE This token of appreciation received numerous thankful comments from Fan Works Design's existing client base. The promotion also got the firm a foot in the door with prospects who, after receiving the package, requested to see more work.

fig. 1.1 The keepsake album comes in a decorative box with a textured finish and custom label.

fig. 1.2 The illustrated front and back covers, a visual collage of personal memoirs, are printed in four-color process, PMS 10 warm gray, and satin aqueous varnish on Mohawk Paper Navajo 180 lb. cover. The warm and inviting presence encourages the recipient to open the piece and look inside.

fig. 1.3 An insert card, printed in four-color process and PMS 10 warm gray plus a satin aqueous varnish on Mohawk Paper 180 lb. Navajo cover in brilliant white, sets the tone of the piece.

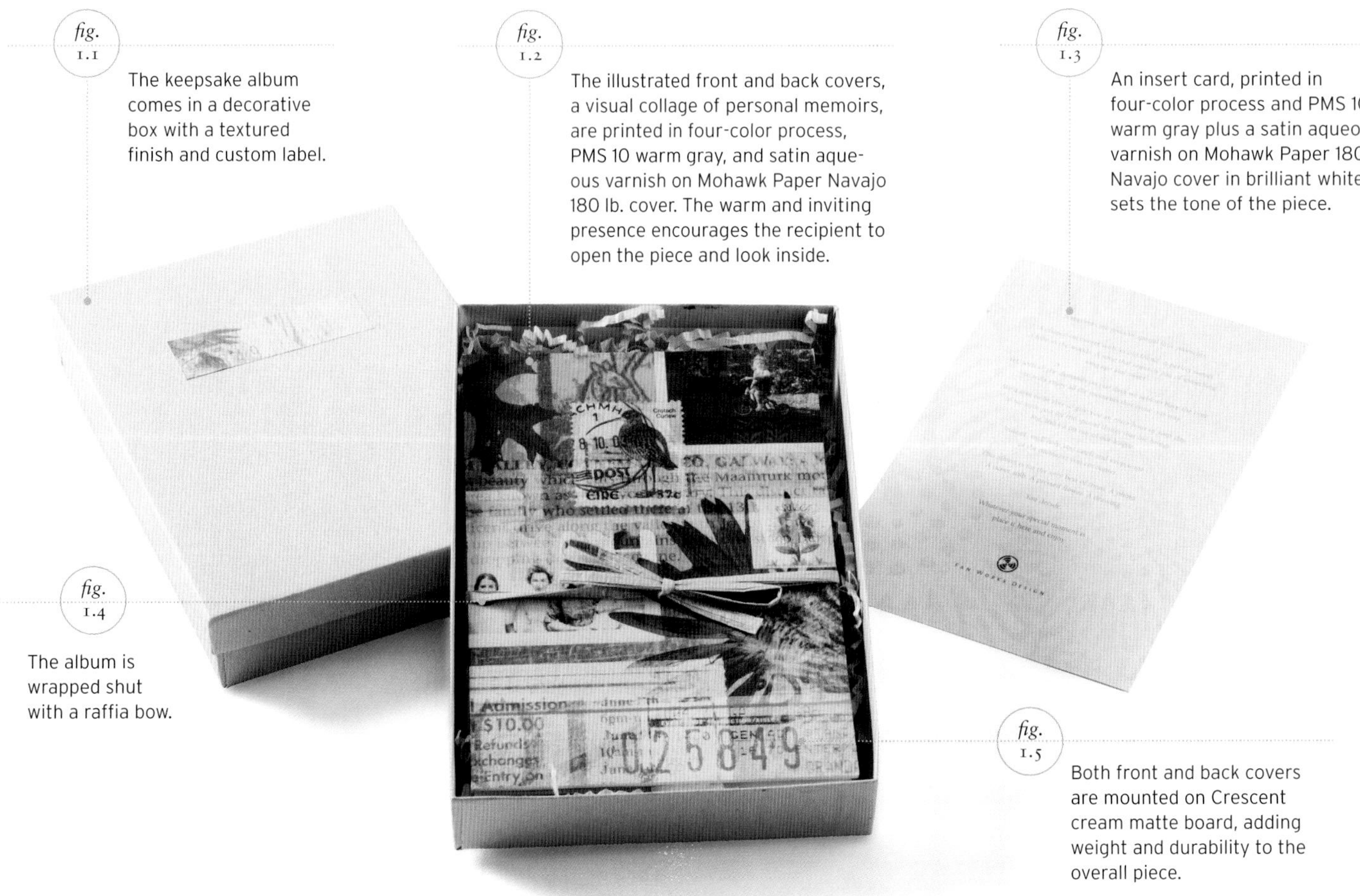

fig. 1.4 The album is wrapped shut with a raffia bow.

fig. 1.5 Both front and back covers are mounted on Crescent cream matte board, adding weight and durability to the overall piece.

fig. 2.1

Once opened, the accordion-folded album becomes self-standing.

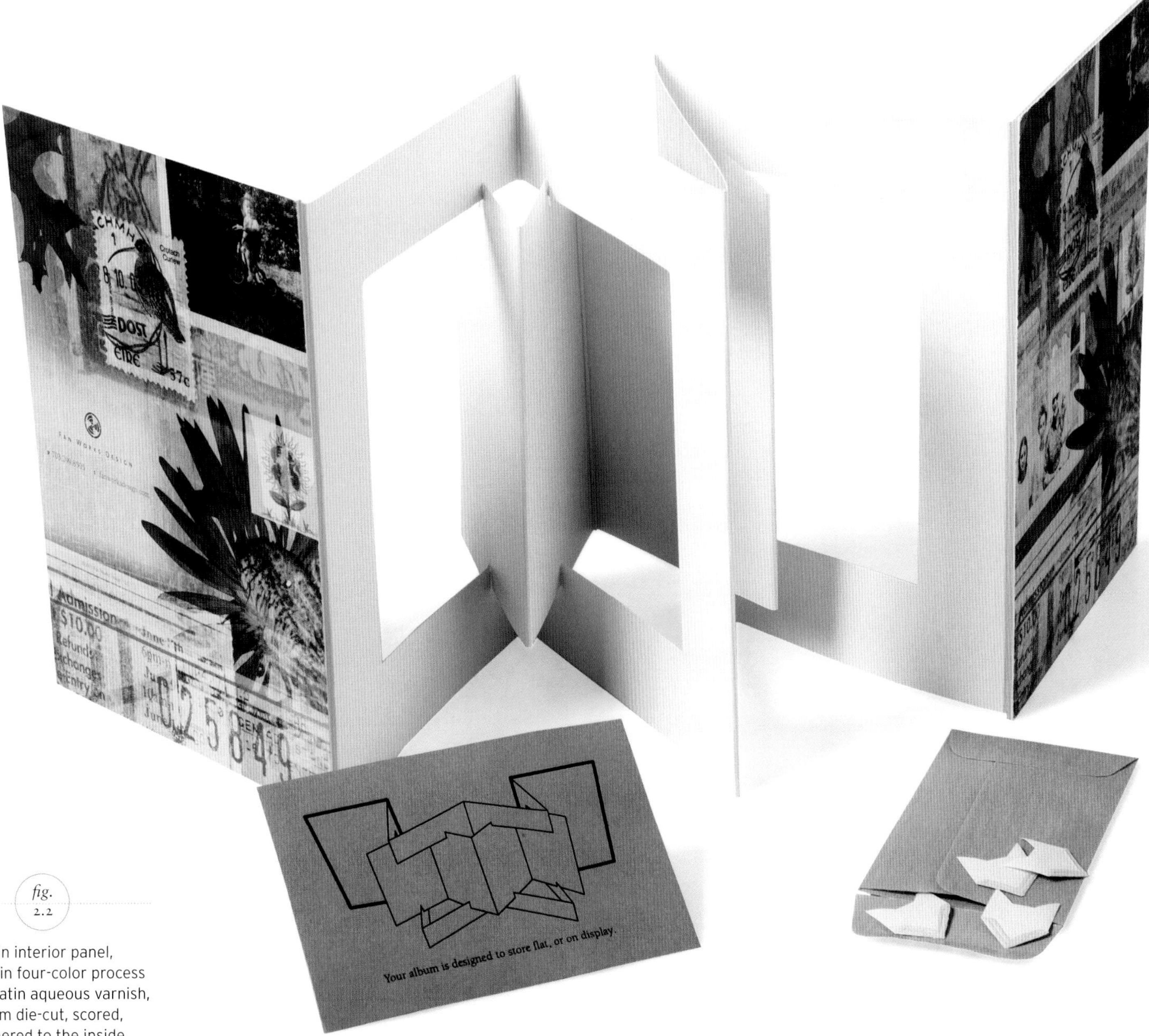

fig. 2.2

The main interior panel, printed in four-color process with a satin aqueous varnish, is custom die-cut, scored, and adhered to the inside front and back covers for stability. Another accordion-folded panel is inserted in the middle, using the same brilliant white cover stock, in the opposing direction as an accent.

fig. 2.3

The scrapbook-like album comes with an instructional insert and cream-colored photo corners stored in a mini sage green envelope.

Venturing Out

Firm Real Art Design Group, Inc.
Creative Direction Chris Wire
Design Jeremy Loyd, Chris Wire, and Kate Rohrer
Printing Patented Printing and Corporate Packaging (pillow pak)
Special Techniques Custom Formed Products (die-cutting)
Manufacturers Corporate Packaging (pillow pak), Woodwright and Lumber Company (wood), Mutual Tool & Die Inc. (metal), and State Line Wholesale (ribbon)

"Designing our own promotions allows us to explore other areas. We can work with new materials and think in different ways that are not necessarily linked to our other projects."

—Kate Rohrer, Real Art Design Group, Inc.

OBJECTIVE For this year's holiday promotion, Real Art Design Group chose to venture outside the norm, pushing their creative and production abilities.

AUDIENCE The target audience included both current and prospective clients as well as vendors and other company contacts. Three hundred and seventy-five kits were produced.

CONCEPT Each year Real Art Design Group produces a unique holiday keepsake. This year the firm focused on creating a custom light for which clients could participate in the creative process by customizing the look and feel of their keepsake. A variety of opaque and translucent shades could be mixed and matched to create a signature look. The promotion was presented in a custom pillow pak wrapped by a brilliant red ribbon.

MESSAGE Happy holidays from the brilliant creative team at Real Art Design Group.

RESPONSE Real Art Design Group's holiday promotions are always highly anticipated. This year was no different. Desks, cubicles, and offices of clients and collaborators are now illuminated with unique custom creations, a radiant reflection on the innovative firm.

The keepsake promotion is presented in a silkscreen-printed plastic package, chosen for the way its overall shape echoes the design and translucency of the lamp. It ties shut with a brilliant red ribbon.

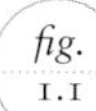

The custom keepsake light is made of baltic birch wood for the sides and black anodized aluminum for support.

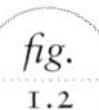

Translucent and opaque shades, printed in four-color process plus PMS 4625 on Glama Natural Translucent 29 lb. cover and Starwhite Vicksburg 110 lb. natural cover, respectively, can be mixed and matched to create a variety of interesting combinations.

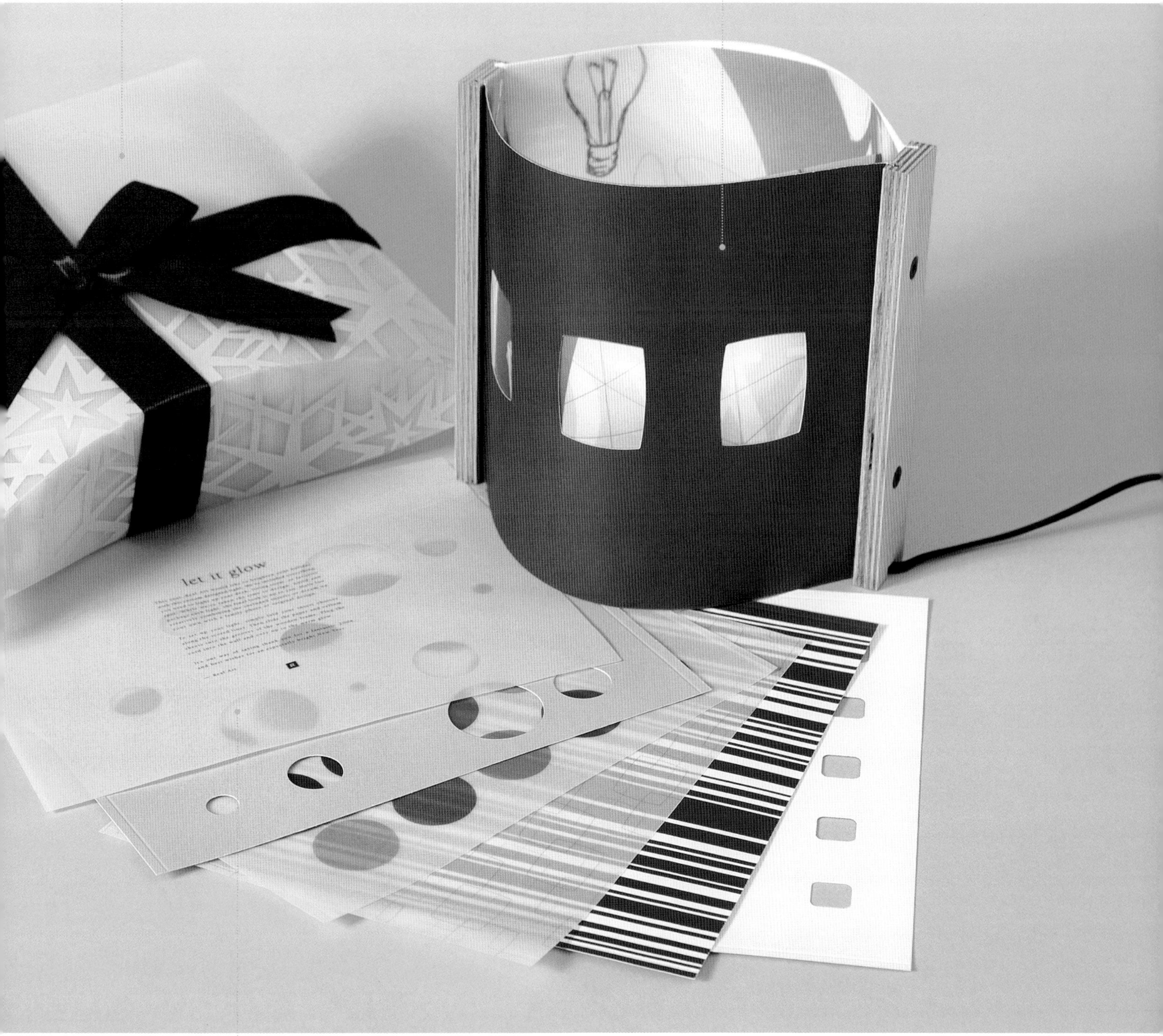

Sending Thanks

Firm KBDA

Creative Direction Kim Baer

Design/Illustration Allison Bloss, Helen Duval, Keith Knueven, Barbara Cooper, and Liz Burrill

Printing Pat Reagh Printing (letterpress)

Manufacturers Taylor Box Company (box)

"Our firm has been blessed with great collaborators, both clients and colleagues. They're what make our work worthwhile."

—Kim Baer, KBDA

OBJECTIVE KBDA was looking to create a heartfelt keepsake promotion as a way to express their gratitude and thanks to clients and collaborators.

AUDIENCE The piece was distributed to existing and prospective clientele as well as colleagues. Seven hundred and fifty were produced and delivered by Thanksgiving.

CONCEPT Under the theme of *giving thanks*, each designer in the studio was given the freedom to create his or her own interpretation. The only restriction in the project was that the design needed to work well in letterpress. The goal was to inspire recipients of the set of thank-you cards to pass on the wishes of gratitude to others.

MESSAGE Don't forget all of the blessings and good fortune in your lives, and remember to thank those around you who have made an impact.

RESPONSE The promotion received tremendous feedback, generating a lot of goodwill for the studio.

fig. 1.1

The cards and mailing envelopes come in a custom-designed box that is wrapped with 70 lb. Finch VHF text and imprinted with the same signature colors as the bellyband.

fig. 1.2

Each of the six thank-you cards is letterpress-printed in either PMS 159 burnt orange, PMS 3975 yellow ochre, or PMS 444 Gray on 100 lb. Starwhite Vicksburg Vellum Tiara white coverstock.

fig. 1.3

The distinctive set of thank-you cards and custom envelopes comes wrapped in a bellyband that is printed in two colors, PMS 159 burnt orange and black, on 70 lb. Finch VHF text stock.

Keeping Time

Firm Huber&Co Design

Creative Direction/Design Anton Huber

Printing/Bindery Werkstatt Höeflich (book) and laser printer (bellyband)

"Good ideas are rare. The worst thing you can do is to overdesign."

—Anton Huber, Huber&Co Design

OBJECTIVE Huber&Co Design was interested in creating a year-end keepsake promotion that could be utilized and enjoyed throughout the year.

AUDIENCE The target market was primarily clients and friends of Huber&Co Design. One hundred and fifty notebooks were produced. The firm continues to hand out the personal journals to new clients.

CONCEPT Huber&Co Design wanted to create something thoughtful yet functional that could be used throughout the entire year. So, they created a limited edition, hand-stamped and -numbered notebook titled *365*. As a vehicle for reflection, the personalized notebook with 365 blank pages, one for every day of the year, beckons recipients to take time from their hectic lives to express their thoughts and ideas.

MESSAGE Seize the day—*carpe diem.*

RESPONSE After the book was launched, the design firm received a stream of phone calls and emails from clients expressing how they have put the notebook to use in their everyday lives. Some clients even requested a second book. The keepsake promotion has also attracted the attention of the design media and industry organizations, generating a magazine feature in *Novum* and an award from the prestigious Type Directors Club in New York City.

Inside the stamped and individually numbered book are 365 blank pages utilizing the same cream-colored stock as the bellyband.

Garamond Amsterdam is the font of choice.

fig. 1.3

The 2 1/4" (5.5 cm)-wide bellyband is printed in black using a laser printer on Buchdruckpapier 80 gsm cream-colored text stock.

fig. 1.4

The cover, made of Keaycolor kodiakbraun 300 gsm, is elegantly embossed with the title *365*.

Growing Goodwill

Firm Iron Blender Studios
Creative Direction/Design Wendy K. S. Berman
Printing Hewlard Packard PSC 1210v inkjet
Manufacturers Alpine Dynamics/Best Containers (round tins), Specialty Bottle LLC (rectangular tin), Staples (Box), Whatcom Seed Company (seeds), Jo-Ann Fabrics & Crafts (maple leaf paper puncher), and Kate's Paperie (pine tree paper puncher)

"It always seems that the simple ideas are sometimes what people appreciated the most."

—Wendy K. S. Berman, Iron Blender Studios

OBJECTIVE In today's increasingly complex world, Iron Blender Studios wanted to create a keepsake promotion that would be a living reminder of the truly important things in life.

AUDIENCE The plant-a-seed promotion was sent to existing clients as a thank-you gift for helping the design firm blossom. Only thirty-five limited-edition holiday promotions were created.

CONCEPT The growing firm wanted their year-end promotion to stand out from the plethora of holiday keepsakes. They decided to give the gift of nature—seeds to plant and prosper for years to come. A fir and sugar maple became the seeds of choice. A miniature booklet reminds the reader that the simplest things can sometimes be the most magnificent, like "the awe-inspiring tranquility of a lunar eclipse on a fall night or the quiet beauty of a tree covered in the season's first snow." Everything in this world has a humble beginning, but with time and effort can blossom into something quite extraordinary. The seeds serve as symbols of the firm's potential, well worth any client's investment.

MESSAGE Plant a seed today and good things will grow tomorrow.

RESPONSE Clients were touched by the reflective gesture. They sent thank-you letters, sharing their plans for the seeds. Many have initiated new projects with the prospering firm.

fig. 1.1 The nature-based promotion is distributed in a white corrugated cardboard box with a custom label.

fig. 1.2 The seeds come in a rectangular tin container wrapped with a mini booklet by two pieces of natural-colored raffia. The tin sits on a bed of crinkled-cut kraft-colored paper.

fig. 2.3

Instructions, printed in-house on Avery inkjet label paper, guide recipients in the planting process.

fig. 2.4

A 3" x 1 3/4" (7.5 x 4.5 cm) booklet, titled *Plant a Seed Today*, is inkjet printed in-house with a nature-inspired palette of black, PMS 463, and PMS 577. It is hand-trimmed and -bound using a single silver brad.

fig. 2.1

Inside the rectangular tin, two tiny round tin canisters are nested inside wood excelsior.

fig. 2.2

The circular tins house the fir and sugar maple seeds. Each container is identified with its respective leaf icon created with a paper puncher using French Speckletone cover and attached to the lids using double-sided tape.

fig. 2.6

Throughout the promotion, the fonts ITC American Typewriter and SpillMilk from Fonthead Design are used. Flower Show is employed for the various leaf art accents at the end of the booklet.

fig. 2.5

French Paper Speckletone Starch Vine 100 lb. cover was used on the outside of the mini booklet; Hewlett Packard 24 lb. inkjet paper was employed for the interior pages.

Blossoming Relationships

OBJECTIVE The objective behind this client-specific keepsake promotion was to plant a seed with the creative department at Marshall Field's, a chain of retail stores, in hopes that a relationship would blossom.

AUDIENCE This promotion was targeted specifically to the Marshall Field's Creative Group. It was given as a thank-you after an appointment. The three-dimensional promotion has also been distributed to other prospective clients. Eight were created in all, each hand-delivered. The firm plans to continue with the keepsake promotion in the future.

CONCEPT The project was based on the theme *Now in Bloom*, planting the seeds of growth. The planter promotion not only was appropriate for the season but also helped to convey the recent growth of the Curb-Crowser team and their eagerness to build a relationship with the chain of retail stores. The clay pot, symbolic of a solid foundation, is accompanied by soil, bulbs, forget-me-not seeds, trowel, and floral identification stick: the necessary tools for success in the growing process. All the items are branded with the same theme.

MESSAGE Curb-Crowser is growing and able to tackle larger projects.

RESPONSE The firm walked out of the appointment with work, the beginning of a growing relationship.

Firm Curb-Crowser

Creative Direction Tracie Curb-Crowser

Design Caitlin Nugent and Chris Van Ert

Photography Joe St. Onge

Printing Xerox Phaser 7750

Manufacturers Bachmans (soil, stick, seeds, bulbs and planter) and Restoration Hardware, Inc. (trowel)

"Almost all of our promos are three-dimensional because we don't want them to be filed in a folder. Even if the prospect does not respond immediately, we know the promotion is being used or is sitting on someone's desk to remind him or her of us."

—Tracie Curb-Crowser, Curb-Crowser

fig. 1.1

A green metal trowel with a wooden handle is tied to the top of the planter with twine.

fig. 1.2

The bottom of the clay planter is used as a cover to seal the promotion.

fig. 1.3

A custom hangtag, tied on with a leather strap, is made of two printed labels adhered onto 20 pt. board for added durability.

fig. 2.1

A lime green and yellow color palette is used throughout for its ability to symbolize spring growth.

fig. 2.2

The clay planter, soil, and identification stick are all customized with labels printed in-house on Epson premium bright white 24 lb. paper and applied with Xyron adhesive.

fig. 2.3

Century Gothic, AT Clearface Gothic, and Trade Gothic are the fonts used throughout.

fig. 2.4

The custom-designed seed packet is printed on a Xerox Phaser 7750, hand-trimmed, and adhered with double-sided tape. The front features the forget-me-not flower in bloom while the back details planting instructions.

Bon Appétit

Firm Hornall Anderson Design Works

Creative Direction Jack Anderson

Design/Illustration/Photography Sonja Max, Henry Yiu, Leo Raymundo, Andrew Wicklund, and Elmer dela Cruz

Printing/Bindery Metropolitan Fine Printing (dining guide) and Canon Color Laser Copier 1140 (bellyband)

"We hope to capture people's attention by sending them something that is useful. We find that the best way to do this is to figure out what we like to keep on our desks or take home and save."

—Sonja Max, Hornall Anderson Design Works

OBJECTIVE Hornall Anderson Design Works wanted to create a tasteful keepsake promotion to celebrate their twenty-second anniversary.

AUDIENCE The dining guide was distributed to employees, friends, and existing clients at Hornall Anderson Design Works' twenty-second anniversary party. It was also mailed to prospective clients as a promotion. About 1,500 were produced.

CONCEPT The handheld dining guide, titled *22 Entrées to the Soul*, was produced as a useful resource to celebrate the firm's twenty-two years in business. Restaurants were profiled, showcasing many of the firm's favorite hot spots and hideaways. To break up the feature spreads and aid in the overall pacing, humorous food-related quotations were interjected in a whimsical yet sophisticated fashion.

MESSAGE Come visit Seattle and experience great food, friendship, and, of course, design—Hornall Anderson style.

RESPONSE The commemorative book generated a great response, with many requests for more. It also provided out-of-towners with a taste of Seattle, the hometown of Hornall Anderson Design Works.

fig. 1.1

The resourceful dining guide is foil-stamped on the front and back cover with the firm's corporate color, orange. A muted brown, textured finish stock, Gilbert Oxford bronzed 100 lb. uncoated cover, is used to draw attention to the foil imprint.

fig. 1.2

The perfect-bound, pocket-sized guide is wrapped with a custom bellyband. If the piece is to be mailed, it is sent in a clear plastic envelope.

fig. 2.1

Inside the dining resource, two colors, PMS 448 deep brown and PMS 4515 muted khaki, are printed on Mohawk Superfine 80 lb. text in a myriad of ways to activate each spread.

fig. 2.2

UV inks are used throughout—a richer alternative to standard inks when printing on an uncoated stock.

L.A. Adventure

Firm KBDA
Creative Direction Kimberly Baer
Design Keith Knueven
Printing/Bindery ColorNet Press
Manufacturers G2 Graphic Service (plastic sleeve)

"L.A. is a rich resource. Angelenos spend a lot of time going from point A to B, often missing the abundance of quirky finds in between. We have uncovered a few gems."

–Kimberly Baer, KBDA

fig. 1.1

Adobe Caslon and Frutiger are the fonts of choice.

OBJECTIVE KBDA was looking to communicate the studio's culture and approach to problem solving by developing a functional keepsake promotion that recipients would want to use, enjoy, and hold onto.

AUDIENCE The L.A. guide was distributed to existing and prospective clientele as well as collaborators, colleagues, and design publications. About 2,000 booklets were produced.

CONCEPT Located in the heart of Los Angeles, KBDA chose to produce a promotional piece that addressed their city's culture and scenic venues—from shopping, nightlife, dining, and entertainment to outdoor vistas, spas, and tranquil getaways. The mini travel guide provided an inside look into L.A.'s sites. The handy manual, designed to fit in any glove box, slips conveniently into a plastic sleeve for protection.

MESSAGE You don't have to travel afar. Sometimes the most exciting adventures can be right in your own backyard.

RESPONSE The piece has generated a lot of positive feedback from clients and colleagues alike. There has also been a great deal of interest in merchandising the pocket-size travel guide in retail outlets.

fig. 1.2 A plastic sleeve, open on both ends, adds protection.

fig. 1.3 Throughout the portable travel book, a system of icons is used to communicate the offerings and neighborhood of each venue.

fig. 1.6 To give the piece a satin finish, an overall aqueous coating is applied.

fig. 1.4 The screw-bound, die-cut book fans open for quick reference to numerous locations simultaneously, making planning and selection that much easier.

fig. 1.5 The 6" x 3" (15 x 7.5 cm) travel guide is printed in PMS 432 gray, PMS 174 rich brown, PMS 346 mint green, PMS 277 pale blue, PMS 128 yellow, and black on Topkote 130 lb. coverstock. Solid light gray, PMS 421, is printed on the back.

Creative Correspondence

Firm Art & Anthropology

Creative Direction Jason C. Otero

Design/Illustration Wendy Brookshire, Joe Lamarre, Paco Proano, and Jason C. Otero

Printing Art & Anthropology (letterpress) and Xerox Phaser 3400 (insert sheet)

Manufacturers Office Depot (seals and clear acetate) and ClearBags.com (envelopes)

"We decided to allow the project to grow organically in phases rather than define a specific finished piece. Each designer was given an opportunity to affect the previous designer's contribution in a continuum, letting go of expectation and opening up the project for true creative experimentation."

—Jason C. Otero, Art & Anthropology

OBJECTIVE Art & Anthropology wanted to create a keepsake promotion that would highlight both their studio creativity and letterpress printing technologies. They also wanted to produce a functional item that could be sold to the consumer market through retailers, diversifying their market.

AUDIENCE The primary audience was existing and prospective clientele as well as boutique card and stationery retailers. This endeavor, titled *Envelope Project: Open*, is part of an ongoing collaboration. A total of 250 sets were produced.

CONCEPT A set of four uniquely sized postcards were created. The overall concept centered on coded forms of language and icons that build meaning through familiarity and use. The graphic symbols and shapes were a result of three years of collaborative fine-art and installation work with artist Paco Proano. The iconic shapes were purposefully meant to be ambiguous, allowing recipients to construct their own interpretation. The title *Envelope Project: Open* had a double meaning. Its purpose was not only to direct the audience to physically open the piece but also to enlighten them, opening their minds to the idea of correspondence.

MESSAGE Share your thoughts through letter writing was the primary message. The secondary message was to revel in the creative work and letterpress printing capabilities of Art & Anthropology.

RESPONSE Clients who received the promotional package really enjoyed the overall design as well as the tactile quality of the letterpress printing. The cards are currently being sold through Composition, a boutique retailer of modern design office products.

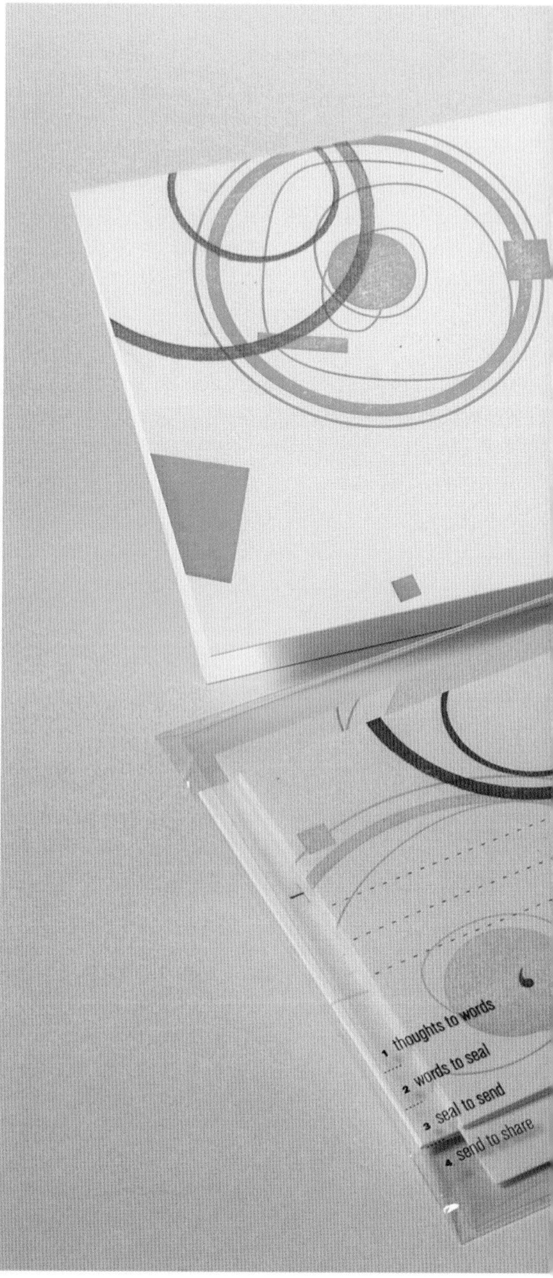

fig. 1.1

The set of four cards, clear inserts, and seals come in a clear 5" x 7" (12.5 x 18 cm) plastic envelope.

fig. 1.2

Each uniquely sized, signature-style card is letterpress-printed on Mohawk Superfine 100 lb. eggshell coverstock.

fig. 1.3

The palette employs all special-mix colors for this limited edition run.

fig. 1.4

Alternate Gothic No. 2 is the font of choice.

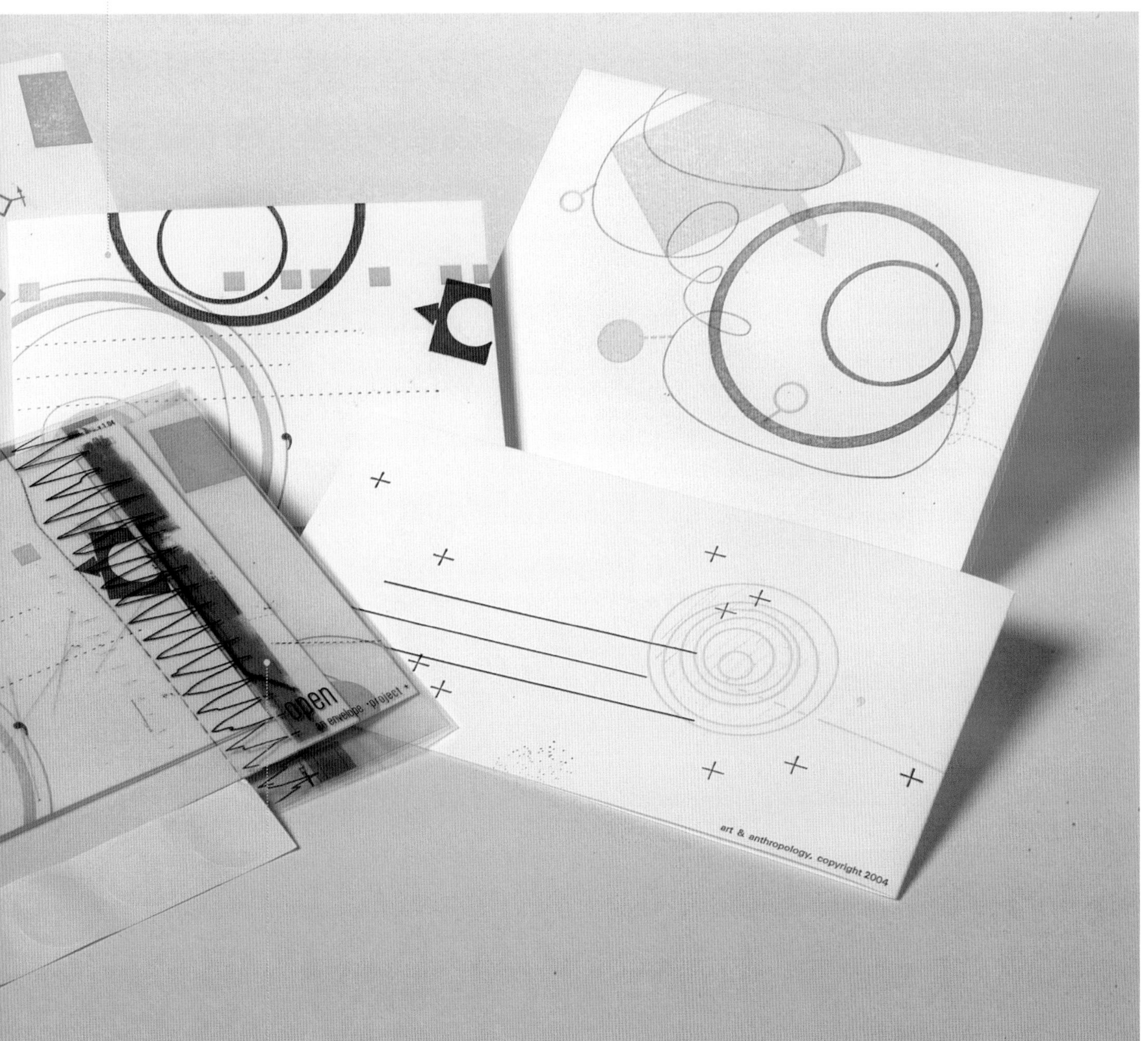

fig. 1.5

A clear insert sheet, printed in black on a laser printer, shares poetic words to encourage the recipient to correspond through letter writing.

fig. 1.6

Clear circular seals are enclosed to be used by the recipient for their correspondence.

Power of Design

Firm ALEXANDER ISLEY INC.
Creative Direction ALEXANDER ISLEY
Design TARA BENYEI AND GEORGE KOKKINIDIS
Printing JORNIK (BASEBALL) AND RTO GROUP (TISSUE PAPER, LABELS, AND STICKERS)
Manufacturers JORNIK/SUNRISE BUSINESS PRODUCTS

"An effective promotion needs to inspire, encouraging clients to accept your way of thinking."

—Alexander Isley, Alexander Isley Inc.

OBJECTIVE Alexander Isley Inc. wanted to create a keepsake promotion to promote their business and to draw attention to the strength and power of great design.

AUDIENCE The baseball-inspired promotion was distributed to existing and prospective clientele, primarily marketing and corporate communications executives. Three hundred were produced. Roughly 150 to 200 were given away as holiday gifts; the rest were used throughout the year in new business promotional efforts.

CONCEPT The design team chose the baseball because of its strength in design for both form and function. It was also a well-known object that everyone would relate to. Its smooth white leather juxtaposed against a highly textural, scarlet-red stitching is not only stunning to look at but also highly functional, a mastery in aerodynamics. The ball is imprinted with the firm's name redrawn in a way that is reminiscent of baseball graphics. By having the entire team—from design and production to account management and bookkeeping—sign the ball, the object became personalized.

MESSAGE The main message was to get clients to think about the power of great design. A secondary message positions the firm as team players.

RESPONSE The firm has received numerous thank-you notes and phone calls, generating new business for the team.

fig. 1.1

The 3" x 3" (7.5 x 7.5 cm) adjoining booklet is printed in two colors, PMS red and black, on Plainfield Opaque smooth 100 lb. text.

The baseball is wrapped with onionskin paper imprinted in PMS 1797 red. The graphics play off the ball's aerodynamic design while the text makes references to the game of baseball.

fig. 1.2

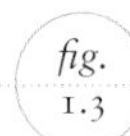

Belizio and Century Expanded BT, the firm's corporate fonts, are used throughout.

fig. 1.4

The package is personalized with two custom die-cut labels printed on Starliner 70 lb. text label stock in blinding white.

The promotion comes in a cylinder-shaped tin wrapped with natural cardboard stock.

Once the screw-off metal container is opened, a hand-signed, custom-imprinted baseball is revealed.

Luminous Objective

Firm Orlando Facioli Design
Creative Direction Orlando Facioli
Design Orlando Facioli
Printing Confetti (serigraphy on lamps) and TAYO (serigraphy on packaging)
Manufacturers Confetti (polypropylene for lamps) and TAYO (polypropylene for packaging)

"Everyone is tired of the same solutions. This type of work brings us to a different level of creativity where the solutions can come from any kind of material. We are not arrested to paper."

—Orlando Facioli, Orlando Facioli Design

OBJECTIVE Orlando Facioli Design wanted to create a promotion that would illuminate their market niche, an interesting combination of graphic and object design.

AUDIENCE The innovative package was targeted toward prospective corporate clientele. It was used to establish the firm as a leading player in the design industry. Initially 400 were distributed. The promotion is still used as a gift given to every new client.

CONCEPT To really communicate their uniqueness in the marketplace, Orlando Facioli Design wanted to not only incorporate two- and three-dimensional thinking but also utilize alternative materials and techniques. It was also important to involve the recipient in some way. In the promotion, the use of light symbolically represents creativity and imagination. Six patterns were created, three in orange and three in green.

MESSAGE Experience brilliant design that breaks away from traditional approaches.

RESPONSE This inventive keepsake attracted client work from such companies as Absolut Vodka, L'Oreal, and Avon, each with an interest in creating work that uses alternative materials. The promotional package also generated interest with both graphic and object-design publications. The piece has received various international awards, including the grand prize in the London International Awards for design.

fig. 1.1

The plastic polypropylene assembles to a 7" x 8" (18 x 20.5 cm) cube light. The transparent plastic material creates a vibrant, almost fluorescent glow when a light source is added.

fig. 1.2

The luminous promotion is mailed in a clear recyclable, polypropylene packaging. The only point of contact is a website listing.

fig.
2.1

An interesting array of circular patterns adorns each of the cube light objects. To imprint the surface, serigraphy is employed. Orange and green are the colors of choice.

Picture Perfect

OBJECTIVE Real Art Design Group wanted to develop a keepsake that would make a unique connection to the spirit of the holiday season.

AUDIENCE The keepsake promotion was distributed to current and prospective clientele as well as vendors. Three hundred and fifty were produced.

CONCEPT Focusing on the sharing of memories, the firm decided to develop a photo kit, containing a handcrafted mini photo album and Holga 120S camera. The theme for the initiative was *Photo4: A Picture Perfect New Year.* The medium-format Holga 120S camera is like no other. Its lack of sharpness, constant distortion, accidental double exposure, and other such mishaps give the pictures it takes character. To help recipients with their picture-taking experience, the firm included operating instructions and helpful hints on the back of the custom wrap. To carry the initiative further, the design firm held a photo contest, asking recipients to send in their favorite image. The firm even offered to handle the processing of their first roll film. Once all entries were in, they were posted to the firm's virtual gallery called HolGallery. The winner, chosen by a panel of judges, received a professionally framed 16" x 20" (40.5 x 51 cm) archival print of the prize image. The online gallery helped to showcase what other clients were doing with their Photo4 kit. It also drew people to the design firm's website.

MESSAGE Share memories and the magic of creativity.

RESPONSE The response to the holiday promotion was one of excitement and interest. One client was particularly intrigued, because the promotion inspired a derivative assignment project.

Firm REAL ART DESIGN GROUP, INC.
Creative Direction CHRIS WIRE
Design JEREMY LOYD AND KATE ROHRER
Production CRYSTAL RHODES, PATRICE HALL, JAIN WATSON, AND BETSY MCFADDIN
Printing PATENTED PRINTING
Special Techniques CUSTOM FORMED PRODUCTS (DIE-CUTTING)
MANUFACTURERS W.C. SIMS CO. (TIN BOX) AND FREESTYLE PHOTOGRAPHIC SUPPLIES (CAMERA AND FILM)

"These projects not only challenge us to try new printing and manufacturing techniques but also give us an opportunity for a team-building experience, because we do all the fulfillment and assembly in-house."

—Kate Rohrer, Real Art Design Group, Inc.

fig. 1.3

The matchbook-style cover, printed on Strathmore Script 130 lb. smooth cover, completely wraps around the album, protecting the interior French-folded pages.

fig. 1.1

The 2004 handcrafted photo album, cleverly titled *photo4*, is bound with silver grommets and a red ribbon, adding a festive touch.

fig. 1.2

Inside the custom album, printed on Pegasus 100 lb. text in midnight black, are die-cut windows, each sized to fit 6" x 6" (15 x 15 cm) prints created by the Holga 120S.

fig. 2.1

A Holga 120S serves as a fun and creative add-on to the "Picture Perfect New Year" promotion. The camera's optical imperfections make every picture it takes a surprise.

fig. 2.2

The picture-perfect promotion, packaged inside a tin box and closed shut with a custom die-cut and embossed wrap, is accented with a square hangtag. Both the wrap and hangtag are printed on Strathmore Script 130 lb. smooth cover.

Think Local

Firm Innovative

Creative Direction/Design Lars Lawson

Photography Arnie Benton, Kent Esmeier, Patrick Laurent, Conrad Piccirillo, Tom Stahl, and Lars Lawson

Production Matrix Imaging (film process and digital scanning)

Printing/Bindery Print Exchange (calendar) and Xerox Phaser 7300 (label and hangtag)

OBJECTIVE Innovative was looking to produce a multipurpose promotion. First and foremost, it had to serve as the design firm's year-end holiday gift to clients. Second, it needed to appeal to the local retail market as a desirable product. Last, whatever was created needed to involve the entire design staff.

AUDIENCE The weekly planner was distributed to existing and prospective clients as well as suppliers. It was also sold locally through retailers. Five hundred were produced.

CONCEPT The firm chose to create a weekly planner, something that many people rely on every day to keep organized. The black-and-white, horizontally oriented planner features intriguing, journalistic photos of out-of-the-way places in metropolitan Indianapolis. The firm chose to venture far from the typical tourist sites to make their day planner distinctive. With no specific dates featured in the grid, the planner will not be outdated anytime soon, allowing the firm to use the project for a few years.

MESSAGE The design team at Innovative can produce work that not only is creative and distinctive but also performs in a myriad of ways.

RESPONSE The planner has been a big hit among the design firm's existing clientele. The work has also made a strong impression with the local consumer market. If the success of the planner continues, the design firm plans to produce more.

"Every year, Innovative creates a gift or product that reflects our creativity, a symbol of the type of work we do. It means more to our clients and helps sell us as a creative firm."

—Lars Lawson, Innovative

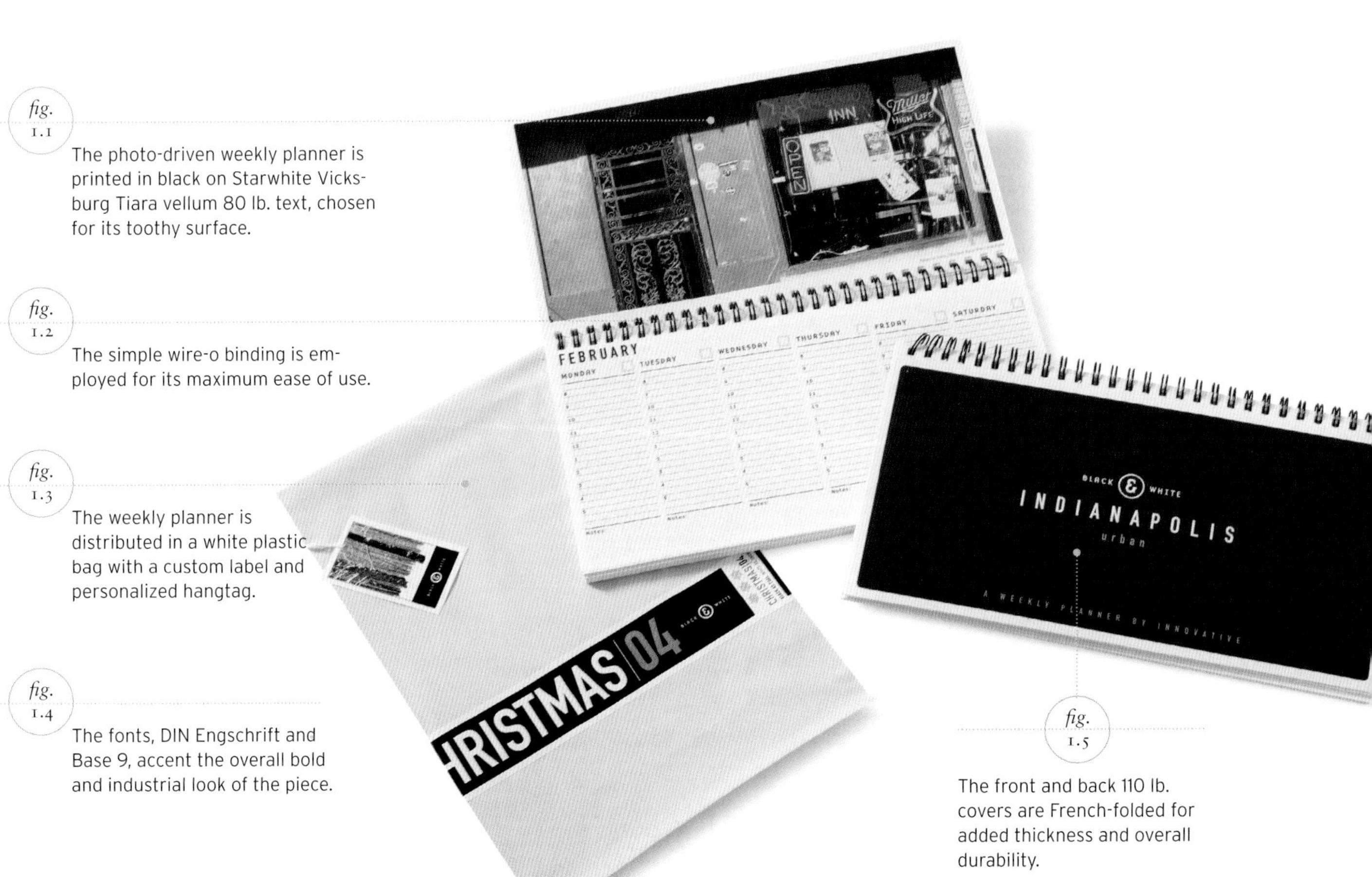

fig. 1.1 The photo-driven weekly planner is printed in black on Starwhite Vicksburg Tiara vellum 80 lb. text, chosen for its toothy surface.

fig. 1.2 The simple wire-o binding is employed for its maximum ease of use.

fig. 1.3 The weekly planner is distributed in a white plastic bag with a custom label and personalized hangtag.

fig. 1.4 The fonts, DIN Engschrift and Base 9, accent the overall bold and industrial look of the piece.

fig. 1.5 The front and back 110 lb. covers are French-folded for added thickness and overall durability.

Worth Noting

Firm Hand Made Group
Creative Direction Alessandro Esteri
Design Alessandro Esteri and Davide Premuni
Printing Nava Press
Special Techniques Nava Press (embossing and hole punching)

"I always try to be innovative, making projects that have an intelligent attitude."

—Alessandro Esteri, Hand Made Group

OBJECTIVE Hand Made Group wanted to create a unique keepsake promotion that would be useful to clients on a daily basis.

AUDIENCE The series of notebooks was sent to existing and prospective clientele as well as the media. Two thousand were produced and hand delivered.

CONCEPT An agenda system was created, something clients would use routinely throughout the year. The series of twelve notebooks includes one book for every month. Each month is distinguished by the number of holes punched in the top-right corner of the notebook. January, the first month of the year, uses one hole, February utilizes two holes, March employs three holes, and so on. The project, titled *One Year of White Pages*, is held together by a black string.

MESSAGE Strong design can be executed in a simple yet elegant manner.

RESPONSE The design firm received a lot of press coverage, as well as a few new business contacts, as a result of the promotional endeavor.

fig. 2.1 The agenda system uses the font Helvetica Neue throughout.

fig. 2.2 The perfect-bound series of twelve notebooks comes wrapped with black cotton thread tied in a bow.

fig. 1.1 Each cover, printed on Fedrigoni Arcoprint Edizioni in black, is embossed with the title, *One Year of White Pages*.

fig. 1.2 Each book is uniquely punched in the top-right corner: one hole for January, two holes for February, and so on.

fig. 2.3 Inside, the notebooks contain mostly white space except for the first page, which features the firm's contact information and a space for the recipient's name. It is printed in PMS 7 warm gray.

A *New* Spin

Firm Hornall Anderson Design Works
Creative Direction Jack Anderson
Design Sonja Max, Leo Raymundo, Henry Yiu, and Andrew Wicklund
Illustration Andrew Wicklund and Sonja Max
Printing G.A.C./Cenveo Seattle

"There are people who have their Christmas gifts wrapped by Thanksgiving and will not have the fun of using wrapping paper that is sent to them in early December. Start designing sooner!"

—Sonja Max, Hornall Anderson Design Works

OBJECTIVE The design team at Hornall Anderson Design Works wanted to create a promotion that would not only provide them with an opportunity to explore but also serve as a functional gift to distribute during the Christmas holiday season.

AUDIENCE The collection of wrapping papers was sent to clients, friends, and employees as a holiday gift. A quantity of 1,500 was printed of each sheet.

CONCEPT The design team created a collection of wrapping papers that puts a new spin on Christmas paper graphics. Using a nontraditional approach, one of the designs presents a sophisticated grid of numbers with twenty-five, the date of Christmas, embedded in random intervals. Another uses a well-known Christmas carol and repeats the lyrics in an interesting and graphic way. The other two designs are much more freeflowing and whimsical. One uses various popular gift items and arranges them into smiling faces, while the other makes a humorous comparison of tree owners and the Christmas trees they buy.

MESSAGE Happy holidays from your friends at Hornall Anderson Design Works!

RESPONSE Clients and friends loved the collection. Many positive comments were made on the unique twist of each design. Hornall Anderson Design Works' employees also enjoyed the paper. Everyone had a lot of fun guessing which colleague designed each sheet.

fig. 1.1

The collection of wrapping paper is distributed in a 9" x 11" (23 x 28 cm) clear envelope with a custom label.

fig. 2.1

The various wrapping papers are printed on Husky Smooth Book 60 lb. uncoated text stock, a nice contrast from the typical high-gloss commercial gift wrap.

fig. 2.2

Two dominant colors, PMS 1807 deep burgundy and PMS 5787 steel green, are used throughout the collection. The white of the paper is employed as an accent.

New Orleans Style

Firm H, Strategic Graphic Design
Creative Direction Winnie Hart
Design Winnie Hart and Suzy Rivera
Printing/Bindery Harvey Press (catalog, bellyband, notecards, file folders and, journal covers), Sir Speedy (labels), and Brennan's (line sheets for journals)
Manufacturers Packaging Services Corporation (plastic boxes) and Envelopemall.com (envelopes)

"We wanted to develop expertise in the product-design market and felt the only way to learn was to have the experience ourselves, expanding our boundaries by developing a new creative channel. We learned a lot, and it has helped us to remember to think beyond the client and into the mind of the consumer in everything we do."

—Winnie Hart, H

OBJECTIVE As a way to sharpen their expertise in the product-design market, H wanted to develop a product line of their own that could be given away as keepsakes to clients as well as sold in the retail market.

AUDIENCE As a keepsake promotion, the work is continually distributed to the firm's existing client base. In the retail paper product arena, the line targets the style-conscious consumer.

CONCEPT The firm decided to develop a line of New Orleans-inspired stationery. In addition to the file folders, notecards, and journals, the stationery collection consists of thank-you cards, greeting cards, letterhead, note pads, and gift wrap. A catalog, featuring several lines of stationery, was also developed.

MESSAGE Experience the essence of historic New Orleans.

RESPONSE As a result of the promotional initiative, the firm secured several product-design opportunities from corporate and retail chains requesting exclusive brands for their businesses. The exquisite line of stationery is now sold in more than sixty retail locations. In addition, the work has been profiled in six major retail magazines.

fig. 1.1

An 8 1/2" (21.5 cm) square catalog is printed on accent opaque 65 lb. white smooth cover in nine colors—PMS 124, 1817, 257, 550, 552, 5797, 612, 704, and 9123—plus black.

fig. 1.2

The catalog is sealed shut with an embossed bellyband made from the same stock. The vertically striped bellyband is imprinted with seven colors: PMS 124, 9123, 704, 612, 399, 257, and 552.

fig. 2.1

The set of eight $6^1/4$" (16 cm) square notecards, printed in yellow ochre—PMS 124 and PMS 9123—on 80 lb. smooth pure white cover, come with white envelopes packaged in a clear plastic box with a custom label that wraps around to the back.

fig. 2.2

The matching journal employs the same trim size, stock, and ink as the notecards, while the interior sheets are printed in PMS 430 gray on 70 lb. Glacier opaque smooth white text.

fig. 2.3

The set of nine file folders, printed in the line's two signature colors on manila tag, is packaged inside a clear plastic bag that seals shut on the side. It employs a custom label that is imprinted with five colors: black, PMS 612 olive green, 704 cranberry red, 550 slate blue, and 124 yellow ochre.

fig. 2.4

The series of keepsakes uses various forms of Franklin Gothic and Trade Gothic typefaces.

From 2D to 3D

Firm Fan Works Design, LLC

Creative Direction/Design Dawn Ripple McFadin

Illustration Dawn Ripple McFadin and Kevin McFadin

Printing York Graphic Services (wrapping paper and origami manual covers) and HP LaserJet 5000dn (origami manual interior)

Manufacturers York Graphic Services

"We know that clients are hit with promotions and mailings on a regular basis. That's why we always strive to design something a bit different, something with a twist. The concept of wrapping paper and origami provided a good framework for us to generate illustrations in."

—Dawn Ripple McFadin, Fan Works Design, LLC

fig. 1.1

The collection of decorative papers and the origami booklet front and back covers are printed in four-color process with a satin aqueous varnish on Mead Westvaco Sterling Ultra C1S 70 lb. stock, chosen for its excellent folding ability in multiple directions with minimal cracking.

OBJECTIVE Fan Works Design was looking for a creative way to showcase their illustration capabilities. The team liked the idea of producing decorative wrapping paper but felt, as a standalone, it was not engaging enough. To make the illustrated paper more interesting and dynamic, they decided to produce a companion origami booklet, changing the two-dimensional promotion into an interactive, three-dimensional work of art.

AUDIENCE The target audience was primarily existing clientele. The paper was also used as a giveaway to prospects at The Illustrators Club of Washington D.C., Maryland, and Virginia's Portfolio Show. About three hundred were produced.

CONCEPT So that the origami paper could be used at any time during the year, the firm opted to illustrate a variety of themes. The cover and back sheets are the only holiday-based sheets created. The origami manual provides fully illustrated, step-by-step instructions on how to fold the assortment of decorative papers to make various objects, further encouraging interaction with the promotion and its illustrations.

MESSAGE The main message to clients is two-fold. The first is heartfelt thanks for their business over the year; the other is to call attention to the firm's diverse illustration capabilities.

RESPONSE The origami wrapping paper project received positive response, with many requests for additional sheets by both existing clients and prospects. It also helped to inform clients about the range of illustration styles offered in-house by Fan Works Design.

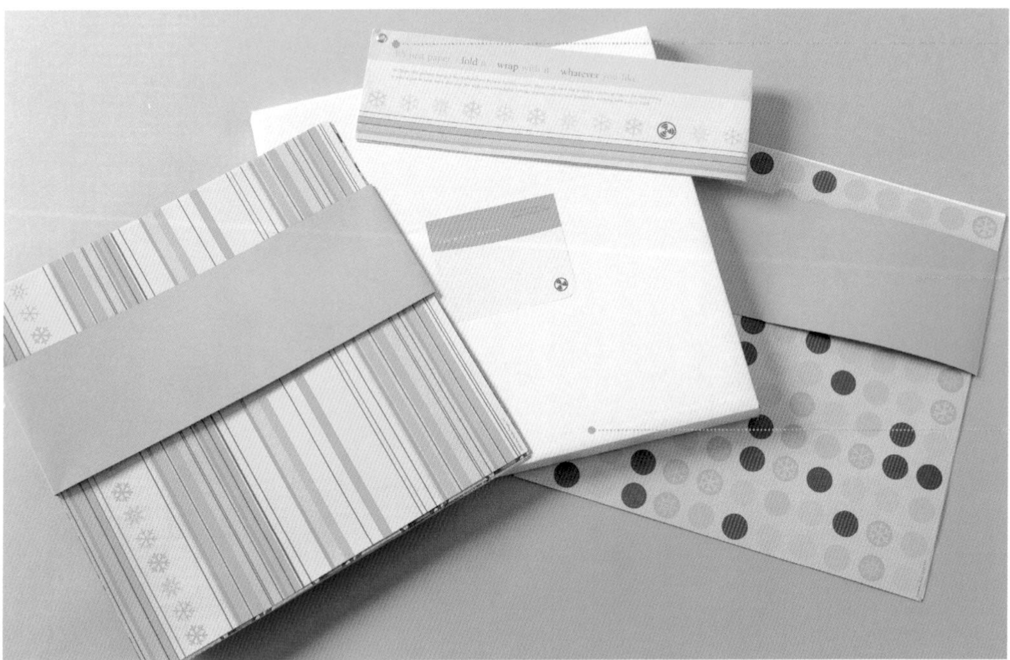

fig. 1.2

The rivet-bound origami manual is imprinted with the same graphics and color scheme as the lead cove sheet. The firm's logo, cleverly integrated in the pattern, works as a nice accent.

fig. 1.3

The wrapping papers are held together by a matching blue bellyba made of Fraser Brights 65 lb. cove

fig. 1.4

The entire package is mailed in a white corrugated box with a label.

fig. 2.1

The origami wrapping papers are illustrated in two distinct styles, one as a step-and-repeat pattern and the other as a layered montage.

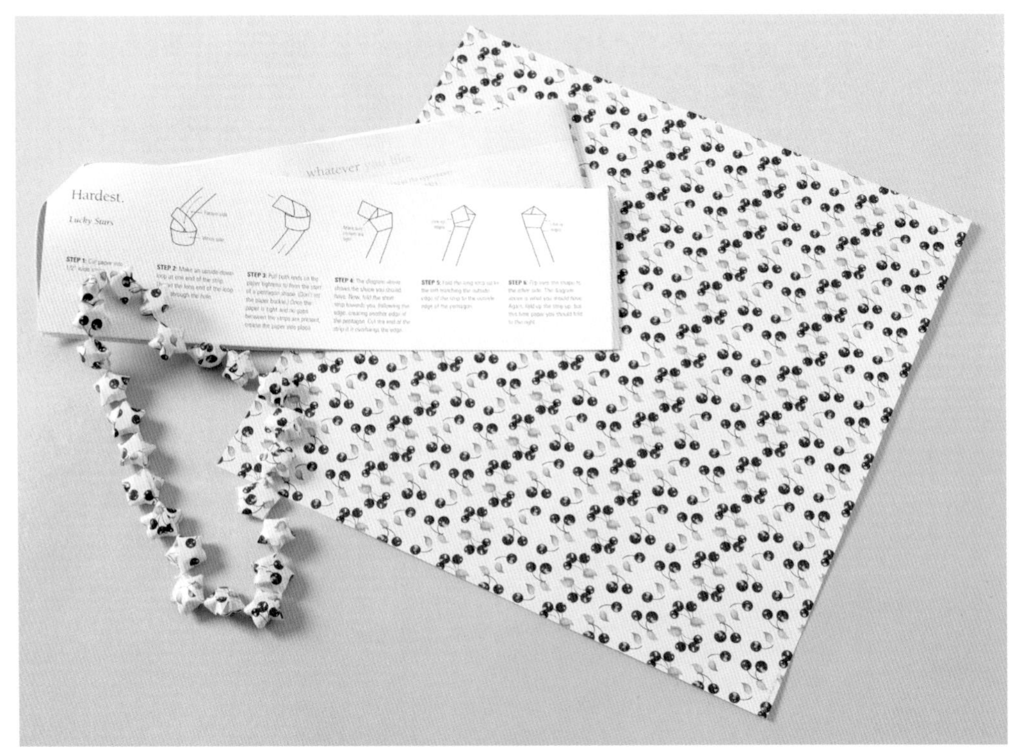

fig. 3.1

The manual's interior pages are printed in-house in black and white on a laser printer.

fig. 3.2

Each booklet is hand-trimmed and bound between two French-folded cover sheets with a rivet.

Yearly Endeavor

Firms FrankSturgesReps, Salvato Coe & Gabor Design, and Baesman Printing Corporation

Creative Direction/Design Layne Peters

Illustration Noma Bliss, Daniel Chang, Josef Gast, Matt Curtius, The Heads of State, David Hollenbach, Roman Klonek, Franklin Hammond, Rich Lillash, Michael Miller, Gina Triplett, and Walter Vasconcelos

Printing Baesman Printing Corporation

"I always think it's a good thing when creative minds get together. It allows for a different perspective, ultimately producing a better finished product."

—Layne Peters, Salvato Coe & Gabor Design

OBJECTIVE For six years, FrankSturgesReps, Salvato Coe & Gabor Design, and Baesman Printing Corporation have collaborated to produce a theme-based wall calendar promotion to draw attention to their various services.

AUDIENCE The primary target audience for the artist representative was advertising agencies, graphic designers, book publishers, magazines, and record companies, while the design firm and printer targeted more corporate accounts. Five thousand calendars were split between the three firms.

CONCEPT This year's theme was *Oxymoron*, two words that seemingly contradict one another. *Miserable bliss, same difference, wise fool, buried alive*, and *pretty ugly* are just some of the familiar oxymoron phrases used throughout the illustrated keepsake calendar. Each of the participating firms received calendars and envelopes customized with their mailing address.

MESSAGE Remember FrankSturgesReps, Salvato Coe & Gabor Design, and Baesman Printing Corporation for your illustration, design, and printing needs.

RESPONSE After six years, recipients look forward to what the collaborators will come up with next. Although there has been significant work generated for each of the participants as a result of the calendar, the promotion serves more as a constant reminder of each firm's presence in the market.

fig. 1.1

The 8 3/4" x 8 3/4" (22 x 22 cm) calendar, entitled *Oxymoron*, is printed in four-color process on Unisource porcelain ultra 100 lb. silk cover and text and hole-punched for hanging.

fig. 1.2

An aqueous coating is used throughout for durability.

fig. 1.3

The primary font is a custom-designed typeface created to work with the overall graphic look and feel of the calendar. It is supported by the Mrs Eaves family of fonts.

fig. 1.4

The illustrated calendar comes in a custom-designed envelope made of Williamhouse and Unisource 28 lb. white wove.

fig. 2.1

Inside the whimsical calendar, familiar oxymoron phrases are used. This highly stylized image by artist Josef Gast features the oxymoron *same difference*.

fig. 1.1

The set arrives with a custom insert card, imprinted with PMS 871 gold metallic on one side, wishing holiday cheer.

fig. 1.2

Each coaster is printed in four-color process on heavy Fibermark absorbent paper on the front and PMS 477 brown on Curious Collection Lightspecks Sky 80 lb. uncoated cover on the back. The front and back sheets are glued together with chipboard in the center for additional stability.

fig. 1.3

The series are cost-effectively gang-printed six up, two rows of three, on the same offset press sheet.

fig. 1.4

The entire package is mailed in a 5" x 5" (12.5 x 12.5 cm) white envelope imprinted with PMS 477 brown to match the backside of the coasters.

Coastal Inspired

OBJECTIVE After moving into a newly renovated space located on Pacific Coast Highway in Hermosa Beach, California, the team at IE Design + Communications decided to share their excitement about their new locale.

AUDIENCE The series of coasters were mailed to prospective and existing clients as well as vendors, the press, friends, and family. Two thousand were produced.

CONCEPT By creating a set of six coasters, naturally titled *Pacific Coasters*, the design firm was able to build awareness not only of their new location but also of their creativity and ingenuity. To create a series of fashion-savvy coasters, the team researched interior design and home decorating trends. They noticed that coral and shells were very popular as were the colors blue-green and salmon-red. This knowledge helped pave the way for their beach-infused theme. Each *Pacific Coaster* is hand-illustrated in an abstract, ocean-inspired fashion by a different member of the creative team. On the back, poetic, thought-provoking quotes inspire and motivate. The keepsake promotion demonstrates to clients how image, word, form, and function can work together successfully.

MESSAGE What do you get when you move a graphic design firm to the Pacific Coast Highway in Hermosa Beach?

RESPONSE The design firm received tremendous response from their holiday keepsake promotion, including several projects that came in as a direct result of the mailer. The West Coast firm has also received numerous emails and phone calls thanking and complimenting them on their exquisite work. Several people even framed the coasters. The firm is still receiving requests for more.

Firm IE Design + Communications
Creative Direction Marcie Carson
Design/ Illustration Marcie Carson, Cya Nelson, Amy Klass, Jane Kim, and Nicole Lehmann
Printing Roadrunner Press
Manufacturers Spicers Paper (paper)

"When you can combine creative talent, unique designs, and functional items, you always have a successful mailing."

—Marcie Carson, IE Design + Communications

Spice It Up

Firm Capsule
Creative Direction Brian Adducci
Design Brian Adducci
Illustration Anchalee Champbundabongse
Printing Diversified Graphics (spice labels) and Art-house (T-shirt)
Manufacturers Wayzata Bay Spice Company (spice blend), Fruit of the Loom (T-shirts), and Uline (anti-static bags)

"Outerspice, created as a way to maintain a relevant position in the mind of the audience, is an example of the Capsule brand coming to life in the form of a product."

—Brian Adducci, Capsule

OBJECTIVE Capsule wanted to produce a unique and memorable holiday keepsake promotion, one that clients would savor for months after the holidays.

AUDIENCE Outerspice was distributed to current and prospective clients as well as friends and family. Initially 500 units were produced. The spicy endeavor is now available for purchase on the Web.

CONCEPT The design firm chose to venture outside what might be seen as typical or expected when it came to their year-end promotion. To tie into the Capsule brand, the firm chose an outer-space theme presented in a fun, whimsical fashion. Outerspice, a bold and spicy steak rub, became the brainchild of their efforts.

MESSAGE Experience the Capsule brand in a fun and delectable way.

RESPONSE Everyone who received the spicy mix began to inquire about purchasing the product. After experiencing tremendous success with the steak rub, Capsule launched a full line of Outerspice products, including T-shirts and desktop screensavers available for purchase on the Web at www.capsuleshak.com. To continue their retail success, Capsule has launched another product called Cocoa Mang. It is currently being considered for full-scale distribution by a regional retail grocery chain.

fig. 1.1

Screensavers, called desktops, are yet another part of the growing Outerspice line.

fig. 2.1

The Outerspice steak rub, a unique blend of ten spices, comes in a round tin customized with a signature label.

fig. 2.2

The Outerspice label, printed in four-color process plus an overall aqueous coating on 60 lb. pressure-sensitive semigloss label stock, boasts a custom logotype accented by the Capsule corporate font Akzidenz Grotesk.

fig. 2.3

The out-of-this-world meat enhancer is distributed in a silver antistatic bag that seals shut. The brown label that accents the silver package is offset printed in PMS 7540 on 60 lb. Fasson brown kraft uncoated paper.

fig. 3.1

T-shirts, an extension of the Outerspice line, are silkscreen-printed with the signature Outerspice character in three colors: PMS 374 light green, PMS 376 green, and white on dark gray.

fig. 3.2

The imprinted shirts also come in a silver antistatic bag with a custom label.

Get Production Savvy

No.
01

REDEFINE THE VISUAL EXPERIENCE

WHEN IT COMES TO CAPTIVATING AN AUDIENCE, creatives are beginning to redefine the visual experience. Because of advancements in technology, opportunities to be truly creative abound. No longer are there limitations on what can be produced. Unconventional materials and techniques are finding their way into promotional initiatives in inventive combinations. Metal, wood, leather, fabric, and a vast array of plastics are being employed as interesting alternatives to paper where processes such as transfers, etching, laser-cutting, serigraphy, sculpted embossing, and stitching are the imprints of choice. Print is adopting a more animated and three-dimensional surface, especially with the use of lenticular tip-ins and anaglyphic stereo usage. Even the application of ink has become more dynamic. It is glowing in the dark, glitter-infused, thermo-sensitive, and layered in alternative ways to create intriguing effects. New forms of bindings and fasteners are being employed. Buttons, bones, elastics, magnets, feathers, clasps, sticks, screws, and wire are all being repurposed as bindery. "New materials must be introduced for people to touch, manipulate, and get involved with," shares Orlando Facioli of Orlando Facioli Design. "We need to go far from the common places." Formats have also come a long way. From custom-molded containers, welded packages, inflatable objects, and intricate die-cut boxes and books to multipieced assemblages that pop up, fold out, perforate off, assemble, and light up, today's promotions are putting a new face on the once static mailer. "We're always seeking out new materials and resources. We have folders and bins of samples that might work in the future," shares Robert Clancy of Spiral Design Studio. "Nothing is outside the realm of possibility. It all depends on what we're trying to say and who we're trying to target." The architecture of the promotional package is evolving, and creatives no longer feel locked into traditional approaches.

From custom-molded containers, welded packages, inflatable objects, and intricate die-cut boxes and books to multipieced assemblages that pop up, fold out, perforate off, assemble, and light up, today's promotions are putting a new face on the once static mailer.

No.
02

INNOVATE WITH PURPOSE

Experimental production should never triumph over effective communication. The clever use of techniques and materials is effective only when it visually enhances the overall messaging. Employing alternative production for the sake of being different is not innovative but a gimmick and should be avoided. "We see lots of promotions that try to disguise a poor concept with great production," says Rule29's Justin Ahrens. "In the end, concept is always king." Lars Lawson of Innovative agrees, "Beauty is only skin deep. The idea always has to come first. Meaningful, profound design must have an inner layer of depth and purpose behind it." When the message drives the design, innovative production can truly enliven the visual experience.

If budget constraints are an issue, consider repurposing a ready-made container as a cost-effective way to package your promotion. Sometimes the addition of custom printing, labels, or handmade accents onto an existing substrate or container can make a promotion really stand out. "Custom add-ons lend an air of exclusivity," adds Maureen Mooney of Spiral Design Studio. "Recipients get the sense that the piece was made especially for them." In addition, advancements in inkjet printing have opened the door for everyone, seasoned to newcomer, to explore, even when budgets are tight. The decreasing cost of equipment along with the substantial increase in quality has encouraged many to bring the production of their promotional materials in-house. This cost-effective approach has significantly changed print runs to well-targeted quantities, ultimately eliminating the need for storage of offset promotional items that become outdated as soon as they get off the press. The flexibility of print-on-demand from the desktop printer allows for customization and up-to-date changes for each printing. Desktop technology has also allowed creatives to produce high-quality promotional materials using a variety of surfaces from canvas to watercolor paper. "The real beauty of being able to print in-house is experimentation. I can test out new formats, concepts, and materials quickly and easily, without relying on an outside vendor," shares Wendy K.S. Berman of Iron Blender Studios. "It also allows me to personalize promotional materials, especially leave-behinds. Desktop printers are bringing the world of fast-food to our office but without the guilt!" Inkjet printing on unconventional surfaces such as wood, metal, tile, or plastic requires treating the surface first. You will also need access to a large-format, flatbed printer with high head clearance. For more in-depth information on utilizing inkjet printing in innovative ways, go to www.DigitalAtelier.com. The three partners—Dorothy Simpson Krause, Bonny Lhotka, and Karin Schminke—share years of experience integrating inkjet printing with traditional tools and processes. Print-on-demand using desktop printers is an area that that will continue to expand as time goes on. "It offers flexibility, providing better design with smaller budgets," says Mike Tuttle of Planet 10. "It begins to level the playing field." Technology has revolutionized the way promotions are produced.

No.
03

VENTURE OUTSIDE THE NORM

To source unusual materials and techniques, many are looking outside the traditional venues. From local hardware, building, and office supply outlets to suppliers for the automotive, medical, fashion, and craft industries, engaging solutions are being discovered. "Take materials out of their common application and reinvent them, combine materials, and try new mixtures and formats," suggests Lars Harmsen of Starshot. "It is a real challenge, but the results are surprising." To be truly innovative, you must give yourself the freedom to take risks. Realize that without risk there is no reward. "Keep a keen eye, a curiosity about everything, and don't be afraid to experiment and confront failure," advises Nelida Nassar of Nassar Design. "Sometimes accidents make for the best creative encounters. They teach us new skills. Try to listen and be attentive to the muse of creativity that strikes at the most unexpected moments." Discovering new ways to combine different materials and techniques can be challenging, but it can give your promotion the edge that it needs to penetrate the marketplace.

Chapter Four

"A self-promotional publication has to have something substantial to offer, beyond being a show-and-tell piece. You have to be tactful about content, keeping it interesting and balancing it with compelling images. Besides building your profile, it provides an opportunity to partner with a variety of associates."

—Ric Riordon, Riordon Design

PUBLICATION AND NEWSLETTER PROMOTIONS

When it comes to ongoing communications with a target audience, a trend toward an editorial sensibility is evident. This content-driven focus has initiated promotional initiatives that speak to the audience in ways they value. Publication promotions inform, inspire, and entertain. Their storytelling nature engages an audience into participating in the overall messaging. "A self-promotional publication has to have something substantial to offer, beyond being a show-and-tell piece. You have to be tactful about content, keeping it interesting and balancing it with compelling images," offers Ric Riordon of Riordon Design. "Besides building your profile, it provides an opportunity to partner with a variety of associates." Books, magazines, newsletters, e-zines, and weblogs are being explored as alternative ways to connect with an audience.

To create interest, promotion-based publications are experimenting with alternative formats and bindery. The engaging folds, clever inserts, and interesting die-cut shapes create distinction and encourage interaction. Many publications are even boasting unique design and production details that vary depending on the content, making each issue a welcomed surprise. "In my opinion, design must have rough edges to create momentum, making the observer get caught," suggests Lars Harmsen from Magma. "By analyzing the competition and looking at the norm, you will know how to cancel the usual practice." With a premium product, top talent and vendors from paper companies to printers want to participate by donating their time and services. "Once we had the first issue of *In Plain View* in hand, it was easy to get collaborators on board because they could see the quality of the end product and how it could benefit their own marketing efforts," adds Matt Ralph of Plainspoke. By bartering, creatives can collaboratively develop a promotional publication that goes far beyond what their own resources could produce.

Promotional publications not only provide an opportunity to highlight new work and recent endeavors but also serve as a vehicle to introduce innovative and experimental concepts into the culture. "*Plazm* magazine (see page 136) is a laboratory for exploring ideas about form, process, and content, including work we generate, things we want to publish, and collaborative efforts we've done with other designers and artists," shares Joshua Berger of Plazm. By covering content not shown in any other mainstream design publication, *Plazm* magazine was able to establish a niche in the marketplace. The success of the publication became a showcase for the firm's other initiatives, like Plazm Fonts and Plazm Design. When ATTIK developed *Noise* (see page 150), it allowed them a platform from which to really experiment, pushing boundaries outside the limits of client-based work. Every page challenges the viewer to open his or her mind and imagination to new forms of expression. "*Noise* forces us to continually evolve as creative individuals," admits Simon Needham of ATTIK. "It is how we test ourselves to design something that is fresh and unique." Creatives are beginning to reexamine the fundamental methodology in which they promote and showcase their work. Through publication-based initiatives, new pathways are being established in what is possible when it comes to attracting buyers.

Visual Journalism

Firm STVARNIK
Creative Direction/Design SAŠO URUKALO
Copywriting BRINA SVIT
Illustration SAŠO URUKALO
Printing TISKARNA TIPOS
Special Techniques TISKARNA TIPOS (FOIL STAMPING)
Manufacturers TISKARNA TIPOS (BLACK BOX)

"Fish might speak. The fact that we don't understand them doesn't mean that their language doesn't exist. There exists a space to understand them. Words and patterns communicate and capture the world of interpretation."

– Sašo Urukalo, STVARNIK

OBJECTIVE STVARNIK, a design and advertising studio, was in search of an engaging way to present their unique vision and approach to graphic design.

AUDIENCE The target audience was primarily the design community. Three hundred hand-numbered and -signed pieces were produced.

CONCEPT Working in collaboration with author and journalist Brina Svit, creative director Sašo Urukalo developed a bibliophilic artist book called *Silence of the Fishes*. The intricate layering of text and image creates a new language, one that is universal. The book reflects new possibilities in letterforms, design, and storytelling. The text appears in three languages: Slovene, French, and English.

MESSAGE Experience storytelling in a unique way.

RESPONSE The book has generated quite a bit of attention. It was exhibited at the Llys Gallery in Paris and the Visconti Fine Art Kolizej in Slovenija. It has also traveled to the International Graphic Design Biennial in Brno, Czech Republic, as well as the DesignMai Berlin. At the first Biennial of Slovenian Visual Communications held in Ljubljana, the work ranked among the finalists, receiving the award of excellence in book design. The project is also in the library collection at the Cooper-Hewitt National Design Museum in New York City.

fig. 1.1

The artist book comes in a 13 1/2" x 14 1/2" (34.5 x 37 cm) custom black box imprinted with a signature logo.

fig. 1.2

Inside the box sits a three-panel letter-folded wrap with a 1/4" (0.5 cm) spine on the right and left. It is securely cushioned with white thick acrylic felt on all sides.

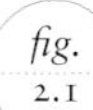

fig. 2.1

Inside the custom wrap is a hand-numbered and -signed book titled *Silence of the Fishes*.

fig. 2.2

The cover features a solid bleed of orange accented by a ruby red hot-foil stamp.

fig. 2.3

A series of single and fold-out illustrated pages, printed using both silkscreen and offset printing techniques, helps to tell the story in a unique way.

Window of Opportunity

Firm Starshot GmbH & Co KG

Creative Direction Lars Harmsen and Tina Weisser

Design Lars Harmsen, Tina Weisser, Steffi Harder, and Axel Gärtner

Illustration Lars Harmsen (*Useless 02*)

Photography Kai Stuht, Gerard Rancien, and Olaf Unverzart

Copywriting Florian Glück and Kai Stuht (*Useless 01*); Melanie Schönthier and Stephan Bernhard (*Useless 02*) with Bill Connors and Luke Lalor (translations for *Useless 02*)

Printing/Bindery Peschke Druck

Special Techniques Storelite Leuchtfarben (glow-in-the dark ink) and Arbeitskreis Prägefoliendruck (embossing)

Manufacturers Schneider Söhne (velvet cover stock for *Useless 02*)

OBJECTIVE Starshot had reached market saturation in the biking industry, peaking in 2003 with their work for the world-renowned Tour de France. To open new markets and enlarge the field of action, the design team decided to target the fashion industry. The idea was to arrange joint ventures between sporting and fashion companies, yielding a much higher budget to create and produce something really exciting. While designing a catalog for the International Trade Fair for Sports Equipment and Fashion (ISPO), Starshot saw its window of opportunity, and the first issue of *Useless* was born.

AUDIENCE The primary target for the publication is major sporting goods and fashion brands. More than 30,000 free copies of *Useless* are distributed twice a year, winter and summer. About 50 percent are distributed during the ISPO with the remaining issues mailed to select shops all over Germany, many now clients of Starshot. The publication is available in both German and English.

CONCEPT To capture the attention of both the fashion and sporting markets, Starshot knew they had to create something really different. It had to be exciting and certainly something that an enthusiast would want to hold onto. Throughout each issue, high-action photography is supported by captivating editorial interviews with top-notch athletes. The publication's show-stopping presentation boasts innovation: foil stamping, embossing, glitter-infused varnish, glow-in-the-dark ink, and metallic and fluorescent colors layered in highly creative ways. The overall format and eye-catching covers make *Useless* stand out from the typical sporting or fashion magazine, truly creating a buzz.

MESSAGE Dazzle the eye and stimulate the mind with engaging, behind-the-scene profiles of well-known athletes posed in high-fashion clothing.

RESPONSE There is nothing like *Useless* existing in Europe, and for Starshot the market was theirs for the taking. By the time *Useless 01* came out, clients were knocking down their door to advertise in the next issue. To further increase profitability, Starshot designs many of the ads that grace their publication. It not only allows them to control the overall look but also gives them a foot in the door for future work with an entirely new client base.

"Many of the companies we worked with while doing *Useless* are now commissioning us for other projects. This magazine has opened a lot of doors for us."

—Lars Harmsen, Starshot

fig. 1.1

Useless 02, on the other hand, has a look and feel all its own. The highly tactile, plush cover is charmingly imprinted with a silver emboss—not an easy thing to do on velvet.

fig. 1.2

Useless 01's eye-catching cover features a strong graphic using both foil embossing and tightly registered glow-in-the-dark ink. These extraordinary finishing techniques give a high-end, luxury feel to the overall book.

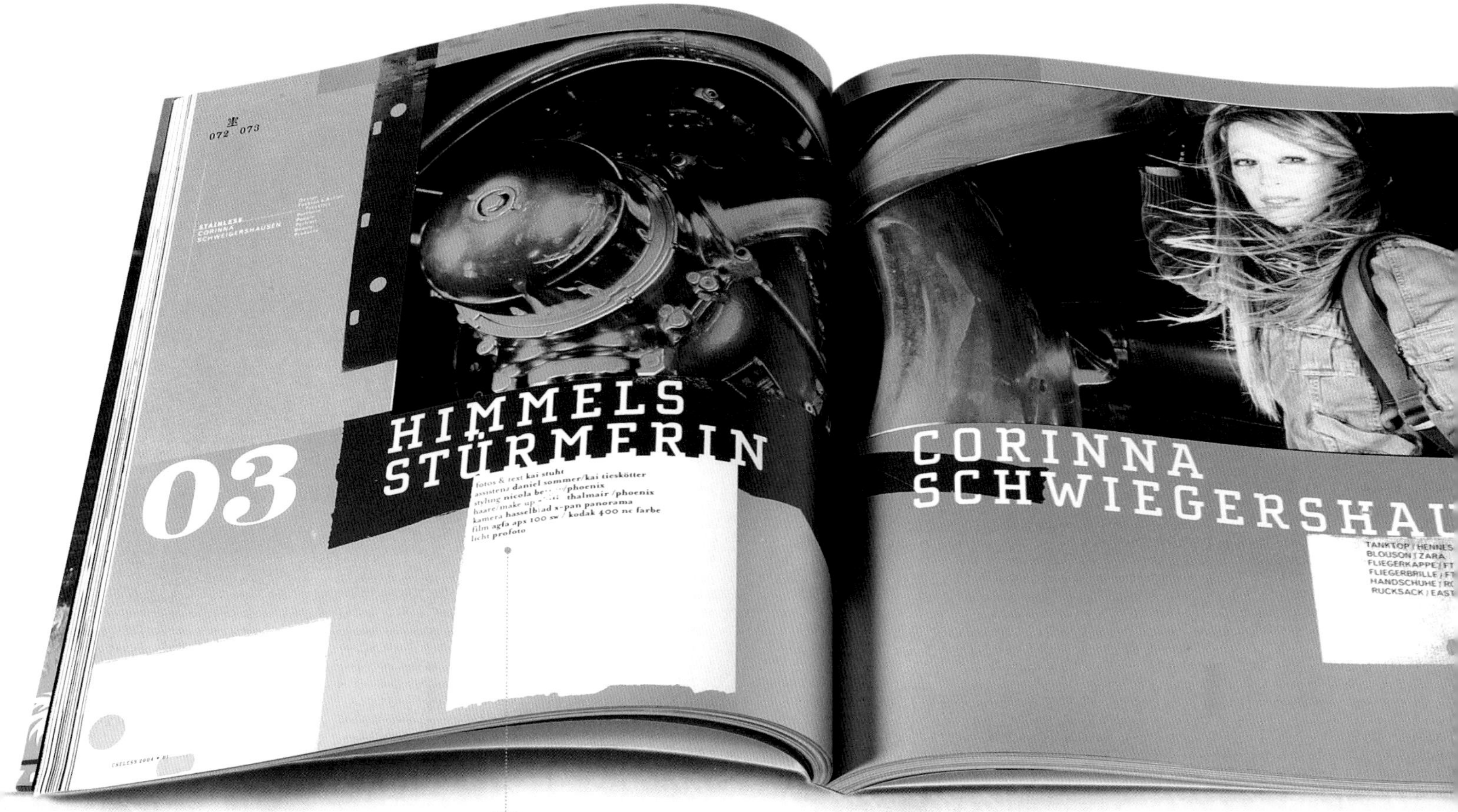

fig. 2.1

In *Useless 01*, cutting-edge graphics and text are overlaid with metallic and fluorescent inks to add excitement to each spread.

fig. 3.1

Useless 02 employs glitter-infused varnish to activate its spreads. Throughout the publication, images are overlaid with varnish, contrasting matte and glossy to get dynamic effects.

An Inside Look

Firm Mirko Ilić Corporation
Creative Direction/Design Mirko Ilić
Photography Various
Copywriting Marci Sutin Levin and Adam D. Tihany
Printing/Bindery Mondadori Printing SpA (book) and Darby Printing & Litho (notecards)
Special Techniques Mondadori Printing SpA (die-cut)
Client Tihany Design

"Adam's work is never on the outside of a structure but on the inside. Typically, one must walk into the door and through the lobby to find what he has created. So, it was important that the book show layers, a peeling back or entering into to his work."

–Mirko Ilić, Mirko Ilić Corporation

OBJECTIVE Tihany Design was interested in producing a publication that would feature the work of their studio. Principal Adam D. Tihany, a widely recognized, internationally known hospitality designer, sought out Mirko Ilić to develop an engaging and eye-catching format. Because the two designers had worked together on many projects, Tihany felt Ilić was the perfect choice to capture his vision.

AUDIENCE As a promotional book, the primary target market was existing and prospective clients, including operators and developers of five-star hotels, restaurateurs, and leading chefs. The book is also being sold in trade book outlets and online. Fifteen hundred were produced. This is the second book in a series.

CONCEPT *Tihany Style: Hospitality Design* is a custom publication with a special die-cut cover and end pages, featuring the initials of Adam Tihany. To add distinction, three fluorescent color schemes were created. The layered design uncovers Tihany's most significant projects from late 1999 to 2004. Throughout the book, Tihany's world-class hospitality designs are profiled. Quotes from design's leading visionaries follow each project. A traveling line of biographical text sits at the bottom of each spread, bringing the back matter to the front. The book closes with a distinguished picture of hospitality designer Adam D. Tihany. Each book is sent out to clients gift-wrapped in black or silver paper.

MESSAGE Come experience the unique vision of Adam D. Tihany.

RESPONSE As a promotional device, the book has been well received and serves as a visual showcase of sophistication and refinement. It also provides insight into the hospitality designer's practices and philosophies in an interesting and engaging way. Many professionals as well as students have purchased the book as a source of inspiration.

fig. 1.1

A series of three custom die-cut books are available in florescent PMS 805 red, 804 orange, and 802 green. Each custom cover is silkscreen-printed on Pouché black stock wrapped over board.

fig. 1.2

A matching set of notecards was created to complement the distinctive publication, each printed in the same fluorescent colors as the books.

fig. 2.1

The endpapers boast a full coverage of florescent ink, each matching the cover accent color.

fig. 2.2

Inside the highly visual book, each spread was printed in four-color process.

fig. 2.3

A traveling line of text sits at the bottom of each spread and functions as the biography.

fig. 3.1

The overall shape of the accent quote mimics a strong design element on the opposing page. In this particular spread, the copy is structured to play off the strong orange-and-red graphic image featured on the left.

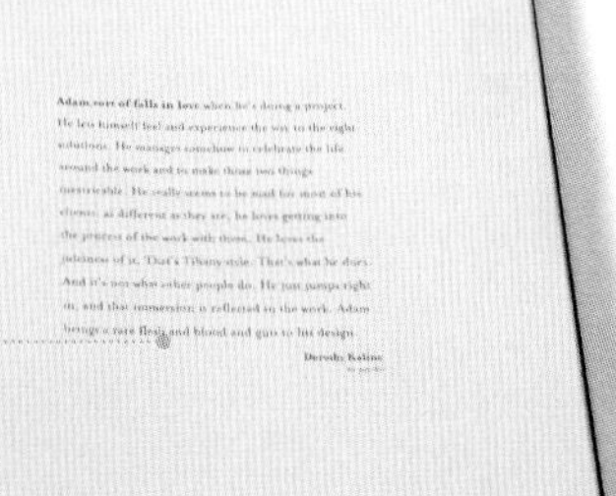

fig. 3.2

Each featured location begins with a strong image and ends with a complimentary quote by a well-known industry authority. The quotations help separate each feature and also serve in the pacing of the book.

fig. 3.3

Throughout the book, images bleed a bit differently each time, creating energy and movement.

fig. 3.4

Small thumbnail pictures, featured at the bottom of each spread, refer to projects highlighted in the hospitality designer's first book, *Tihany Design*.

Type Savvy

Firm MAGMA [Büro für Gestaltung]

Creative Direction Lars Harmsen

Design Ulrich Weiß, Sandra Augstein, and Lamosca

Illustration André Rösler, Katharina Gschwendtner, Paul Hoppe, and Tim S. Weiffenbach

Photography Christian Ernst

Interviews Stefan Sagmeister, Jean François Porchez, Kimberly Lloyd, Wiesbaden (M Publications), Jürgen Siebert (FontShop), Fons Hickmann, Pieter van Rosmalen, Eindhoven (GarageFonts), Dirk Uhlenbrock, Essen (Typetype), Vier 5, and Leslie Cabarga

Copywriting Peter Reichard, Angela Lau, Thomas Mettendorf, and Lars Harmsen

Printing/Bindery Hirsch GmbH

"Being creative as an editor is something wonderful, because reflecting about design and typography enriches perception, making a positive impact on my work."

—Lars Harmsen, MAGMA [Büro für Gestaltung]

OBJECTIVE After the success of their weblog, www.slanted.de, the most up-to-date German-language website regarding typography, MAGMA decided to publish a print publication.

AUDIENCE The target audience was drawn from the readership of the weblog. For the inaugural issue zero, 600 copies were produced and handed out at Typo Berlin 2005. Future issues will be published twice a year with a circulation of 15,000 to 20,000.

CONCEPT By developing a magazine, MAGMA is able to showcase their custom fonts called Volcano Type in an engaging and content-driven way. Each issue of *Slanted Magazin* has a main area of focus. In addition, the publication presents interviews, illustrative interpretations of a font namesake, photo essays, type analysis, and student work. Content related to the weblog is included as back matter and presented in a different paper color and finish.

MESSAGE Typography is not just a mere collection of shapes, curves, and internal space. It is also about life and culture—typography is everywhere.

RESPONSE The first issue was presented at the international typography conference Typo Berlin 2005 and had an immediate impact. Weeks after Typo Berlin, the firm had a 26 percent increase of traffic on their weblog. They also got people interested in contributing to the newly formed publication.

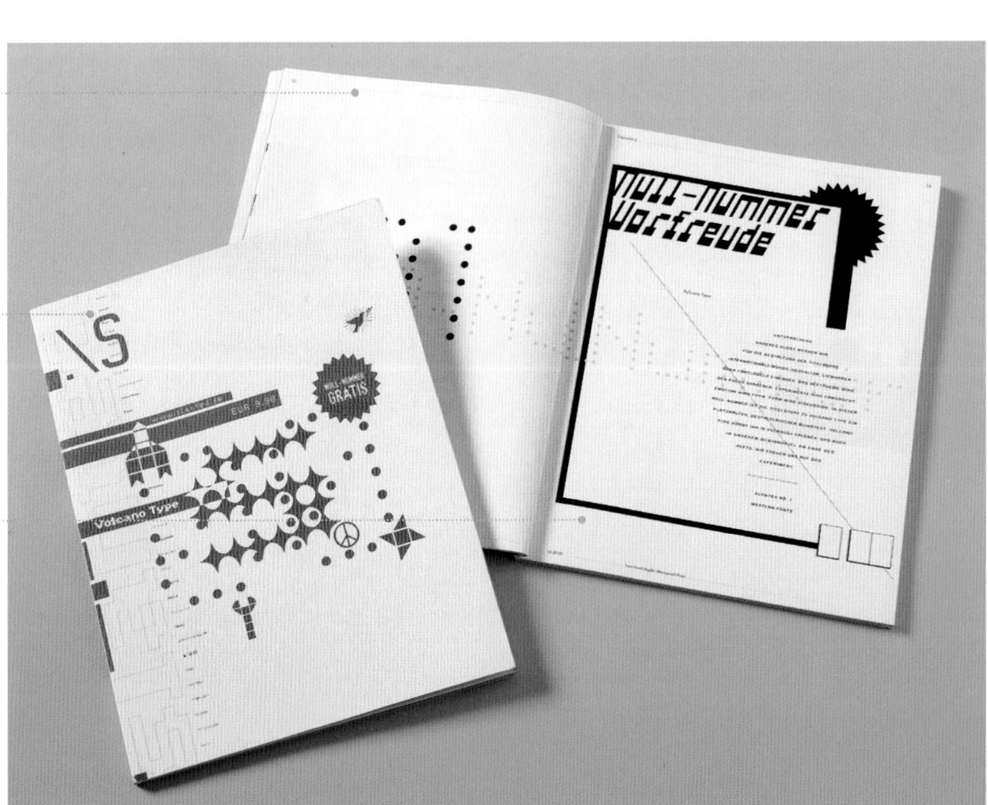

fig. 1.1

The cutting-edge typographic publication is formatted very closely to an American format rather than the European format DIN A4 (8 1/2" x 11 1/2" [210 x 297 mm]).

fig. 1.2

The cover of *Slanted Magazin* issue zero is printed in florescent orange on a highly textural Römerturm Feinstpapier Upgrade weiβ welle 285 gsm stock.

fig. 1.3

The inside is printed on LuxoSatin 115 gsm white stock in black ink only, because the classic look and feel of typography doesn't need additional colors to show its quality.

fig. 1.4

Throughout the publication, MAGMA's own Volcano Type fonts are employed.

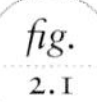

Presented in a well-designed format, interviews with leading industry visionaries inspire and educate.

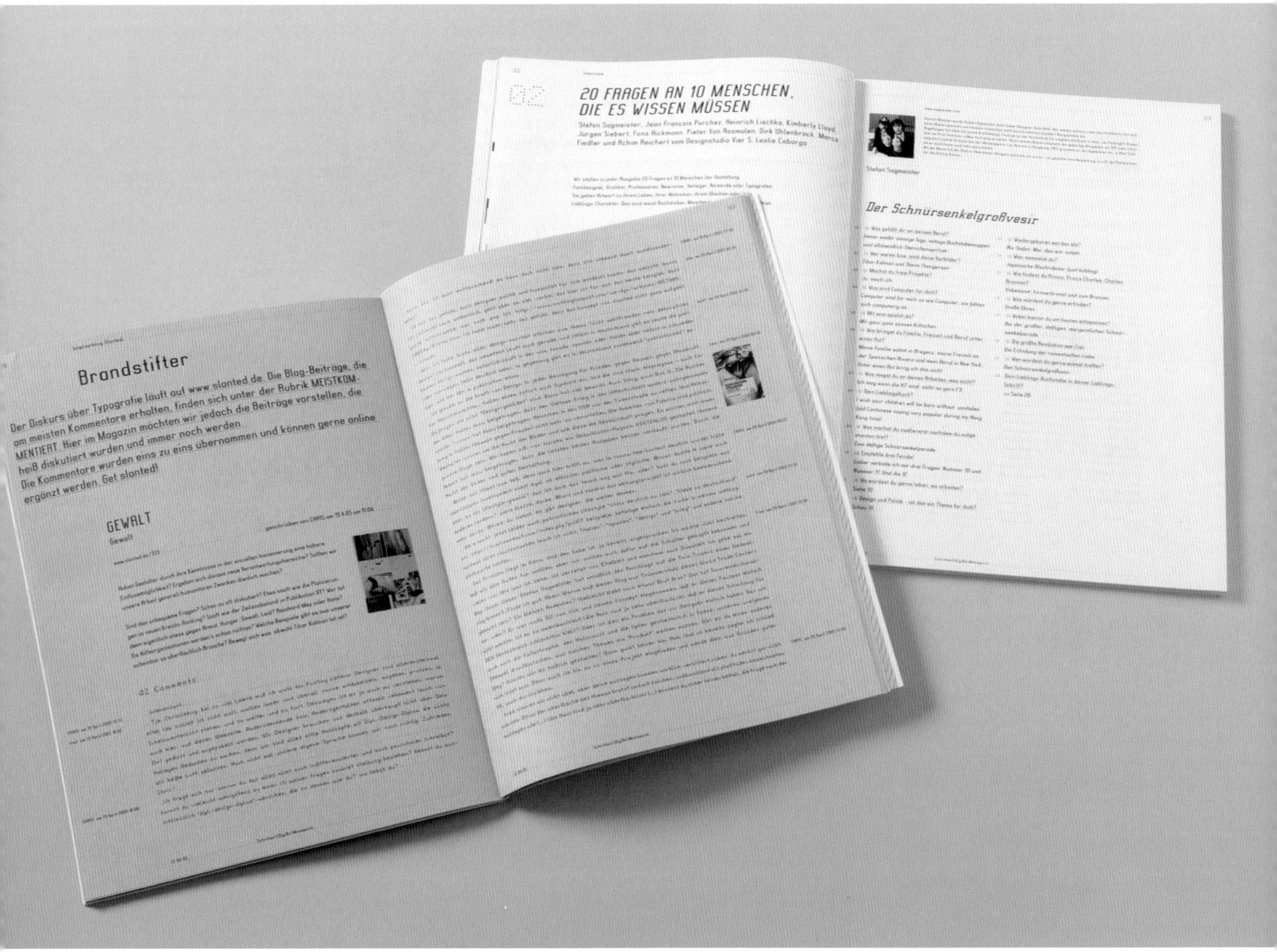

fig. 2.2

Back matter, printed on Caribic 90 gsm purple uncoated stock, makes reference to content profiled on the weblog, allowing for cross-promotion.

Alternative Approaches

Firm Plazm
Creative Direction Joshua Berger, Niko Courtelis, and Pete McCracken
Art Direction Joshua Berger
Design Milton Glaser (cover) and Joshua Berger (table of contents)
Illustration Milton Glaser (cover), Katie Kunesh (table of contents), and Melina Rodrigo (feature)
Editors Jon Raymond and Tiffany Lee Brown
Printing/Bindery Dynagraphics

"*Plazm* magazine's existence has helped draw attention to other things we do, like Plazm Fonts and Plazm Design. In addition, it has acted as a laboratory for us to experiment with form, process, and content, which we can then apply to our other projects."

—Joshua Berger, Plazm

OBJECTIVE From an interest in creating a forum for the exploration of ideas, *Plazm* magazine was born. Since its launch in 1991, *Plazm* has served as a laboratory for investigating alternative concepts and approaches that the firm can then apply to their other endeavors.

AUDIENCE The target audience is composed of designers, artists, writers, photographers, art directors, creative directors, and snowboarders. Approximately 7,500 copies of each issue are produced and distributed through the Internet, newsstands, and subscriptions.

CONCEPT The theme chosen for *Plazm 28* was *luck*, a highly appropriate message for a magazine whose very existence is based on taking chances. The issue contains a lot of handmade works, banned drawings, and protest graphics with an undercurrent that communicates a kind of raw energy. Like most issues, it does not adhere religiously to the chosen theme, allowing for a bit of flexibility in content.

MESSAGE *Plazm* magazine gives a voice to all forms of creative expression not found in the mainstream media.

RESPONSE In the beginning, Plazm conducted open-ended meetings discussing topics such as media accountability and artistic representation. Creatives from a plethora of disciplines were eager to get involved, each sharing a common dissatisfaction for the available avenues of expression. The evolution of this discourse can be found in the fifteen-year history of *Plazm* magazine.

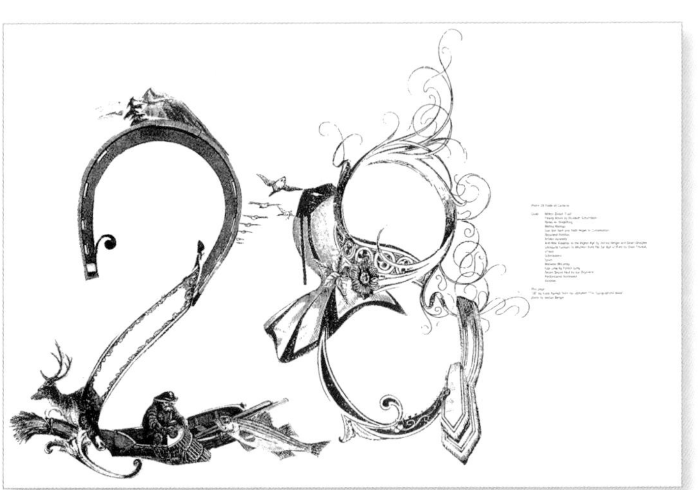

fig. I.1

The perfect-bound, 9" x 12" (23 x 30.5 cm) publication is printed in four-color process throughout on Scheufelen PhoeniXmotion stock. It uses 110 lb. for the cover and 90 lb. for the inside.

fig. I.2

For durability, a UV coating is applied to the cover.

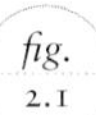
fig. 2.1

Each profile or feature exposes work that does not fit in the mainstream media. Artist Melina Rodrigo's work, personal and political in nature, draws from her 'zine titled *AW* (www.awzine.com). The subject of the short narrative featured is "less." The character feels weighed down by the past. The fire that appears symbolizes the destruction of an overbearing existence and the birth of something new.

Editorial Slant

Firm Storm Editions, Inc.

Creative Direction John Duffy/The Fin Company (issue 1 and 2); Robert Louey/Louey Rubino Design (issue 3)

Design Tim O'Donnell (issue 1) and John Duffy (issue 1 and 2); Javier Leguizamo, Robert Louey, Daniela Fahrig, and Juliana Suterman (issue 3)

Production Management The Actualizers, Inc.

Editorial Illustration Celia Calle and Bob Shea (issue 1); Luba Lukova (issue 2); Shawn Barber, Brad Holland, Jo Tyler, and John VanHamersveld (issue 3)

Cover Photography David Robin

Editorial Photography James Smolka, Graham McIndoe, Micheal McLaughlin, Henrik Knudsen, Dave Barry, Sian Kennedy, Greg Miller, Perkin Lovely, and Chris Buck (issue 1); Paul Bielenberg, Karen Collins, Charles Gullung, Julian Hibbard, Glen Luchford, Martien Mulder, David Robin, and Paul Warchol (issue 2); Richard Avedon, Michael Grecco, Steven Meisel, Max Vadukel, Albert Giordon, Jill Greenberg, Sam Jones, Pete Tangen, and Gregory Crewdson (issue 3)

Copywriting Mary Fichter, Todd Levin, Michael Moses, Bob Shea, and Alex Villasante (issue 1); Ben Byrne, Lisa L. Cyr, Laurel Harper, Cynthia Jones, and Ronald Tierney (issue 2); Barry Berg, Lisa L. Cyr, Susan Emerling, Tiffany Meyers, and Juliette Wolf Robin (issue 3)

Printing/Bindery Jet Lithocolor, Inc.

"The premier issue of *ALT Pick* magazine featured stories about New York. We wanted the magazine to reflect the quirkiness and craziness of the city. This issue set the tone that we were creating a different kind of publication. After the launch, we were able to get feedback from the community and really hone in on what the format and direction would be for future editions."

—Juliette Wolf Robin, Storm Editions, Inc.

OBJECTIVE With an established sourcebook and website, Storm Editions was looking for another innovative way for commercial photographers, illustrators, and designers to feature their work and stand out in the minds of buyers.

AUDIENCE *ALT Pick*, a biannual publication, is distributed to prospective buyers, primarily creative directors, art directors, art buyers, editors, and designers. For each issue, approximately 15,000 copies are printed. Copies are also sold in select cities throughout the United States and abroad.

CONCEPT Storm Editions wanted to present commercial talent to buyers in a format that would be not only attractive but also informative. By producing an editorial publication, the firm was able to provide interesting content in an engaging, well-designed manner. Behind-the-scenes profiles, insightful industry articles, and cutting-edge talent all come together in a dynamic package. Each issue focuses on the creative output of a specific geographic locale, from national to international in scope.

MESSAGE Celebrate the creative collaboration between commercial talent and the buyers of their work.

RESPONSE Since the initial launch, feedback from the creative community has been extremely positive. The publication has helped Storm Editions to further strengthen their brand, making a niche in the industry.

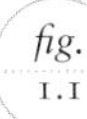
fig. 1.1

Each publication is printed in four-color process on Domtar paper with a different spot color on the masthead logo for each issue. For the first two issues, there is a spot lamination on the inside covers. The third issue has a scratch-and-sniff ad on the inside back cover.

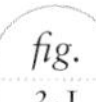
fig. 2.1

Throughout the cutting-edge publication, high-end design, photography, and illustration are employed in an engaging and exciting manner.

Creative Freedom

OBJECTIVE The Pushpin Group's owner Seymour Chwast wanted to produce a publication that would allow him to experiment without boundaries, something that would not only promote his illustration and design work but also serve as a medium for self-expression.

AUDIENCE The primary target audience is composed of art directors, designers, editors, and colleagues. *The Nose* is published twice a year with a print run of 4,000 copies.

CONCEPT Each issue of *The Nose* supports a different theme and boasts custom illustrations by Seymour Chwast. For issue 8, *The Nose* deals with fear as a source of inspiration and insight. In the ninth issue, truth and lies becomes the point of departure; while trickery and deception fill the eleventh issue. Each publication of *The Nose* is unique in both design and production. Throughout the theme-based magazine, clever die-cuts, custom gatefolds, and surprising inserts help support the content in a fun and engaging way. The Pushpin Group collaborates with paper companies that contribute the selection of paper for each issue in exchange for a custom ad designed by Chwast.

MESSAGE Experience the extraordinary work of Seymour Chwast.

RESPONSE Since the initial launch in 1997, *The Nose* has received positive response from the design and illustration community. The work has also been accepted into many industry competitions.

Firm The Pushpin Group, Inc.
Creative Direction Seymour Chwast
Design Carol Chu (no. 8 and 9) and Clinton Van Gemert (no. 11)
Illustration Seymour Chwast
Editor Steven Heller
Printing/Bindery Berman Printing Co. (no. 8 and 9) and Steve Woods Printing Co. (no. 11)

"Most of the assignments I get from publications involve illustrating for editors, who in turn accept or reject my solutions. *The Nose*, on the other hand, gives me complete freedom to conceive and execute to my liking."

—Seymour Chwast, The Pushpin Group, Inc.

fig. 1.1

The Nose is printed in four-color process with an additional spot color employed as an accent.

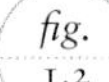
fig. 1.2

The 7" x 11" (18 x 28 cm) saddle-stitched publication uses varnish on the front, back, and inside covers.

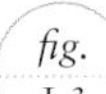
fig. 1.3

For issues eight and nine, *The Nose* is printed on Finch Fine White 100 lb. cover and 80 lb. text for the interior pages; issue nine is printed on Utopia One X silk 120 lb. cover for the outside and 80 lb. cover for the inside.

fig. 2.1

Each issue incorporates some kind of special production accent. In *The Nose* 11, the inside cover folds out to mask half of the character's face. A circular die-cut allows the left eye to pierce through. The intro page, shown on the right, is printed on Curious Touch Soft 80 lb. cover.

fig. 2.2

In the middle of the publication, a miniature book on magic is presented, featuring five tricks of the trade. It is printed on Curious Touch Wet 80 lb. text.

fig. 1.1
The newspaper-style format was printed in four-color process for one half of the publication and black-and-white for the other half on Bruk Norcke Kog Nornew 45 gsm newsprint.

fig. 1.2
The font Mulabeg, regular and bold, is used throughout.

fig. 1.3
The exhibition catalog is packaged in a clear plastic bag and vacuum sealed.

Under Pressure

OBJECTIVE Trio, a design studio, and Fabrika, an advertising agency, were in charge of creating a publication to announce a solo exhibition of the work of designer, illustrator, and author Mirko Ilić.

AUDIENCE The target market ranged from design professionals, artists, and the media to the general public. Five thousand copies were distributed.

CONCEPT The exhibition title, *Mirko Ilić Under Pressure*, emerged from the urgency of quick deadlines and high demands that have been a part of Ilić's politically driven editorial work over the duration of his thirty-year career. A tabloid-sized newspaper packaged inside a clear plastic bag compressed using a vacuum packing machine was the perfect combination to carry the message. Throughout the publication, the designer's philosophies on design are accented by his illustrative work from the 1970s to present. The exhibition was held at the Arts Gallery of Bosnia and Herzegovina, the designer's birthplace.

MESSAGE Mirko Ilić, who has been working editorially for more than thirty years, has been given the honor of getting a newspaper dedicated to his work.

RESPONSE The public was thrilled by the unconventionality of the catalog and the energy that was put into every project by the artist. It was also nostalgic for the public to see Ilić's work again locally, more than twenty years later.

Firms Trio and Fabrika

Creative Direction Bojan Hadžihalilović

Design Amer Mržljak

Illustration Mirko Ilić

Copywriting Mirko Ilić (Rules for Designers) and Milton Glaser (Interview with Mirko Ilić originally written for *Graphis* magazine)

Printing Unioninvestplastika

Manufacturers Local meat packer (plastic bags and vacuum packing)

"With a good idea and creative concept one can make an original publication, which in production terms costs less than forty cents."

—Amer Mržljak, Fabrika

fig. 2.1

Throughout the publication, controversial images and insightful quotes work together to convey designer Mirko Ilić's design philosophy and vision. This particular spread reads: "A good designer should analyze and draw inspiration from all other kinds of art, except for design. Music, painting, sculpture, and such arts inspire more innovative design than design itself."

Inform and Inspire

OBJECTIVE Riordon Design wanted an innovative way to not only profile recent work but also provide strategic insight into how they address client-based business objectives.

AUDIENCE The newsletter promotion was distributed to both existing and potential clients, primarily corporate CEOs and upper-management executives. In addition, each issue was posted on the firm's website for cross-pollination marketing.

CONCEPT The design team chose to showcase work in an editorial-style format. The uniquely shaped newsletter is eye-catching, making it stand out from other publications. The overall curvature echoes the brackets used in the firm's tagline "(inform) inspire." The signature die-cut shape is also used on many of the firm's corporate communications collateral.

MESSAGE Get a behind-the-scenes look into Riordon Design's unique approach.

RESPONSE This annual news magazine has been well received, assuring the development of new business for the strategically creative firm.

Firm Riordon Design

Creative Direction Alan Krpan and Ric Riordon

Design Alan Krpan (vol 1, 2, and 3), Cori Hellard (vol. 1 and 2), Dan Wheaton (vol. 2), and Dawn Charney (vol. 3)

Illustration Tim Warnock (vol. 1), Dan Wheaton (vol. 1 and 2), Jack Diamond (cover vol. 2), and Jeff Elliott (cover and spots vol. 3)

Photography David Graham White (vol. 1), Gary Gerovac (vol. 1, 2, and 3), Alan Krpan (vol. 3), Ric Riordon (vol. 3) and various stock

Copywriting Ric Riordon, Cathy McMahon, Alan Krpan, and Cheryl Dangel Cullen (vol. 1); Ric Riordon, Dan Wheaton, Tim Turnbull, and Harry Cornelius (vol. 2); Ric Riordon, Rachael Bell, Alan Krpan, Cathy McMahon, and Cori Hellard (vol. 3)

Printing/Bindery C.J. Graphics

"The publication really expresses who we are and how different we are from other design and communication firms. It also seeks to demystify the process of creativity to the business sector, or at least bring the two perspectives to an understanding of mutual benefit."

—Ric Riordon, Riordon Design

fig. 1.1

Each issue is stochastically printed in four-color process and PMS 550 slate blue with an overall satin aqueous coating applied throughout.

fig. 1.2

Mead Westvaco Sterling ultra dull 100 lb. white text stock is the paper of choice.

fig. 1.3

The custom die-cut promotional newsletter is sent as a self-mailer.

fig. 2.1

In a fun and informative way, *CultureCue* serves as a vehicle to share business savvy and marketing insight behind projects produced by Riordon Design.

fig. 2.2

Trade Gothic and Proforma are the primary fonts used in each issue.

Sayles and Marketing

Firm Sayles Graphic Design
Creative Direction John Sayles
Design/Illustration John Sayles
Photography Bill Nellans
Copywriting Sheree Clark and Kristin Lennert
Printing Artcraft Inc.

"*Sayles and Marketing* is a vehicle that makes clients feel like they know us personally while still detailing the wide range of projects we've done. People will actually read a newsletter if it is engaging to them."

—Sheree Clark, Sayles Graphic Design

OBJECTIVE Sayles Graphic Design wanted to create an ongoing newsletter to share the firm's successful endeavors and personal interests in a fun and engaging way.

AUDIENCE The newsletter targeted prospective and existing clientele as well as friends of the firm. The inaugural issue is featured here.

CONCEPT The publication, entitled *Sayles and Marketing*, draws from the design firm's name, Sayles Graphic Design, as well as their corporate look and colors. The eight-page, tabloid-size newsletter features a variety of national and local client promotions as well as profiles on various staff members and the things they love to do outside of work. A business reply card is enclosed for recipients to request more information about the firm and their services.

MESSAGE Take a look inside Sayles Graphic Design.

RESPONSE As a result of the first issue, the firm received a significant number of new business relationships. Several existing clients called to say things like "I didn't know Sheree was a runner," or "Wow, I take tai kwan do, too," in response to articles about individual staff members.

fig. 1.1 The tabloid-style newsletter, printed in four-color process on Boydon Silk 80 lb. text stock, is warm and inviting.

fig. 1.2 Coronet MT BD along with various forms of Futura are the chosen typefaces used throughout the eight-page newsletter.

fig. 1.3 The publication is sent out folded in half as a self-mailer. A business reply card is enclosed for feedback and follow-up purposes.

Molding Decor

Firm PRINCIPLE, INC.
Creative Direction/Design PAMELA ZUCCKER
Photography NICHOLE SLOAN PHOTOGRAPHY AND ROB BRINSON PHOTOGRAPHY
Copywriter LYNN FEY
Printing/Bindery CARACTÉRA
Client LARSON-JUHL

"Leveraging Larson-Juhl's superior artistry, we shifted their brand image to showcase the stylish partnership between frame and home decor. We embraced color palettes, fabrics, surfaces, and decorative accessories. The right custom frame creates a dialog between art and decor, a visual bridge that becomes a backdrop of personal expression."

—Pamela Zuccker, Principle, Inc.

OBJECTIVE After a seven-year run with the same campaign, Larson-Juhl recognized the need to update their brand and marketing strategy. They turned to Principle to breathe new life into their beautiful line of custom moldings.

AUDIENCE The collection of books was distributed internally to the sales team and delivered by hand to select partners. Three thousand sets were printed, and the design firm plans to produce an additional booklet that will fit in the original slipcase.

CONCEPT Rather than just providing factual information about molding, Principle decided to appeal to the audience by sharing designer tips and ideas on how to create several custom interiors, using the Larson-Juhl framing collections as accents. A series of eight mini books were created as inspirational and educational tools. The series, titled *Interior Identities*, helps make the connection that custom framing can accent personal style and expression. From *Urban Loft, Cottage Casual, Metropolitan Noir*, and *Luxe Lodge* to *Southwest Zest, Classic Club, Golden Grandeur*, and *Global Origins*, there is an environment that will please anyone's taste. The series fits nicely into a custom slipcase—something that cannot be tossed in a folder with hundreds of other brochures. In addition to the books, Principle has applied the imagery and messaging to a series of nine ads, a press kit, T-shirts, in-store signage, direct mail, and a new corporate identity.

MESSAGE Larson-Juhl can help customers achieve the look they want through a wide range of selections.

RESPONSE Larson-Juhl was so excited by the mini books that they printed larger booklets to use in demos. Because of the initiative, Larson-Juhl captured the attention of production designer Kelly Van Patter of *The Apprentice*. Select frames were used to decorate the walls in "the suite" of the popular TV show for season 3. The series of books and ad campaign truly led to an exciting shift in product awareness for Larson-Juhl.

fig. 1.1

The set of eight interior design books, printed in four-color process plus PMS Cool Gray 10 on Productolithe matte 100 lb. text, are held together with a bellyband and inserted into a matching slipcase. A water-based, satin varnish is applied throughout.

fig. 1.2

Each 4 1/4" x 5 3/4" (11 x 14.5 cm) staple-bound book conveys a different look and feel, easily referenced by color.

fig. 1.3

Futura Book, Copperplate, and Goudy are the fonts employed throughout the series.

Collaborative Effort

OBJECTIVE “Build it and they will come” is the strategy that Plainspoke has taken with this distinctive publication. To produce each issue, the design firm collaborates with talented photographers, artists, and writers. It is a perfect venue for both the design firm and its various collaborators to feature their personal work. One issue is published every year.

AUDIENCE To broaden their reach in the institutional market, Plainspoke created this ongoing series of mini fine-art publications to reach out to museums, art galleries, and art publishing clientele. In addition, each of the collaborators received copies to send out for their own promotional use.

CONCEPT The self-published periodical is titled *In Plain View*, a play on the design firm’s name, Plainspoke. The main premise behind the series is to provide an opportunity for the firm to showcase their ability to create a fine-art-quality publication annually using innovative printing and binding techniques. Even though each issue is distinctive and unique, they all maintain the same trim size—5 1/2" x 8 1/2" (14 x 21.5 cm)—for consistency purposes.

The first issue of *In Plain View* highlights the work of photographer Kellie Walsh. The journalistic-style portraits shown throughout the book were taken during the photographer’s travels throughout the United States and abroad. The second issue features the on-location work of photographer Brian Wilder. Beautiful panoramic views with soft-focus edges grace every page of this well-crafted, horizontally oriented book.

MESSAGE Plainspoke creates high-quality, image-driven fine-art publications.

RESPONSE Since its launch, *In Plain View* has opened the door for the design firm to bid on exhibition catalogs for two major museums. The visual journal of sorts has also been a huge success with existing clientele. They are drawn to the quality and care that went into the making of each issue.

Firm Plainspoke
Creative Direction Matt Ralph
Design Matt Ralph
Production Connie DiSanto
Photography Kellie Walsh (issue 01) and Brian Wilder (issue 02)
Printing Penmor Lithographers (issue 01), Millennium Graphics (issue 02)
Bindery Penmor Lithographers (issue 01), Millennium Graphics (issue 02)

“To appeal to high-end clientele in the fine arts sector, you need to produce pieces of equal or better quality than what they are producing in order for them to take serious notice. Each issue of *In Plain View* is an opportunity for us to explore.”

—Matt Ralph, Plainspoke

fig. 1.4

Spot gloss varnish is used on the images and the areas of solid dark coverage to give them an additional depth.

Each black-and-white photograph is reproduced as a tritone of two blacks and PMS 408 gray, creating depth and a wider tonal range overall.

The perfect-bound publication, printed on Domtar Solutions Thai Gold 80 lb. cover and Scheufelen Job Parilux Silk 115 lb. text, boasts French-folded pages and a short trim cover. This innovative bindery adds an additional color and surface texture to the overall cover presence.

Inside, images from one page are carried over the fold to the next, creating an interesting juxtaposition.

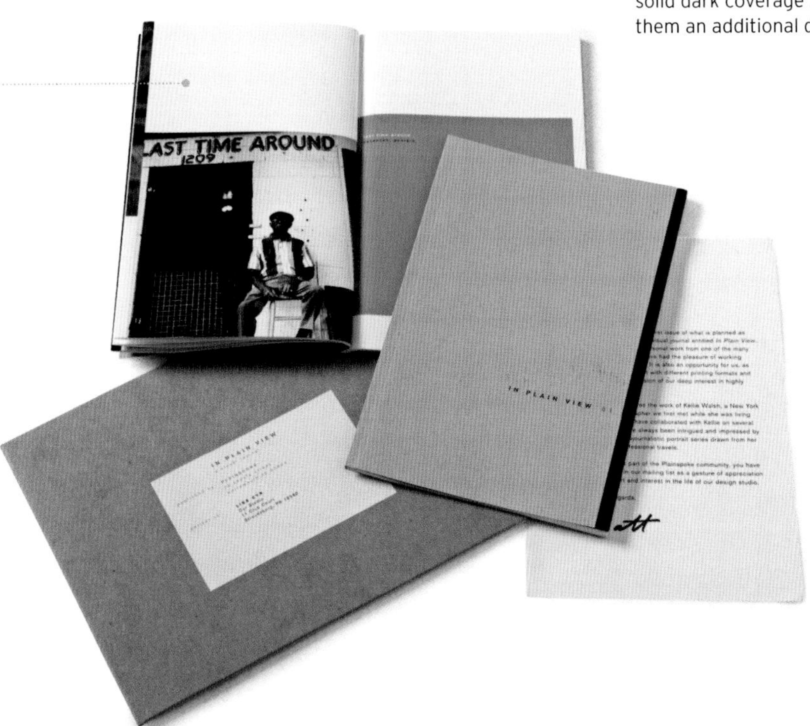

fig. 2.1

The mini publication employs two separate runs of wire-o binding, an interesting spin on the typical single run.

fig. 2.2

The warm color scheme includes black and two hits of PMS 876 metallic printed on Fraser Papers Synergy Green 80 lb. cover.

fig. 2.3

It is sent in the same brown kraft envelope as the first issue, continuing the overall look and feel of the brand.

fig. 2.4

Inside, photographic images are reproduced as process quadtones on Scheufelen Phoenixmotion Silk 100 lb. cover. Adjacent to the panoramic scenes, full-bleed accent pages are printed in PMS 8002 metallic.

fig. 2.5

Spot gloss varnish is applied onto the images and areas of dark solid coverage.

Pushing Limits

Firm ATTIK

Creative Direction Simon Needham

Design Miguel Castro and Stuart Wilson

Illustration Various Artists

Photography Richard Moran, Alfonso Smith, Dave Smith, Max Doyle, Dean Tirkot, and Ben Telford

Copywriting Barry Truax (introduction), Elton Greig, Hugh Ballantyne, Ture Liilegraven, Flynn Larson, and Martin Hennessey

Printing/Bindery HBI (Harper Collins Publishers)

"*Noise* offers us the opportunity to develop, test, and explore new modes, sensibilities, and experiences outside the commercial environment. It's a chance to show how we think and how we create. *Noise* is a tangible manifestation of the creative force that propels ATTIK forward."

—Simon Needham, ATTIK

OBJECTIVE For ATTIK, *Noise* is a vehicle for experimentation and a physical manifestation of their passion, vision, and creativity without limitations.

AUDIENCE The target audience is prospective clientele as well as design professionals, educators, students, and enthusiasts. The publication is sent out as a credentials book to clients. It is also available for sale at bookstores and other retail outlets.

CONCEPT With *NoiseFour*, the design team decided to be more pronounced with the themes they used throughout the book when accompanying their visual experiments, which have become a trademark of the cutting-edge publication. *NoiseFour*, like its predecessors, provides a venue to publish ideas and concepts that are unconventional, more abstract, and metaphorical in nature. Every page presents a new idea and direction in creative thinking, posing thought-provoking challenges to the reader. The book is divided into three sections, *NoiseLab, CutureLife,* and *RealityArchive. NoiseLab* showcases the firm's experimental work, *CultureLife* communicates its personality, and *RealityArchive* houses client applications and real-world work. To launch *NoiseFour*, each office held several art-based events that tied in performance and sculpture, mirroring the *NoiseFour* theme of unrestrained creative expression.

MESSAGE A fresh perspective can be discovered when boundaries are transcended.

RESPONSE In the beginning, *Noise* was created as a vehicle to call attention to what makes ATTIK tick. It was given away, but people loved it and were eager to purchase the publication. Today, the experimental publication is distributed worldwide. In the creative industry, it has made ATTIK a force to be reckoned with. When *NoiseFour* launched, the firm was approached by several organizations to use the artwork featured in the book. ATTIK graciously declined each opportunity, because it was never their intention to use the publication in that way.

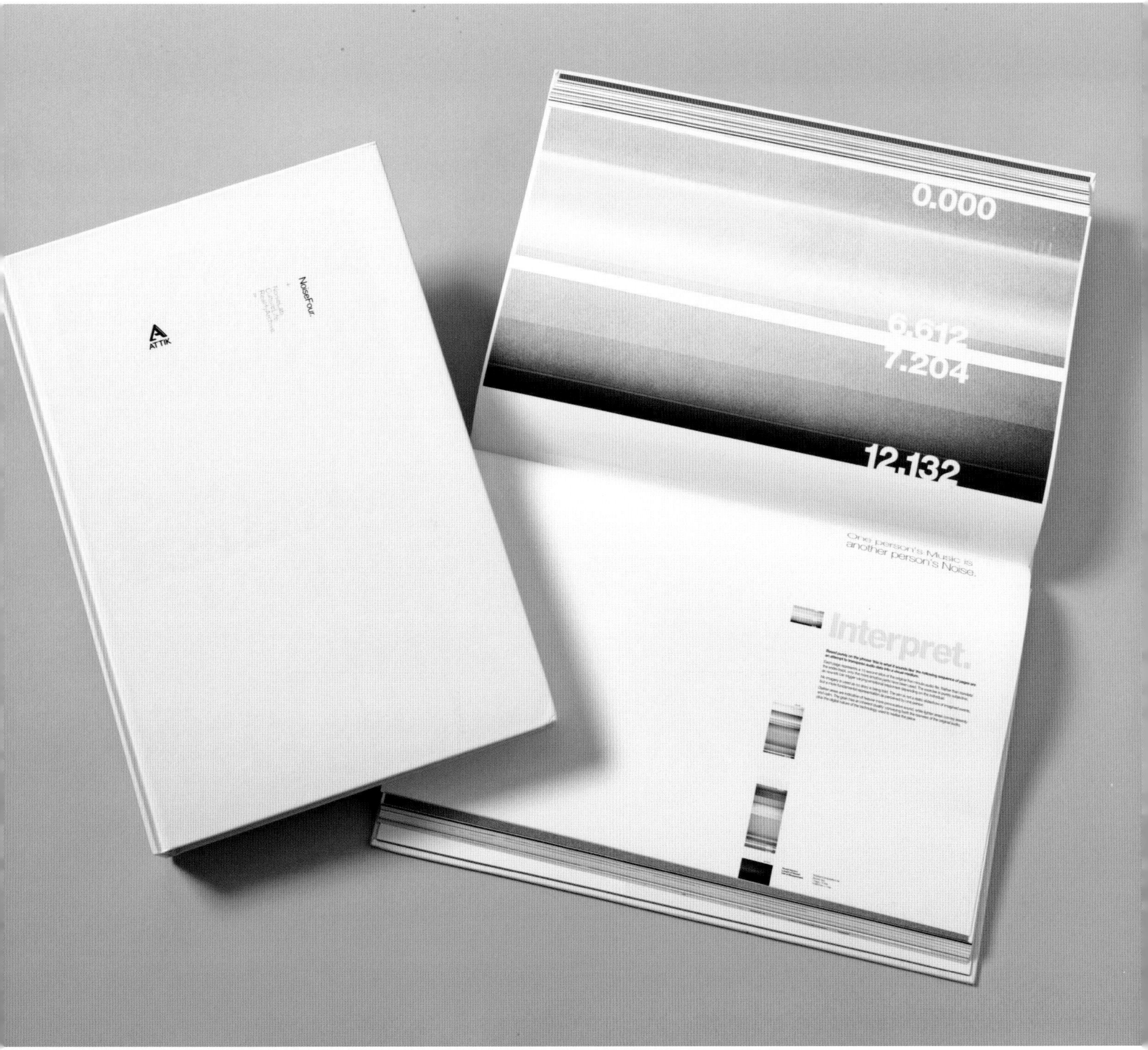

NoiseFour, ATTIK's latest experimental design publication, is a hardcover, 9" x 13 1/4" (23 x 33.5 cm) perfect-bound book with 500 pages of conceptual-based content.

Throughout the cutting-edge publication, more than fifty unique concepts such as *Cause and Effect*, *Innocence Lost*, and *Interpret* are presented in a well-designed, thought-provoking manner.

Treading New Ground

No.
01

EXPLORING NEW MARKETS

To remain viable in an ever-changing marketplace, creatives are using innovative promotional initiatives to explore new market opportunities. When multimedia artist Matt Frantz of the Independent Opposition wanted to create concept-based work for the music industry, he needed to have something that would actively demonstrate his design, editing, and producing capabilities. The artist came up with the idea to produce his own CD, a musical compilation that interpreted what the end of the world might sound like. Using the Internet, Frantz was able to send a call for submissions to a global audience, soliciting musicians from around the world who would believe in his vision. Intrigued by the project and its content, collaborators came from all around to participate. In exchange for their efforts, each partner received copies of the finished CD to distribute and sell at concerts and performances. In addition to the sound compilation, an interpretive video, gallery installation, and postcards were also created to complete the campaign (see page 168). Since its launch, the initiative has generated interest from both the music and film industries. "I believe it is important for creative people to produce self-initiated projects," remarks Frantz. "I think too many commercial artists get into the rut of thinking about utilitarian purposes and lose sight of the larger scope of art." Riordon Design shares their experience in breaking into the music industry, "We created a portfolio promotion of fake groups and projects, elaborately photographed and presented, to showcase our enthusiasm, imagination, and abilities. We also included a few samples of projects for real clients," recalls principal Ric Riordon. "This won us confidence with a couple of record labels in Nashville and opened up the opportunity for our first breakthrough. We then set to work on earning a reputation through industry awards with subsequent promotions on our accomplishments in the music industry." Since the launching of the inaugural initiative, Riordon Design has produced more than 600 music CDs for various clients. By creating promotions that served as demonstrators, each firm was able to get a foothold in a market that they could not have otherwise.

Interactive initiatives are at the forefront in finding new ways to capture an audience. Sound, motion, and storytelling work in tandem to produce exciting, high-end, signature communications. Messaging that has been integrated into a game experience entertains and captivates, a direct shift from the hard-core sales approaches of years past.

No. 02

ENTREPRENEURIAL APPROACH

KEEPSAKE PROMOTIONS not only call attention to new skills but also provide a perfect opportunity to test the waters for other potential endeavors, especially in the direct-to-consumer arena. As a way to enhance their capabilities in product design, the firm H developed a series of paper product keepsake promotions to be given to their existing client base. The success of the endeavor encouraged them to launch their own line of stationery to the retail market (see page 116). "The paper products line is a lateral development into the product design market, while integrating product design as part of the comprehensive strategic services we offer," explains Winnie Hart of H. "The more we understand our client's business concerns, the better we can deliver solutions as designers and partners. It has also helped us to remember to think beyond the client and into the mind of the consumer in everything we do." The firm now distributes a full line of paper products through reps, e-commerce, and tradeshows like the National Stationery Show and the Gift Show.

After the overwhelming success of a holiday keepsake called Outerspice (see page 122), the design firm Capsule launched an online store targeted to the consumer market (www.capsuleshak.com). "We are constantly trying to push limits to make our promotional projects more memorable and unique," offers Capsule's Brian Adducci. "The Capsuleshak website is an example of this. It is one part online retailer, one part experimental lab, and one part marketing theater." The interactive site offers a full line of Outerspice products, including the spicy steak rub, T-shirts, and desktop screensavers. With the Outerspice line in place, Capsule has launched another productlike keepsake. Cocoa Mang, a spicy Mexican cocoa, is now being considered for full-scale distribution by a regional grocery chain. With an established market tapped, the entrepreneurial design firm plans to continue growing its family of product lines. Successful keepsake initiatives can open doors for creatives to diversify their offerings, essentially becoming their own client.

No. 03

NEW MEDIA INITIATIVES

PROMOTIONS ARE ALSO EMBRACING NEW MEDIA. Interactive initiatives are at the forefront in finding new ways to capture an audience. Sound, motion, and storytelling work in tandem to produce exciting, high-end signature communications. Messaging that has been integrated into a game experience entertains and captivates, a direct shift from the hard-core sales approaches of years past. Blockdot, considered by many to be one of the forefathers of advergames (advertising-based games), launched their first interactive promotional initiative in the late '90s. *Elf Bowling* was created and served as the company's holiday greeting. It was installed 7.6 million times in one month. "The phenomenal success of the game made us the first developers to break into Media Metrix Top Ten Games with a game that did not come bundled within the Microsoft operating system," shares Blockdot's Dan Ferguson. "We are still entertaining and engaging millions of people every month through our game portal Kewlbox (www.kewlbox.com)." Kewlbox serves as the launching pad for the firm's client-based advergames. To date, the innovative firm has generated more than 350 million game plays, totaling 60 million hours plus of active interaction (see page 172). The overwhelming success of the advergame experience has led to the acceptance and utilization of interactive games as a viable and highly effective promotional tool. With downloading available from the Internet, this new form of communication has allowed businesses to cost-effectively penetrate a worldwide market. When it comes to new media promotional initiatives, the market is just seeing the tip of the iceberg in this emerging arena. "We live in a highly interactive society that thrives on a steady flow of information and communication," details Ferguson. "To set our promotional message apart from the pack, we must continue to find ways to incorporate interactive elements in relevant ways that have an impact and meaning to the audience." Limited only by their imagination, creatives are pushing the envelope to what is possible. Their eagerness to experiment has opened the door for new, more engaging ways to communicate. The industry is evolving, and a new generation of artists is redefining what it means to promote. It is an exciting time.

Chapter Five

"Within the last few years, markets have become much more complex, requiring us to design more strategically. More than any other time in recent history, there is a challenge to custom-tailor the experience in a promotional effort."

—Ric Riordon, Riordon Design

CAMPAIGNS

RATHER THAN RELYING ON ANY ONE VENUE to deliver their message, creatives are penetrating an audience on many fronts. Well-crafted campaigns are being employed as an effective way to make a long-lasting impact. "If you meet me once, chances are you may forget me. If you meet me three or four times, you are more likely to remember, and not only that, I've probably formed some unforgettable impression in your mind—good or bad," acknowledges Ric Riordon of Riordon Design. "Making the right impression has a lot to do with being sure you've carefully planned for it."

When designing a campaign, think in terms of creating an experience for the audience. Like a director of a theatrical performance, you need to set the stage, define the main characters and their roles, and ensure that the storyline plays out in a captivating way. "Within the last few years, markets have become much more complex, requiring us to design more strategically," observes Riordon. "More than any other time in recent history, there is a challenge to custom-tailor the experience in a promotional effort".

Instead of approaching a broad spectrum of clients with a series of generalized promotions, narrow your targets to a select group, creating a more personalized initiative that speaks to clients in ways that matter to them. "People like to be addressed personally," comments Aleksandar Maćašev of Black Pixel (Folie a Trois). "Communicate to someone you know, and your audience gets a message from a friend." The best campaigns customize to the needs of the recipient.

"Focus on your target audience," advises Blu Concept's Richard Klingle-Watt. "Get inside their head and turn them on in an unexpected way. Get them excited about the possibilities and opportunities that you can offer."

Through collaborative endeavors, creatives are unfolding new-found promotional possibilities when it comes to campaign initiatives. Group-inspired promotional endeavors draw from the collective energy, skills, and wisdom of each participant involved. Because the financial and work responsibilities are divided among the group, a collaborative campaign allows for the exploration of avenues far more outstanding than what any one participant would have the budget, time, or resources for. When illustrator Chris Sickels of Red Nose Studio collaborated with the designers of Planet 10 and the high-end printers Quality Printing and D.E. Baugh (See page 156), the results were nothing shy of inspirational, uplifting, and rewarding for all involved, garnering a great deal of attention both nationally and internationally "Working with the right people with the right passion for good work can push your work above and beyond," says Sickels. "Everyone involved in the project made it better. The designers helped me see the project as a whole while the printers had the ability to create a piece with the attention to detail that would carry my vision throughout." With a captivating and engaging design, a personalized and distinctive message, and an accurate and well-targeted mailing list, campaign initiatives can be a great way to go after new prospects as well as generate repeat business from existing clientele.

Inventive Storytelling

OBJECTIVE Planet 10, Red Nose Studio, Quality Printing, and D.E. Baugh were looking to produce an inventive promotional campaign to function as a showcase piece, exhibiting—in an interesting way—innovative design, signature style three-dimensional illustration, and high-end printing and bindery. It also needed to be memorable, something prospective clients would want to hold onto.

AUDIENCE The illustrative campaign was sent to advertising agencies, design firms, and children's book publishers. In addition, the communications industry trade publications were also targeted through competitions and annuals. Two thousand books, posters, and flipbooks were produced and distributed. The collaborative team is currently working on a follow-up piece—a character-based calendar—to round out the distinctive ensemble.

CONCEPT The overall concept was produced to show off excellence in illustration, design, printing, and bindery in a promotional campaign. To generate local attention, an exhibition was created to display the inventive and highly creative work used throughout the project. Flipbooks and posters were sent out as invites to the event. A short stop-motion film was also created and debuted at the exhibition opening.

MESSAGE Experience and be excited by the perfect synergy of design, illustration, printing, and bindery.

RESPONSE The truly creative campaign has been very successful for all involved. It has won numerous awards, most notably the Best of Show in both the *HOW Self-Promotion Annual* and the Society of Illustrators 3D Salon. The work has also won merits in the *Society of Illustrators' Annual, Print's Regional Design Annual, HOW* Perfect Ten Competition, *HOW International Design Annual*, AIGA's Regional Design Competition, and *Applied Arts Annual*. It has also generated calls from clients as diverse as a small regional magazine to a large Hollywood special-effects company. Each collaborator is still receiving requests for this highly coveted project.

Firms Planet 10, Red Nose Studio, and Magnet Reps

Creative Direction Mike Tuttle and Jennifer Tuttle

Design Mike Tuttle and Jennifer Tuttle

Illustration Chris Sickels

Photography Chris Sickels

Printing and Bindery Quality Printing

Special Techniques D.E. Baugh (silkscreen printing, die-cutting, and embossing)

"No one was really paid to be involved. Everyone either traded their time or donated it. We did this project because it gave us an opportunity to collaborate on something special and larger than any of us could have done ourselves."

—Mike Tuttle, Planet 10

fig. 1.1

Invitational posters, machine-stitched closed with red industrial thread, announce the exhibition of original art. The interesting bindery echoes the book binding and helps play off the overall red thread theme.

fig. 2.1

On the inside, engaging pop-ups, interesting die-cuts, clever embossing, and spot and full coverage varnishes bring life to each spread.

fig. 2.2

At the end of the book, a paper doll of the main character is available for interested parties to assemble and enjoy.

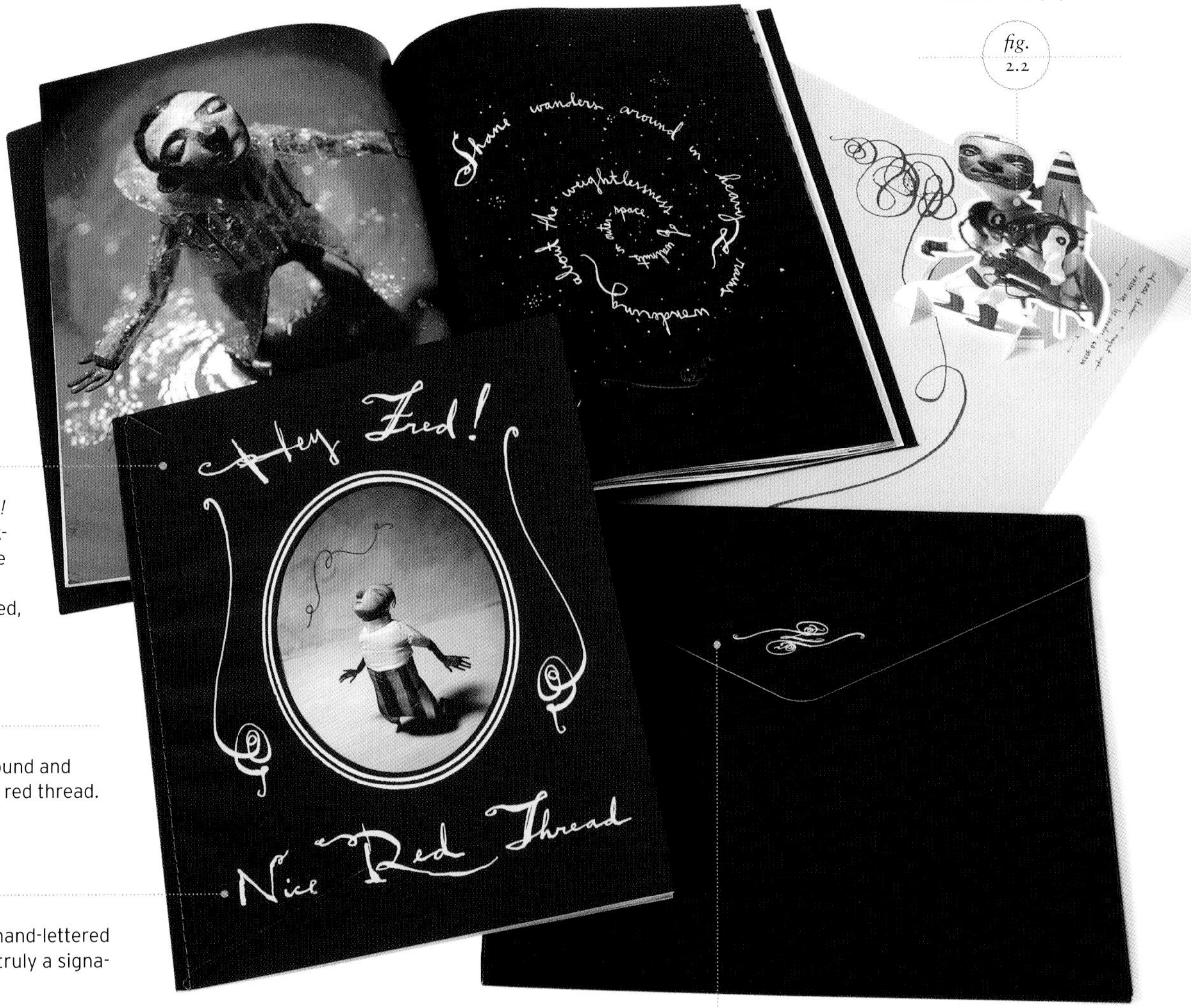

fig. 2.3

The cover of *Hey Fred! Nice Red Thread* is silk-screen-printed in white on 12-point Fibermark Touché Black, embossed, and custom die-cut.

fig. 2.4

The book is perfect-bound and machine-stitched with red thread.

fig. 2.5

The whimsical use of hand-lettered type makes the piece truly a signature work.

fig. 2.6

It is presented in a black case and double hit with ink for a nice even coverage. A Velcro enclosure allows the case to be easily opened and shut on each viewing.

fig. 2.7

A gray envelope with signature graphics is used to house all the materials for shipping.

fig. 3.1

Each engaging, animated flipbook is printed in four-color process throughout. It functions as a follow-up reminder of the exhibition and a sneak-peak into the project.

In Search Of

Firm Spiral Design Studio, LLC

Creative Direction Robert Clancy, Lauren Payne, Neil Wright, Jeanie Guity, Maureen Mooney, Gina Brittain, Anne Hobday, and Liz Katzman

Design/Illustration Robert Clancy, Lauren Payne, Neil Wright, Jeanie Guity, Maureen Mooney, Gina Brittain, Anne Hobday, and Liz Katzman

Photography Various royalty-free stock

Printing Benchemark Printing (postcards) and Xerox Phaser 7700 (vellum interior sheet and insert cover)

Manufacturers The Chocolate Gecko (chocolates), Palacek (red case), JKM Ribbon (cranberry ribbon), Jennifer Papers (pebble paper), Zone 5 (gatorboard), Fire Mountain Gems (leather strap) and Specialty Box & Packaging Co., Inc. (crinkle-cut paper)

"Critical to a promotion's success is its power to provide recipients with a positive, memorable, and multisensory experience. Personalization and handmade elements immediately engage the recipient. We never underestimate the value of a sensory experience and get far greater response with a soft-sell approach."

—Robert Clancy, Spiral Design Studio

OBJECTIVE Spiral Design Studio wanted to develop a distinctive, imaginative year-end promotional campaign that truly expressed the passion and personality of the design team in hopes of inspiring adventurous collaboration with clients.

AUDIENCE The promotional campaign was distributed to current and prospective clientele. One hundred and fifty were created. Additional promotional elements were retained to be used as needed throughout the year.

CONCEPT Inspired by the world around them, the design team set their sights on travel and exploration to entice recipients to take a collaborative journey. The two-part campaign starts with an illustrative travel map sent to intrigue and pique curiosity. It alludes to a worldly journey to come. A customized travel case, personalized with the recipient's name, is sent as a follow-up to reinforce the overall travel theme. Inside the vibrant red leather case is a brass compass asking recipients to discover their true North. Also enclosed is a series of custom postcards of various destinations, beginning with Spiral Design Studio as the stating point. Each card is created in a distinctive style, showcasing the diversity of the design team. Under the compass, a secret message is printed on translucent paper that reads, "Savor the Journey." Behind the message is yet another layer, a delectable array of molded white, dark, and milk chocolates sealed in customized wrappers reminiscent of vintage travel stickers. The entire ensemble encourages recipients to explore a new direction.

MESSAGE Take a journey to discover your true North, collaborating with Spiral Design Studio to assist you in the navigation.

RESPONSE The distinctive promotion received countless emails and phone calls from clients and prospects, complimenting the firm on their ingenuity and creativity. The campaign also generated a substantial increase in client requests for unique, three-dimensional marketing collateral. The promotional endeavor was featured in the *HOW Self-Promotion Annual* and won a NORI award from the Albany Ad Club.

fig. 1.1

A colorful image-driven map, printed in-house on Fraser tallow 80 lb. text, comes hand-tied with a red leather strap.

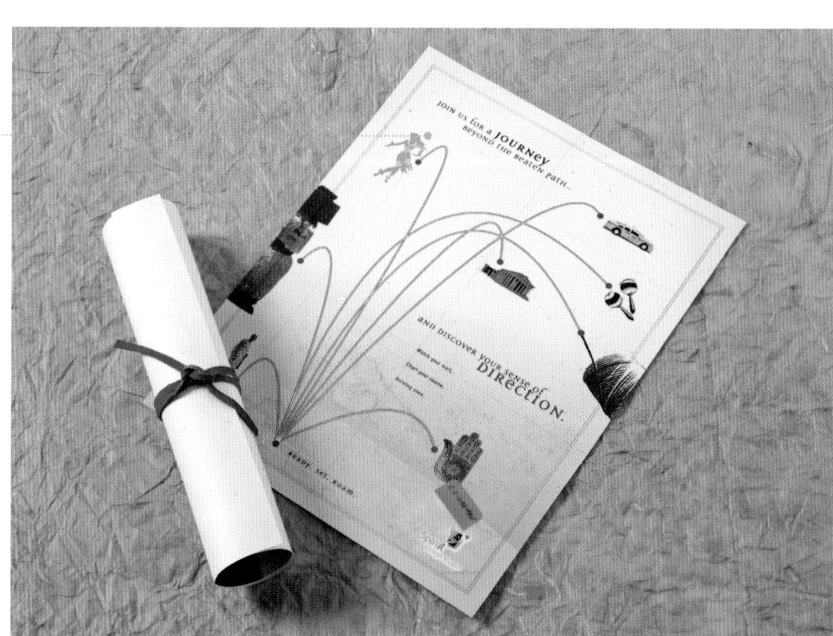

fig. 2.1

Inside the velvet-lined case, a brass compass is embedded into black gatorboard and topped off by a map with motivating copy, encouraging the recipient to discover their true North. A cranberry red ribbon tied on one end accents the piece.

fig. 2.2

The red leather vintage travel case is customized with colorful postage-stamp-size images of various global destinations.

fig. 2.3

To personalize the luggage, a passenger identification tag is attached to each case with a 1/8" (3 mm) black fabric elastic band.

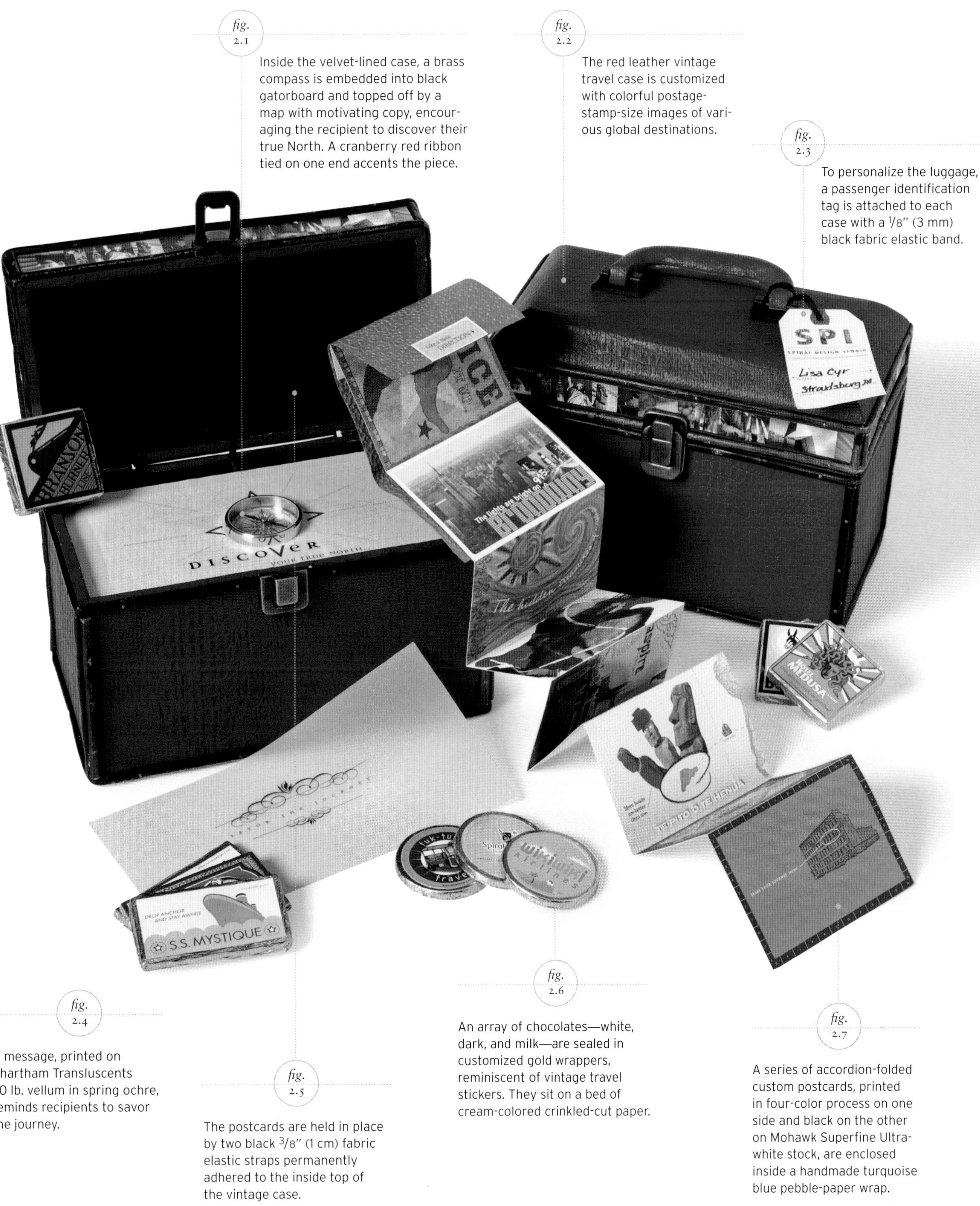

fig. 2.4

A message, printed on Chartham Transluscents 30 lb. vellum in spring ochre, reminds recipients to savor the journey.

fig. 2.5

The postcards are held in place by two black 3/8" (1 cm) fabric elastic straps permanently adhered to the inside top of the vintage case.

fig. 2.6

An array of chocolates—white, dark, and milk—are sealed in customized gold wrappers, reminiscent of vintage travel stickers. They sit on a bed of cream-colored crinkled-cut paper.

fig. 2.7

A series of accordion-folded custom postcards, printed in four-color process on one side and black on the other on Mohawk Superfine Ultra-white stock, are enclosed inside a handmade turquoise blue pebble-paper wrap.

Playful Words

Firm Mucca Design

Creative Direction Roberto de Vicq de Cumptich, Matteo Bologna (Mucca Design), and Ashwini Jambotkar (Adobe)

Design Roberto de Vicq, Matteo Bologna, and Steve Holmes (animator for flipbook and website)

Illustration Roberto de Vicq de Cumptich

Printing/Bindery Andrews Connecticut, a subsidiary of RR Donnelley (book and flipbook)

Copywriting Alyson Kuhn (book, flipbook, and website) and Whitney McCleary, Adobe Systems (book, flipbook, and website)

Website Developer Bo Nielsen (skinnyfish.net)

Manufacturer YUPO Corporation America (paper)

Client Adobe Systems Incorporated

"The project celebrates designers and writers, inspiration and collaboration, passion and discipline, shining a spotlight on the many ways technology—Adobe InDesign and OpenType in particular—serves design."

—Ashwini Jambotkar, Adobe Systems Incorporated

OBJECTIVE Adobe Systems was interested in creating a distinctive campaign to inspire, motivate, and connect with designers, while illustrating the creative and typographical capabilities of Adobe® InDesign® software on Yupo Corporation's synthetic paper.

AUDIENCE The primary target audience was creative professionals. Fifteen thousand books and 10,000 flipbooks were produced. Adobe has dispersed many of the *Words at Play* books and continues to use the project to help demonstrate different aspects of InDesign. The website remains online as long as creatives continue to view and enjoy it.

CONCEPT The *Words at Play* campaign comprises an illustrated book, interactive website, and two-way flipbook, each celebrating the power of words, the beauty of typography, and the creative ingenuity of designers. The illustrative book showcases typographic portraits of well-known authors, with a few exceptions. Each portrait, crafted with a single OpenType® font, is composed using the letters of the featured author's name in a style that is reflective of either his or her work or personality. An insightful quotation by each author not only reinforces a central theme—the power of words—but also alludes to a particular Adobe InDesign feature, cleverly illustrated on each spread. In-depth information on the portraits, typefaces used, and InDesign features that are showcased are all detailed in the back of the book. The *Words at Play* website, on the other hand, animates five of the portraits from the illustrated book in a fun and engaging way. Links to information about the book, OpenType fonts, Adobe InDesign software, and the sponsors of the project are also included on the site. A two-way flipbook draws from two of the animated portraits, Lord Byron and Edgar Allan Poe. It is used as a promotional teaser, creating curiosity and drawing interest to the illustrated book and interactive website.

MESSAGE Adobe InDesign software is a stepping-stone to great design.

RESPONSE The design community has found the work to be not only inspiring but also informative. Both the illustrated book and flipbook have received recognition from industry organizations such as the AIGA and the Type Director's Club, as well as the media, including *HOW* and *Print* magazines. The website landed accolades from The International Academy of Digital Arts and Sciences' Webby and People's Voice Awards.

fig. 1.1

The illustrated, perfect-bound book is printed on Yupo synthetic paper, 100 lb. cover with 78 lb. text for the inside pages. It is wrapped with a translucent jacket, printed on Yupo 104 lb. synthetic paper.

fig. 1.2

The book was printed using four Pantone® spot inks—Pantone® 877 C, 583 C, 1235 C, and Purple C—plus process black, a varnish, and an aqueous coating to help bind the colors and provide a durable finish.

fig. 1.3

The preface, which details the project's intent, features a portrait of the French author Racine. It is created using the OpenType font Ex Ponto®, which boasts organic, flowing letterforms that are tastefully embellished. The spread also illustrates how InDesign handles small caps.

fig. 2.1

Each spread in the book presents a portrait of a writer (with two exceptions) created using an OpenType font that embodies something about his or her personality or work. Margaret Atwood's portrait uses Banshee®, a casual modern script that captures her kinetic imagination, while the one of Evelyn Waugh uses Jimbo®, a period typeface that evokes his rich social commentary.

fig. 2.2

Each spread also illustrates an Adobe InDesign feature. Margaret Atwood's spread demonstrates the value of text threading, while Evelyn Waugh showcases the power of the Adobe Paragraph Composer to improve text composition effortlessly.

fig. 2.3

'he *Words at Play* book is set in Varnock® Pro, an OpenType font lesigned by Robert Slimbach in ıonor of John Warnock, one of he founders of Adobe Systems ncorporated.

fig. 3.1

The flipbook is printed in process black on Yupo synthetic paper, 86 lb. cover for the outside and 58 lb. cover for the interior pages. By using a coverstock for the inside, the flipbook was able to have a hearty snap when the pages are flipped.

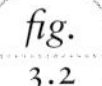

fig. 3.2

The perfect-bound flipbook requires special glue called PUR, which has to cure for twenty-four hours after it is applied.

fig. 3.3

The flipbook cover and bellyband are both printed with a varnish. An aqueous coating is applied throughout to bind the inks to the synthetic page and provide a durable finish.

fig. 3.4

The interactive, small-format book is wrapped by a bellyband, printed in the Adobe corporate red (PMS 486) on Yupo synthetic paper, 68 lb. text.

fig. 4.2

Each portrait on the website is accompanied by a jazz music piece that features a single instrument.

The Book

Words at Play is a book that showcases 21 portraits of well-known authors. It is also a many-splendored, multi-layered typographic *tour d'amour*. Each portrait is crafted from a single OpenType® font, expressive of that writer's personality or work, using all of the letters in that person's name (plus parentheses). Words are at play in every portrait, with letters serving as cravats, coiffures, and character lines.

Each portrait is also paired with a quotation from the author about the power of words or the craft of writing. There's a catch, *natch*: To qualify, each writer's quote had to contain the word *word* or *words*. And, in a punderful twist, each quote had to allude to a specific Adobe® InDesign® feature at play in the book's design.

Who's Who on the Creative Team

A selection of spreads from the book, *Words at Play*

Words at Play is an homage to the beauty of typography and the creativity of designers. It's also a celebration of {InDesign} technology in service to superb typography. Lickety-click, type heaven is within reach. O, text wrapture!

Book at a Glance: *Words at Play*

- Content A limited-run book of type portraits of writers, which also shows off key benefits of InDesign software
- Designed by Roberto de Vicq de Cumptich and Matteo Bologna; written by Alyson Kuhn
- Paper YUPO® synthetic paper (104# translucent for the book jacket, 100# cover, and 78# text)
- Printed on Mitsubishi 40-inch, 6-color, sheet-fed press by Andrews Connecticut, an RR Donnelley Company
- *Words at Play* In Detail: PDF: 2MB

at swordplay

FEEDBACK

Copyright © 2004 Adobe Systems Incorporated. All Rights Reserved.

Terms of Use | Privacy Policy | Permissions and Trademarks

fig. 4.1

The *Words at Play* website (www.wordsatplay.com) is a spin-off of the illustrated book. The typographic portraits of Samuel Beckett, Anne Sexton, Lord Byron, Edgar Allan Poe, and Napoleon Bonaparte are disassembled in Adobe® Illustrator® and then animated using Adobe® After Effects®.

fig. 4.3

An interactive example of an Adobe InDesign feature follows each typographic animation.

fig. 1.1

The laminated bookmarker, presented with a custom hang-tag that is tied on with a silk ribbon, shows how a derivative work can be created to serve a distinctively different format. It is the second in the series.

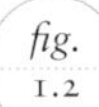

fig. 1.2

The custom marker is sent in a muted-tone envelope that wraps shut with a gold tie.

Licensing Ideas

Firm Cyr Studio
Creative Direction Lisa L. Cyr
Design/Illustration Lisa L. Cyr
Printing Epson 2200 (journal, bookmarker, hangtag, and card)
Bindery Staples (wire-o)
Special Techniques Laminator (USI XL1200)
Manufacturers Kate's Paperie (envelopes), American Ribbon Factory (ribbon and rope) and Fabricland Interiors (beads and cloth)

"It was important to produce a series of stationery-based promotions, each featuring a different usage of the same illustrative work. Sometimes clients can't visualize the variety of ways that a single image can be utilized until you show them."

—Lisa L. Cyr, Cyr Studio

OBJECTIVE Cyr Studio was interested in developing a promotional campaign that would demonstrate how a single illustrated image could be licensed and utilized in a plethora of ways.

AUDIENCE The series of work were distributed to stationery and paper product companies for the purpose of licensing. Only twenty-five of the journals were produced. The bookmarkers and cards are still being produced and handed out to prospects.

CONCEPT It was important to produce a series of stationery-based promotions, each featuring a different usage of the same illustrative work. The wire-o–bound journal cover utilizes a signature illustration in its entirety, while the inside employs several cropped sections of the artwork as tipped-on images, each accenting the six fold-out chapter headers. The bookmarker, sent as a follow-up, shows how a derivative work pulled from the original illustration can be employed when the format changes. The custom hangtag shows yet another cropped version and use of the primary illustration Notecards, the last in the series to be distributed, repeat the use of the original illustration in its entirety to bring the campaign full circle.

MESSAGE The versatile illustration work of Cyr Studio can be used in a variety of formats.

RESPONSE The campaign has been very successful. It has attracted licensees, landing new clients and expanding the firm's presence in the stationery and paper products industry.

fig. 2.1

The wire-o-bound journal, the first in the promotional series, is printed on Epson double-sided matte paper and wrapped over cream matte board.

fig. 2.2

The hangtag that accompanies the bag is overlaid with a vellum sheet imprinted with the artist's name. The hangtag is accented with a set of beads for visual interest.

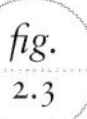

fig. 2.3

The illustrated journal comes in a custom cloth bag that seals shut with a gold cord rope.

fig. 2.4

Inside are a series of six fold-out pages that act as chapters, each highlighted with a different crop of the same cover image to show variety.

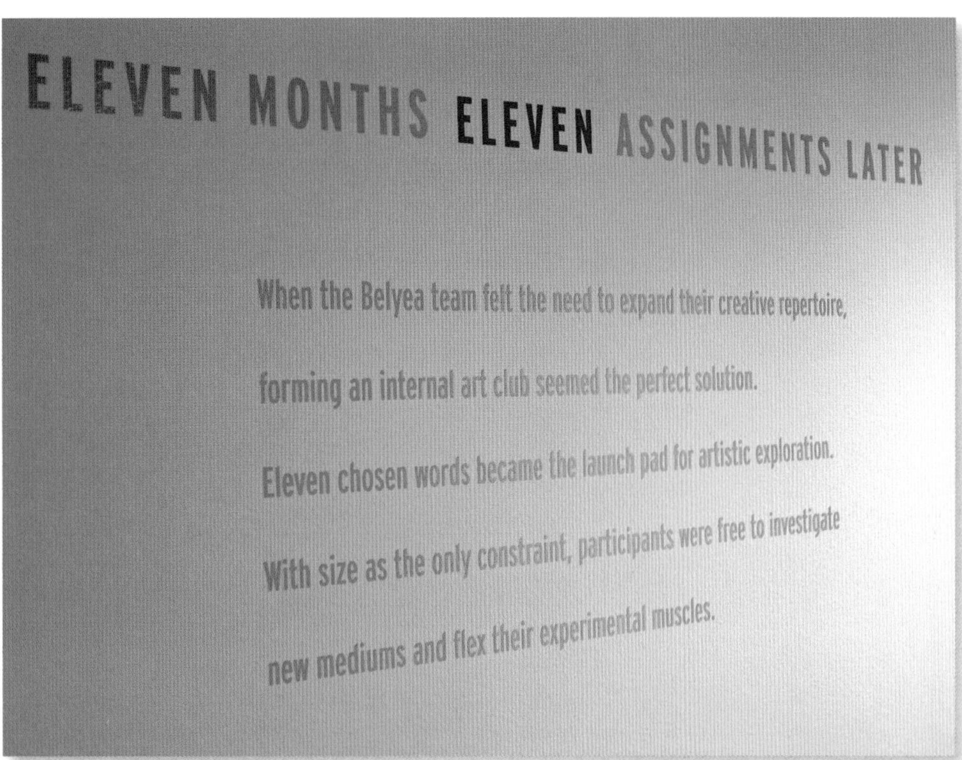

Eleven x Eleven

Firm Belyea

Creative Direction Patricia Belyea

Design Ben Reynolds

Illustration Patricia Belyea, Ron Lars Hansen, Naomi Murphy, Anne Dougherty, and Ben Reynolds

Printing ColorGraphics (cards and envelopes)

Manufacturers Packaging Specialties (ribbon)

"Belyea was working to infuse more creativity in the studio through its art club. This self-imposed project was valuable for inspiring the design team to produce experimental work. The energy in the office was high, and putting an art show together continued to create excitement. Deciding to publish our artwork pushed everyone to work even harder."

—Patricia Belyea, Belyea

OBJECTIVE To keep creativity flowing throughout the workplace, Belyea started its own internal art club. Impressed at what they created, the team wanted to share their vision and experience in a gallerylike exhibition.

AUDIENCE The audience for the exhibition opening consisted of clients and friends. A series of notecards was given as a gift to attendees. The thought-provoking cards were also distributed at the American Marketing Association luncheon, primarily to marketing directors. Belyea is still using the notecards for business and personal correspondence.

CONCEPT For one year, the design team at Belyea developed artwork, exploring materials and techniques and ultimately expanding their creative repertoire. The only requirement for the project was that the work be based on a designated theme and fit in an 11" x 11" (28 x 28 cm) format. A new finished piece of art was presented to the group at the first staff meeting of every month. To share their insight and vision, the design team put together an art exhibition. A set of eleven notecards was developed as a gift for guests to bring home, share, and enjoy. The art ranged from 2-D to 3-D, each quite conceptual in nature. The exhibition, titled *Eleven Months Eleven Assignments*, of original work created under the art club was held on the eleventh of November.

MESSAGE Experience the unique vision of Belyea.

RESPONSE The notecards were enjoyed by all who received them. Many asked for more. After the luncheon event, the design firm received two inquiries from companies interested in starting a working relationship with the creative firm.

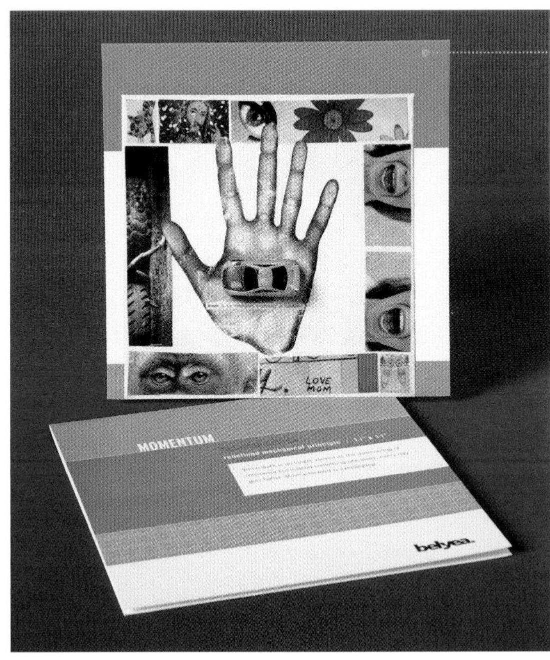

fig. 2.1

Each card has a theme, a piece of custom art on the front, and thought-provoking copy on the back. There is also a brief explanation of the creative concept written by each artist.

fig. 2.2

The accent colors chosen for each notecard help carry the palette of the key image on the front to the back of the card.

fig. 2.3

Under the momentum theme, the art titled *Redefined Mechanical Principle* is explained by owner Patricia Belyea as, "When work is no longer viewed as the overcoming of resistance but instead something one loves, every day gets better. Moving forward is exhilarating." The caution-yellow car rolling across the lifelines of a palm signifies the momentum in one's life.

A signature motif, an abstraction of 11 x 11, is carried throughout the notecards, envelopes, insert card, and bellyband sticker.

fig. 3.3

fig. 3.1

A set of eleven cards, printed in four-color process on Fraser Papers Pegasus brilliant white super smooth cover, is wrapped with a ribbon bellyband and sealed with a custom label.

fig. 3.2

The set is collated using different cards on top to create an interesting display. The ribbon bellybands also alternated from a selection of three colors: steel blue, straw yellow, and sage green.

fig. 3.5

The custom envelopes are printed in four-color process on the inside to produce a selection of four color schemes.

fig. 3.4

An insert card, printed in process colors, helps convey the story behind the artistic endeavor.

fig. 4.1

For the exhibition *Eleven Months Eleven Assignments*, vinyl graphics were created for the studio walls to convey the series of eleven thought-provoking themes.

Selling Luxury

OBJECTIVE Douglas Joseph Partners was looking to selectively expand their client base in the consumer-oriented, luxury-driven markets across the United States.

AUDIENCE The target audience consisted primarily of prospects that deal in luxury goods and services that can benefit from the firm's experience. Fifteen hundred of each custom book have been produced.

CONCEPT The firm chose to penetrate the marketplace with a direct-mail campaign. Designed to introduce the marketing communications firm and its capabilities, the first promotional initiative in the series featured a case study of work produced for a single client, Fraser Papers. The subsequent mailings, a series of books entitled *New Works 1, 2,* and *3*, help to keep the firm's name fresh in the minds of prospects by continuing to show recent projects in an elegant, sophisticated format.

MESSAGE Douglas Joseph Partners produces a wide range of high-quality work.

RESPONSE The campaign has been a tremendous success, landing new clients and expanding the communication firm's presence into the East Coast and Midwest areas of the United States.

Firm Douglas Joseph Partners

Creative Direction Doug Joseph and Scott Lambert

Design Scott Lambert

Photography Rick Brian

Printing Quebecor World George Rice & Sons (case study), Cenveo Anderson Lithograph (New Work 1 and 2), and Graphic Press (New Work 3)

Special Techniques Acme Graphic Arts Finishing (deboss and die scoring) and Jenco Productions (gluing and hand fulfillment)

"The case study reflects our capabilities through work produced for a single client over a period of three years. It demonstrates how we established a brand image and successfully carried it through a myriad of applications on an ongoing basis. The series of *New Work* books were a natural evolution from there."

—Doug Joseph, Douglas Joseph Partners

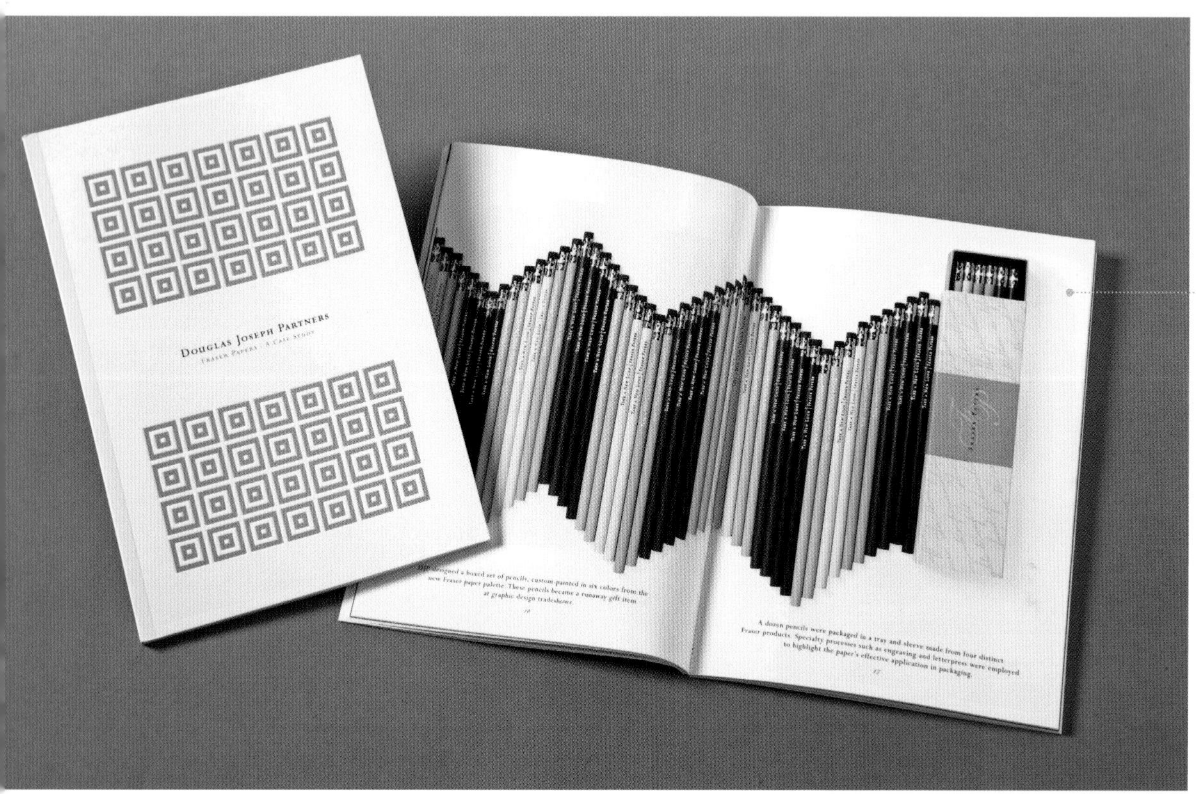

fig. 1.1

The in-depth case study, printed on Fraser Papers (Smart Papers) Pegasus brilliant white super smooth 110 lb. cover and 100 lb. text, is the first book distributed in the series.

fig. 1.2

Perpetua is the font of choice.

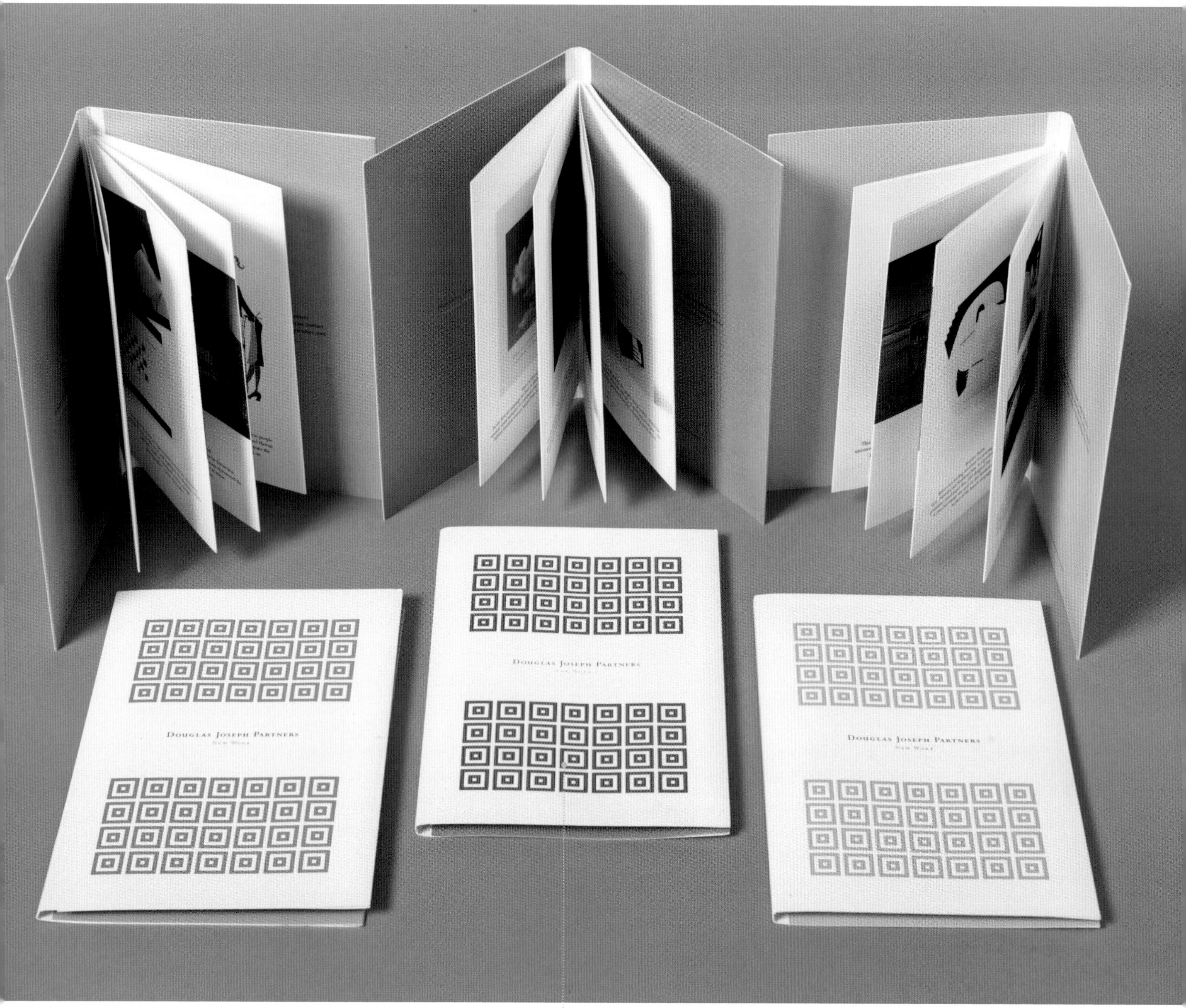

New Work 1 and *New Work 2* are printed on Fraser Papers (Smart Papers) Pegasus briliant white super smooth 110 lb. cover. *New Work 3* employs the same stock but in a different weight, 80 lb.

Each book in the series boasts a highly graphic debossed cover that is printed in its own signature palette of three colors with a dull varnish laid on top.

Inside, each small-format book is printed in four-color process plus one PMS color that is repeated from the back cover. Dull varnish is applied on all the images and areas of solid coverage.

Lasting Sound

Firm Independent Opposition

Creative Direction Matt Frantz

Design/Illustration Matt Frantz

Video Matt Frantz

Music Nectarphonic, Combination No. 10, Panayiotis Kokoras, Ole Peterson, Tat-Gun, Horrendous, Cousin Silas, Tin R.P., Giuseppe Rapisarda, Satyr Oz, Brian Schorn, Cameron Sears, Mystified, Thomas Jackson Park, Dark Audio Project (Aaron Butler, Bill Monson, Hal Dean, Steve Zieverink, Donn Vidmar, Michelle Sierra, Eonju Kim), Brekekekexkoaxkoax, Gates Ensemble, Carmen Resendez, Michael Northan, Moon, Matt Frantz, Bollwerk 81, Signalbleed, Maggi Payne, Tchant, Dave Cupp, Die Bene Tleilax, Mike Pursley, Fridur, Brian Schorn, James Bohn, Planes Overhead, John Salcido, Mike Hallenbeck, Cognition Audioworks (Andrew Duke), R.P. Collier, David Nix, Mobile (Michael Kidd), Porkopolis (Ashley Allen, Dave Duncan, Mike Gregory, Mark Miller, Charlotte Schmitz, Mike Schmitz, Corbett Stepp), Dan Susnara, Whitehall (Jeffrey Patrick Rollason and Fernando Omar Coipel), Greta Nintzel, Bob Arieas, Don Campau, Andrew Greene, and John Salcido

Printing Postcard Press (postcards) and Disk Faktory (CD booklet)

Special Techniques Disk Faktory (CD duplication and imprinting)

"Recent technologies have made it easier than ever before for anyone with a passion for sound to create high-quality records. Developments in Internet communication have given international subcultures a means for passing around news and artistic works. Doing this project, I learned a lot about the high level of talent that exists under the mainstream radar."

—Matt Frantz, Independent Opposition

OBJECTIVE Multimedia artist Matt Frantz wanted to create a promotion that would demonstrate his unique ability to conceptualize, design, edit, and produce thought-provoking work for the music industry. The initiative would serve as the artist's calling card and provide Frantz with a way to stand out from the crowd of traditional composers.

AUDIENCE *The Last Signal* was distributed to video game companies, film production houses, and motion graphic studios in southern California. The CD has been sent to magazines and Internet radio stations for review and play. It was sold as merchandise online and in galleries. The musicians who participated in the project are also distributing the CD through online shops and at performances. For the initial launch, one hundred were produced.

CONCEPT The multitalented artist chose to create a highly conceptual music CD. *The Last Signal* is an international compilation of sonic explorations and creative interpretations of what the end of the world might sound like. The collage of sound blurs the boundaries of music and noise with a variety of conceptual and stylistic approaches. The CD features more than thirty-five tracks from cutting-edge musicians and sound designers from Australia, Canada, France, Germany, Greece, Italy, the United Kingdom, and the United States. The CD showcases a diversity of work in a cohesive listening experience.

MESSAGE The work of multimedia artist Matt Frantz is provocative and cutting-edge.

RESPONSE Through bulletin board postings, emails, Web forums, gallery exhibitions, and direct appeals to disc jockeys, composers, filmmakers, video game companies, and record labels, the artist has been able to generate international attention for the sound collage compilation. The project also generated interest from a director of a feature-length documentary film about experimental musicians.

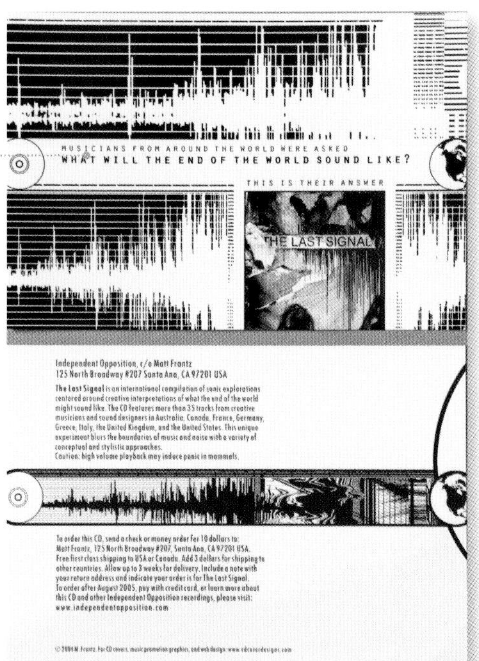

fig. 1.1

A postcard, printed in four-color process on one side and black on the other, introduces the project and solicits orders. A UV coating is applied for protection.

fig. 2.1

The CD insert is reproduced in four-color process on one side and black on the other.

fig. 2.2

Inside the CD case, text is randomly obliterated and distressed, suggesting destruction and doom.

fig. 2.3

The Last Signal CD cover illustration, made from broken and burned CDs and plastic jewel cases left over from the production process, provides a sense of mystery and intrigue as to what is inside.

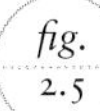

fig. 2.4

The typeface Helvetica is used throughout for its subtle quality, allowing the art to rule.

fig. 2.5

The concept-based music CD comes in a plastic jewel case that is shrink-wrapped shut.

fig. 2.6

The music CD label, silkscreen-printed in four-color process, uses vertical lines to represent audio waveforms graphically. The lines move from left to right, increasing in size until they end in an undefined mass, also known as the last signal.

THE LAST SIGNAL: HANGING HEADPHONES

fig. 3.1

An engaging, highly conceptual wall display with headphones attached is used to promote and sell the CD through galleries. Its artistic, abstract nature can be easily incorporated into any fine-art space.

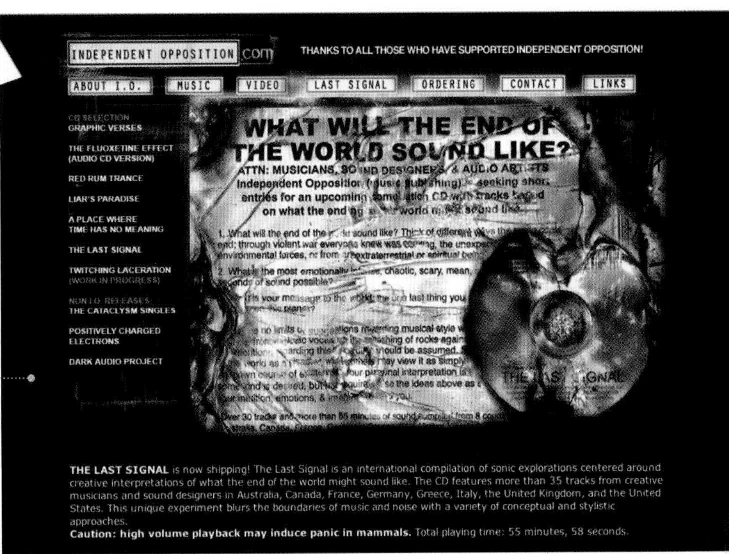

fig. 4.1

A website link, www.independentopposition.com/thelastsignal.html, allows interested parties to sample music from the various tracks as well as the opportunity to view a custom video that was created to further visualize the concept.

Monster Bash

OBJECTIVE Monster, a group of illustrators who joined creative forces to advertise in new and unusual ways, wanted to create a series of promotions that would showcase their creative abilities and establish their brand in the marketplace.

AUDIENCE The target audience ranged in markets. The campaign was sent to existing and prospective clientele of each of the collaborators. Five thousand trading card sets and three thousand flipbooks were produced.

CONCEPT The Monster trading cards feature various monster incarnations on the front and background stats on the back, revealing a bit about each Monster's unique personality. A number of signed, uncut printed sheets are available for collectors on the Monster website, www.monsterillo.com.

The *Fantastique Anatomatique* booklet, designed to be interactive, allows recipients to create their own wacky monster. There is also an online version, where interested individuals can scramble the images endlessly.

MESSAGE We're fun, we're creative, and you should definitely hire us for your next project.

RESPONSE The series of promotions have established the various individual illustrators as a unified group. The Monster collaborative has received substantial press coverage from their efforts. On average, the Monster site receives hundreds of hits a month, generating traffic and new leads. There has also been interest with collectors.

Firm MONSTER

Creative Direction/Design GORDON STUDER (FLIPBOOK) AND BRIAN BIGGS (TRADING CARDS)

Illustration BUD PEEN, GORDON STUDER, MARCOS SORENSEN, MICHIKO STEHRENBERGER, SUSAN GROSS, MICHAEL WERTZ, ISABEL SAMARAS, JAMES A. WINTERS, PAMELA HOBBS, BRIAN BIGGS, DAVE GORDON, AND LLOYD DANGLE

Printing/Bindery BURDISS LETTERSHOP SERVICES (FLIPBOOK) AND COAST LITHO (TRADING CARDS)

Manufacturers A LA CARTE LINE (WHITE PLASTIC BAGS)

"Our concept was to produce different ideas to show our work not only as a group but also as individuals. Because everyone's styles are so vastly different, we don't feel that we're competing for the same projects. As a result, we've ended up establishing a loyal group of art buyers who look forward to our promotions."

—Bud Peen, Monster

fig. 1.1

Each card, printed in four-color process on the front and black on the back, features a wacky monster incarnation. There is a unique monster for each artist in the group. Stats on the back provide insight into the various Monster personalities.

fig. 1.2

The trading cards come as a set of ten packaged in a pearlescent white plastic bag that is sealed on two sides.

fig. 2.1

Sloop ScriptThree is the fancy type used on the cover; Linotype Decoration is employed as an accent.

fig. 2.3

The *Fantastique Anatomatique* flipbook is printed in four-color process on Sundance 80 lb. cover with Quintessence 100 lb. gloss text for the inside.

fig. 2.2

Inside the flipbook, the recipient can make his or her own monster creations using various body parts—a clever way to integrate the group's diverse styles.

Promotions as Demonstrators

Firm Blockdot/Kewlbox.com
Creative Direction/Design Dan Ferguson
Game Development Michael Bielinski, Shane Culp, Andrew Richards, and Don Relyea
Printing/Bindery Imaging Bureau (brochure and CD inserts)
Special Techniques Everest digital printer (CD labels)
Manufacturers US Plastics Corp (cases)

"Our interactive self-promotions show how branding can be integrated into a game experience. By drawing clients into the interactive environment, we can effectively demonstrate our creativity, innovative thinking, and expertise. After spending time playing our games, clients want something similar to promote their brands."

—Dan Ferguson, Blockdot

OBJECTIVE Blockdot, an interactive agency specializing in the creation of advergames (advertising-based games), was looking to produce a series of exciting and entertaining games to use as CD-ROM calling cards for new business development.

AUDIENCE The series of games was distributed to current and prospective clientele, primarily agency marketing executives and corporate brand managers. For the games *Adventure Elf* and *Shrunken Heads*, five hundred were produced. *Action Pack*, a collection of the firm's portfolio of corporate games, was produced in a lot of 1,000.

CONCEPT The theme-based games drew content from two well-known, highly celebrated days. For Halloween, *Shrunken Heads* engages players, encouraging them to stop a zany, out-of control candy-making machine from filling up a pit with nougat-filled shrunken heads. In *Adventure Elf*, a Christmas promotion, Santa's sleigh has been raided by mischievous penguins who mistake the presents for tuna. Players need to help Oliver the elf return the gifts to Santa's sleigh before Christmas Eve. *Action Pack* is, on the other hand, both a dynamic portfolio of mostly client-based games along with informative case studies that demonstrate how advergames can deliver a highly impactful marketing message. It is used year-round as a leave-behind. Players are encouraged to submit their game score to the firm's website at www.kewlbox.com, providing a way to track usage. Once on the site, prospects are able to view a strong track record of advergames produced for a diverse array of companies. To accompany the game initiative, a corporate brochure was created, showcasing the firm's various services. For prospective clients, a promotional insert card is placed inside the CD case to reinforce the firm's offerings. For existing clientele, a thank-you card is included instead.

MESSAGE Interactive games provide content in an interesting and entertaining way.

RESPONSE It is estimated that the various advergames have been played more than 30 million times, generating quite a bit of traffic on the firm's website. In addition, the interactive games have also created a substantial fan following.

fig. I.I
The 8" x 5 1/2" (20.5 x 14 cm) clear, plastic-coil-bound brochure is printed in four-color process with spot applications of both dull and gloss varnish throughout.

fig. I.2
The front and back covers, made of Transilwrap0200 clear matte vinyl plastic, provide a soft-focus feel to the firm's highly graphic presence.

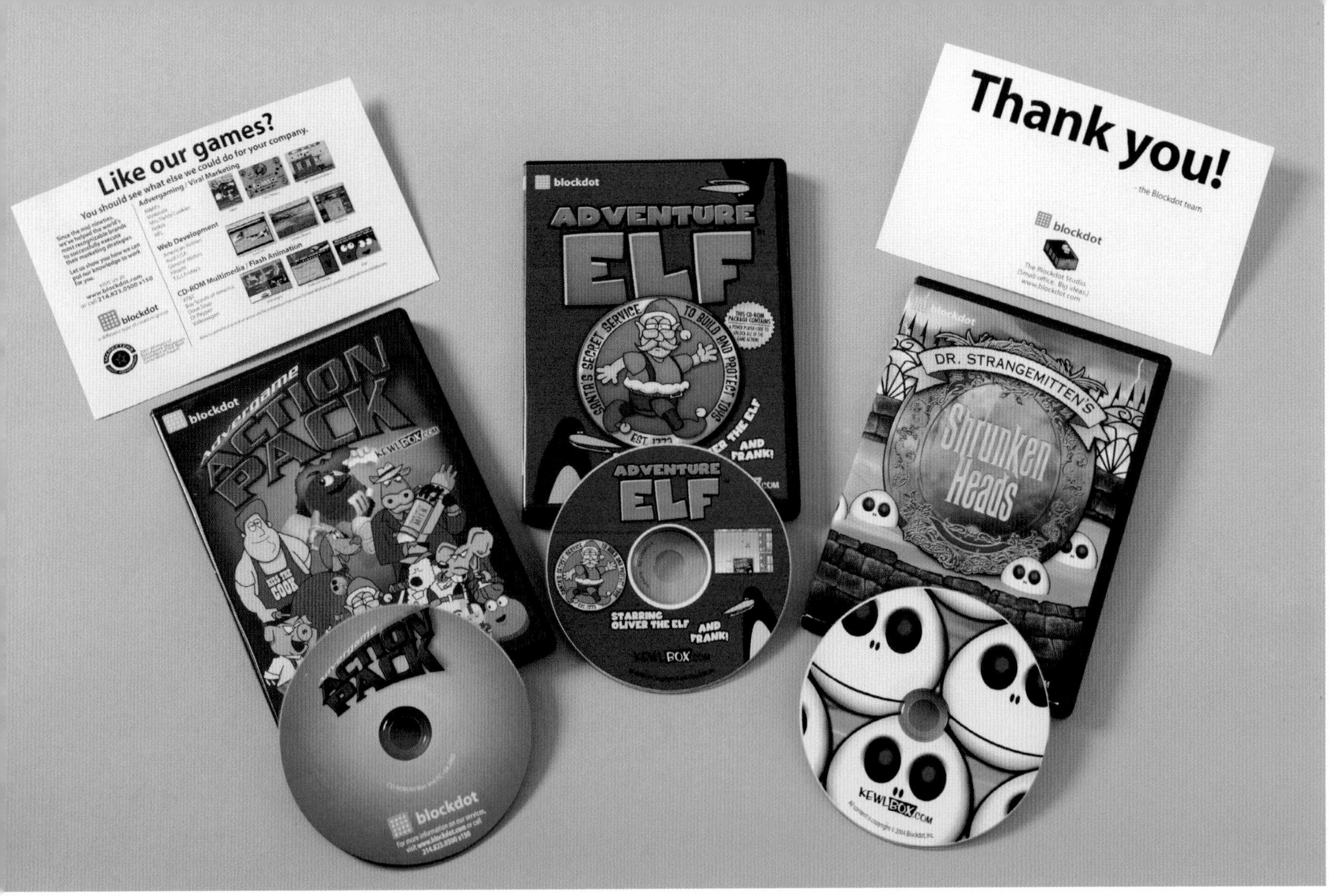

fig. 2.1

Each interactive game comes in a plastic CD case. It is customized with signature graphics on a wraparound insert.

fig. 2.2

Inside the single CD case is a disc with a custom label applied using a thermal process.

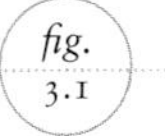

fig. 3.1

Each game is developed using Macromedia Director, Macromedia Flash, Adobe Illustrator, Adobe Photoshop, and Maya.

Images of Power

OBJECTIVE The Museum of History of Yugoslavia was having an exhibition of the work of Yugoslavian-born, world-renown designer Mirko Ilić and wanted to promote the event in a grand way.

AUDIENCE The target audience varied from Yugoslavian youth who haven't been previously introduced to Ilić's work to professionals from the creative industry who have followed the designer's career for many years.

CONCEPT Most of the creative works produced employed designer Mirko Ilić's powerful sociopolitical illustrations. Through the course of the campaign, postcards, bookmarkers, and posters were given away to raise awareness. Billboards and transit posters placed throughout the city also helped to generate a buzz. A TV ad, directed by Stefan Arsenijević, featured some of Ilić's most significant works in a narrative fashion. A Web page and Web banners were also created to promote the exhibition. On the day of the opening, the daily newspaper *Danas*, which means "today," featured a supplement entitled *Sutra*, which means "tomorrow." The clever title referenced a rock-and-roll song written by Ilić during the '80s called "I am a man for tomorrow." The supplement featured Ilić's illustrations and op-ed pages along with personal comments from the designer's friends and coworkers. After the opening, postcards, mouse pads, bookmarkers, and limited-edition hand-signed posters were sold to the general public. Two invitations were created: one for the exhibition and another for an opening reception.

The Museum of the History of Yugoslavia, an old bank building that became a museum during the Communist period, was largely unused until it was revived during the new millennium. It was the perfect setting for an exhibition of an artist who reconnects all parts of former Yugoslavia. The exhibition was divided into sections. The entrance hall featured the designer's earlier works and posters. The main hall was used for works concerning the former Yugoslavia. The central hall was dominated by large prints of Ilić's later works along with original scratchboard artwork, books, packaging design, and several computers showing the designer's animated and interactive work. A large screen was placed at the far end of the third hall so it could be seen from every point of the exhibition, from the entrance to the end. In a side stairway, *Sex & Lies*, which had the look of an intimate peep show, featured Ilić's more controversial work. All the promotional materials were situated at the entrance of the main hall.

MESSAGE Mirko Ilić has returned and wants to inspire others.

RESPONSE The promotional campaign created an incredible euphoria throughout the city, generating a tremendous amount of press coverage, in both print and broadcast. Over the duration of the exhibition, more than 10,000 visitors attended, raising a great deal of interest in Ilić's work and in the issues it addressed. People from former Yugoslavian republics and distant parts of Serbia and Montenegro made special excursions to see the once-in-a-lifetime event.

Firm Folie a Trois
Art Direction/Design Aleksandar Maćašev
Production/Organization Anica Tucakov and Tatjana Ristić
Curator of the Exhibition Anica Tucakov
Director of TV Ad Stefan Arsenijević
TV Production DigitalKraft
Music Darkwood Dub
Illustration Mirko Ilić
Printing Publikum (invitations, postcards, bookmarkers, an posters) Grafix (billboards), Adverto (mouse pads), Big Prin (enlarged exhibits)
Client The Museum of History of Yugoslavia

"In this promotion, we treated the art as a cultural product that needs to be marketed like any other product. In post-Communist Serbia and Montenegro, this is a new practice. Another thing that was done differently was that the entire project was carried out by an independent group of creative individuals and not by a museum or cultural institution."

—Aleksandar Maćašev, Folie a Tro

fig. 1.1

A series of five powerfully illustrative billboards, digitally printed on 140 gsm Rexam blue back stock, commanded the roadways.

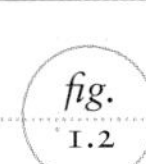

fig. 1.2

Outside the Museum of the History of Yugoslavia, towering banners of Ilić's work greeted guests on their arrival. They are digital printed onto 450 gsm PVC plastic.

fig. 2.1

The invitations, printed in black and white on Stora Enso 300 gsm stock with a matte finish, feature a broken copyright symbol that turns into the strong logo of Mirko Ilić Corporation, a Latin rendering of the Serbian letter ć. The die-cut accent helps draw attention to the break.

fig. 2.2

The primary fonts used are variations of Alternate Gothic.

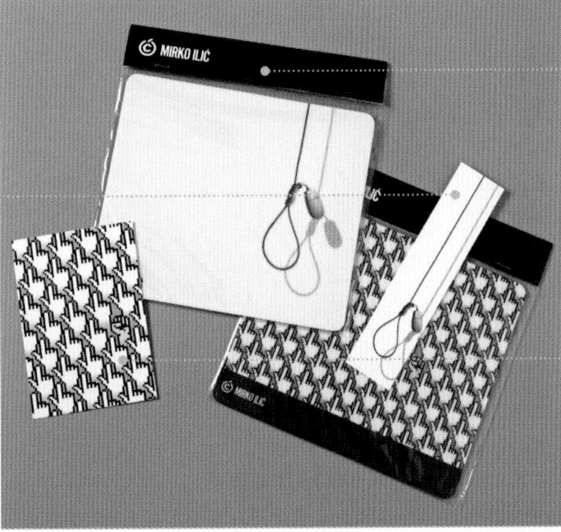

fig. 3.1

Three mouse pad designs, printed on 1/8" (3 mm) foam and packaged in plastic bags sealed with a staple-bound label, showcase Ilić's illustrative work.

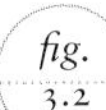

fig. 3.2

Bookmarkers, printed on Stora Enso 300 gsm white stock with a matte finish, are created in three variations.

fig. 3.3

Postcards, produced in nine variations, are each printed in four-color process on one side and black on the other using Stora Enso 300 gsm white stock with a glossy finish.

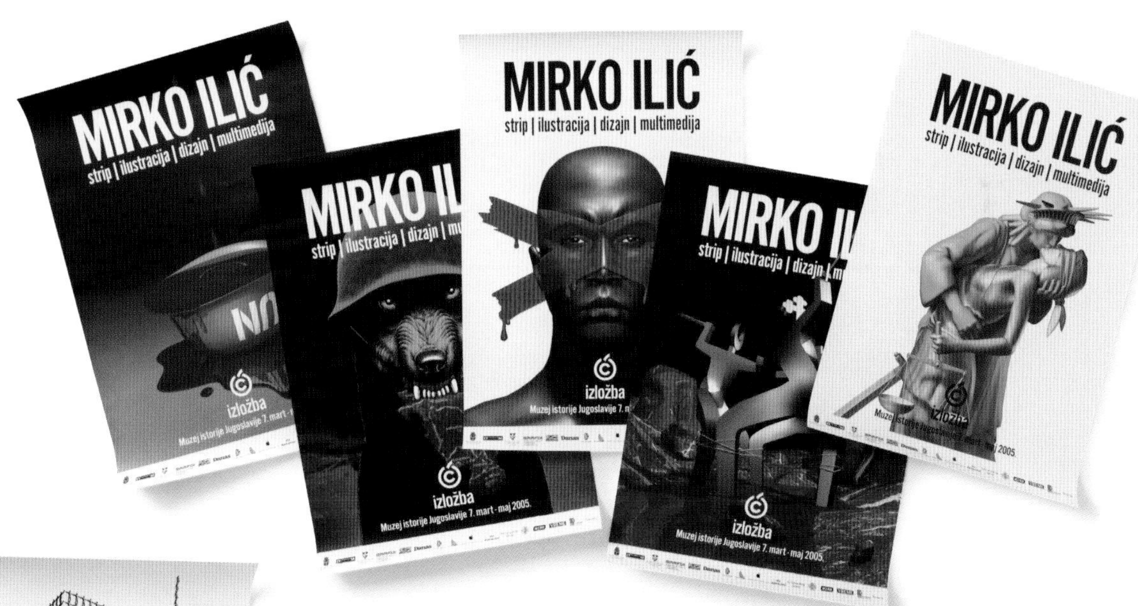

fig. 4.1

The exhibition announcement posters are printed on Stora Enso 200 gsm matte finish stock in six variations and placed in bookstores, cultural centers, schools, and art academies around the city. Transit posters, digitally printed on Ferarri 150 gsm PVC plastic, utilize the same imagery.

fig. 5.1

Limited-edition collectible posters, printed on Stora Enso 220 gsm white stock with a glossy finish, are hand-signed by the designer. One of the images, a concept piece about the tragedy of September 11, does not appear anywhere else.

Proposing Change

Firm Nassar Design
Creative Direction Nelida Nassar
Design Nelida Nassar and Margarita Encomienda
Illustration/Photography Marcella Cajiao, Yuri Suzuki, Leslie Lee, Bonnie Chan, Tobias Armborst, Robert Mercer, Geoffrey Nelson, Bill Haldenby, and Daniel Oh
Printing/Bindery Fit to Print (posters) and Alpha Press (catalog)
Client Harvard School of Design

"It is through repetition, development of the design, and empirical trial that we achieved the correct solution, where all the colors fell into place without ever repeating. The only conscious decision, made at the onset of the design phase, was to start with one series of colors and finish with another."

—Nelida Nassar, Nassar Design

OBJECTIVE Harvard Design School's urban design department wanted to put together a visually compelling proposal package for the redevelopment of the waterfront in Genoa, Italy, to restore the city as a place of culture and historical relevance. Nassar Design was contracted to work in collaboration with students and faculty to make this endeavor a reality.

AUDIENCE The audience for the campaign of posters was quite diverse, from urban designers, architects, environmental engineers, land-use planners, government regulators, conservation authorities, watershed managers, developers, city planners, community managers, psychologists, and lawyers to academic researchers, educators, and writers. Five hundred of a series of eight posters were produced.

CONCEPT The purpose of the proposal was to make a reconnection between the edge of the water and the historic city, transforming sites of former industrial occupation into a more inviting ensemble. The design team used evolution as their primary theme throughout. A map of Italy was abstracted and rotated several degrees clockwise, using Genoa as the point of departure. Each poster displays a different stage of evolution with the final poster revealing the map of Italy in its entirety. There is also a progression in color throughout the series of eight posters.

MESSAGE Let's redevelop this cultural treasure.

RESPONSE The project was deeply engaging for all who participated. The posters have won numerous awards from industry magazines, including *Graphis, Print, Graphic Design: USA*, and *Communications Arts*. The work also won an award for poster design through the AIGA. The series are included in the permanent collection of the Library of Congress. In addition, the urban development series has been exhibited in Genoa, Bologna, Rome, and Milan. The project has positioned Harvard School of Design at the cutting edge, a point of pride for the urban design department and the school.

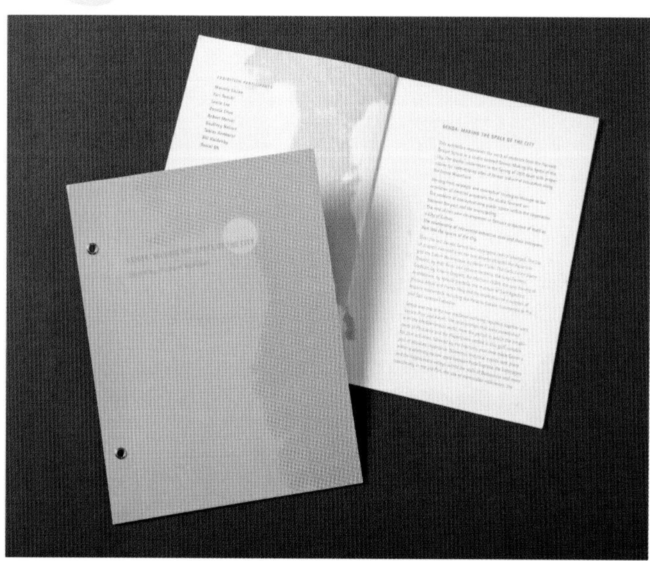

fig. 1.1 An exhibition catalog is printed on Strobe coated 80 lb. cover using PMS 5497 gray and PMS 611 yellow plus gloss varnish.

fig. 1.2 The 6 1/2" x 8 1/2" (16.5 x 21.5 cm) booklet is bound using eyelets, making a connection back to the circular shape dominant in the poster series.

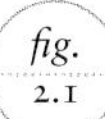

Each poster, printed on Strobe gloss 100 lb. white paper, represents the designs of a different student.

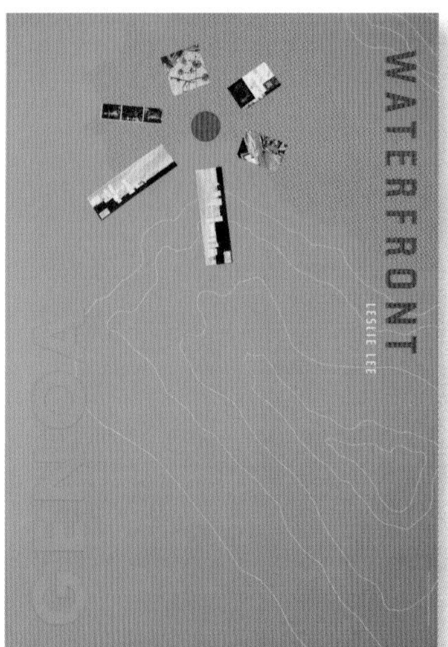

The series of oversize posters are silkscreen- and offset-printed using a complex color sequence—PMS 116, PMS 3005, PMS 247, PMS 533, PMS 172, PMS 376, and PMS 144—that is never repeated. Each poster uses four colors, one acting as a link to the next poster in the series.

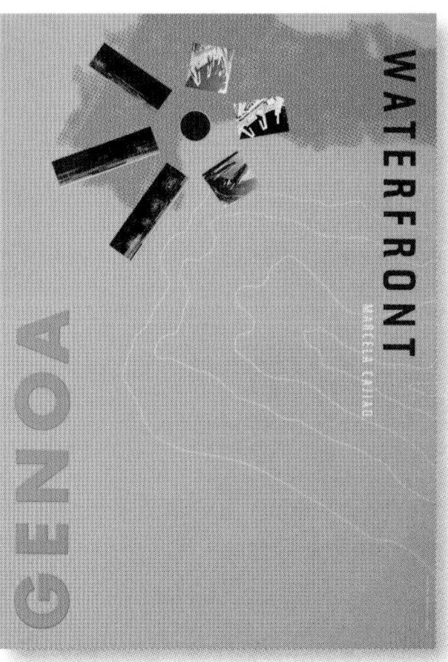

fig. 2.3

Spot gloss varnish is used to bring certain elements forward.

fig. 2.4

The fonts Futura and Tasse are used as complements to the bold graphics.

Soulful Surface

Firms Carmichael Lynch Thorburn and Hatch Show Print

Creative Direction Bill Thorburn

Design David Schrimpf (brochure and booklet), Agnes Barton-Sabo (Blinding White Willy poster), Brad Vetter (White Space poster), Nissa Ellison (Paper Soul Jah poster), and Lori Wilson (Red Text Williams poster)

Illustration/Photography Various stock

Printing Hatch Show Print (posters) and Lake County Press (brochure and booklet)

Manufacturer Towsley's Inc. (guitar pick, buttons, T-shirt, CD case, and tube)

Client Appleton Coated

"I think the more you can surround a campaign with depth, the more opportunity you have to create a full experience. We tried to move from just a brochure to something that penetrates the audience on multiple levels."

—Bill Thorburn, Carmichael Lynch Thorburn

OBJECTIVE Appleton Coated wanted to create an exciting campaign that would draw attention to the design and printing capabilities of their brightest coated paper offering, Utopia One X. Carmichael Lynch Thorburn was chosen to design the campaign's promotional brochure; Hatch Show Print, an historic institution in the letterpress community since 1879, was chosen to create and print the posters.

AUDIENCE The audience varied from graphic design firms and creative businesses to printers, corporate end-users, and high-end paper and printing decision makers. Forty thousand brochures, 60,000 booklets, 2,000 posters, and 1,000 to 2,500 pins, T-shirts, CD cases, and guitar picks were produced. Everything was hand-delivered personally.

CONCEPT To generate excitement and interest, the design team chose to create a multidimensional experience. A fictitious record company, Utopia Recordings, was created as the catalyst for the chosen theme, *Loud, Proud, and Plenty of Soul.* Inspired by music, the promotional brochure boasts a series of album covers from a diverse array of genres, each highlighting various design and printing capabilities on the Utopia One X line. Inside is a record sleeve, showcasing various varnish effects on Utopia One X. The project also employs several custom add-ons, a T-shirt, guitar pick, CD case, and buttons, each contributing to the music-based theme in a unique way. Inside the CD case, a mini booklet highlights the 100 greatest albums of all time. It also includes picks from some of the industry's most prominent designers.

To keep the campaign rolling, a series of posters were also introduced. Four distinctive prints, each typeset by hand with antique wood and metal type, were produced using letterpress printing. The natural irregularities and textural quality inherent in the process give the Utopia One X paper an almost artistic quality. The entire promotional ensemble is fun and engaging.

MESSAGE Experience the design and printing capabilities that can be achieved using Utopia One X.

RESPONSE The response to the music-inspired campaign has been overwhelmingly positive, creating a buzz for Utopia One X.

fig. 1.1

Dull and gloss varnish is used in both spot and flood treatments.

fig. 1.2

The album-shaped book cover is printed on Utopia U1X 120 lb. gloss cover with Utopia U1X 80 lb. gloss and silk cover employed for the inside French-folded pages.

fig. 1.3

Throughout the perfect-bound piece, four-color process plus various match colors are used to achieve certain effects.

fig. 1.4

Inside the brochure, a record sleeve holds six insert sheets, each printed on Utopia U1X 100 lb. gloss text, showcasing a range of varnish effects.

The set comes rolled in a clear plastic tube that is imprinted on both ends.

fig. 2.1

fig. 2.2

The poster *Blinding White Willy* employs the fonts Gothic, Latin Ex, and Tower letterpress-printed on Utopia premium 150 lb. gloss cover.

fig. 2.3

The poster *White Space* uses the fonts Mandy, Gothic, Hardware, and Balderdash letterpress-printed onto Curious Collection Metallics virtual pearl 89 lb. cover.

fig. 2.4

The fonts Sutro Wood, Antique, Radiant Bold, and French Clarendon are letterpress-printed onto Utopia U1X 120 lb. gloss cover for the *Red Text Williams* poster.

fig. 2.5

For the poster called *Paper Soul Jah*, the fonts Rugged, Gothic, Cooper Black, and Stymie Bold are letterpress-printed onto Curious Collection particles silver 80 lb. cover.

fig. 3.1

Inside the CD case is a mini accordion-folded booklet, printed on Utopia U1X 100 lb. gloss text in four-color process plus a special match red and silver on one side and four-color process plus the same match red on the other. An overall aqueous coating is applied on both sides.

fig. 3.2

Music related add-ons—a silkscreen-printed and embroidered T-shirt, silkscreen-printed CD case, silkscreen-printed pick, and buttons—further continue the recording theme.

DIRECTORY OF SUPPLIERS AND MANUFACTURERS

3M
www.3m.com

Acme Graphic Arts Finishing
6133 Malburg Way
Los Angeles, CA 90058
USA
213.622.5181

A.C. Moore Arts & Crafts, Inc.
www.acmoore.com

Adverto
21000 Novi Sad
Serbia and Montenegro
381.63.58.31.73
www.adverto.co.yu

Ainley Fabrication
1450 Radford Rd.
Dubuque, IA 52002
USA
563.583.7615

A La Carte
www.alacarteline.com

Alpha Press
57 Harvard St.
Waltham, MA 02154
USA
781.894.5300

Alpine Dynamics/Best Containers
10939 N. Alpine Highway, Ste. 510
Highland, UT 84003
USA
815.464.7307
www.bestcontainers.com

Alstyle Apparel
1501 E. Cerritos Ave.
Anaheim, CA 92805
USA
800.225.1364
www.alstyle.com

American Ribbon Factory
827B Ann St.
Stroudsburg, PA 18360-1624
USA
570.421.7470

Amsterdam Silkscreen Productions
Zamenhofstraat 150, Unit 228
1022 AG Amsterdam
The Netherlands
31.0.20.6751456
amscreen@xs4all.nl
www.amsterdamsilkscreen.com

Andrews Connecticut
(subsidiary of RR Donnelley)
151 Red Stone Rd.
Manchester, CT 06040
USA
800.627.0382
www.rrdonnelley.com

Arbeitskreis Prägefoliendruck
Nepperberg 3
D 73525 Schwäbisch Gmünd
Germany
49.7171.41834
Fax 49.7171.949337
www.ak-praegefoliendruck.de

Arnies, Inc.
3741 W Houghton Lake Dr.
Houghton Lake, MI 48629
USA
www.basketpatterns.com

Arnold's Bookbinding
Arnold Martinez
915 Linden Ave., Ste. C
San Francisco, CA 94080
USA
650.872.3998

Artcraft, Inc.
P.O. Box 35063
Des Moines, IA 50315
USA
515.285.3550

Arthouse
2300 Kennedy St. NE, Ste. 190
Minneapolis, MN 55413
USA
612.645.5550
www.arthouseprint.com

Associated Bag
400 Boden St.
Milwaukee, WI 53207-6274
USA
800.926.6100
www.associatedbag.com

Bachmans
6010 Lyndale Ave. S
Minneapolis, MN 55419
USA
612.861.7676

Baesman Printing Corporation
4477 Reynolds Dr.
Hillard, OH 43206
USA
614.771.2300
www.baesman.com

Ball Chain Manufacturing Co., Inc.
741 S. Fulton Ave.
Mount Vernon, NY 10550
USA
914.664.7500
www.ballchain.com

Benchemark Printing
1890 Maxon Rd. Ext.
Schenectady, NY 12308
USA
518.393.1361
www.benchemark.net

Berman Printing Co.
1441 Western Ave.
Cincinnati, OH 45214
USA
800.653.5632
www.bermanprinting.com

Cathie Bleck, illustrator
USA
216.932.4910
cb@cathiebleck.com
www.cathiebleck.com

Bliss Wedding Market
P.O. Box 363
Woodbury, NY 11797
USA
866.445.4405
www.blissweddings.com

Big Print
Savski Nasip 9a
11070 Novi Beograd
Serbia and Montenegro
381.11.3016.529
www.bigprint.co.yu

Bill Nellans Photography
3800 Waterworks Pkwy.
Des Moines, IA 50312
USA
515.274.0406
www.billnellans.com

Blue Ridge Communications
826 Bootons Ln.
Orange, VA 22960
USA
540.672.9528

James Bohn
www.bohnmedia.com

Bollwerk 81
www.bollwerk81.de

Boss Print
2 The Works, Colville Rd.
London, W3 8BL
UK

Branders
1850 Gateway Dr.
San Mateo, CA 94404
USA
877.292.4880
www.branders.com

Brekekekexkoaxkoax
2001 Brentwood
Austin, TX 78757
USA

Brennan's Printing and Direct Mail
5612 Blessey St.
Harahan, LA 70123
USA
504.734.7371

Bullseye Disc
3377 SE Division St., Ste. 105
Portland, OR 97202
USA
www.bullseyedisc.com

Burdiss Lettershop Services
14844 W. 107th St.
Lenexa, KS 66215
USA
913.492.0545

Cambridge Silversmiths, Ltd.
116 Lehigh Dr.
Fairfield, NJ 07004
USA
973.227.4400
www.cambridgesilversmiths.com

Don Campau
campaudj@jps.net

Caractéra
1990, rue Jean-Talon Nord, bureau 206
Quebec, Quebec G1N 4K8
Canada
514.289.9191

Cenveo Anderson Lithograph
3217 S. Garfield Ave.
Los Angeles, CA 90040
USA
323.727.7767
www.andlitho.com

Cenveo Seattle
480 Andover Park E
Seattle, WA 98188
USA
206.575.3500
www.cenveo.com

C.J. Graphics
134 Park Lawn Rd.
Toronto, Ontario M8Y 3H9
Canada
416.588.0808

Clearbags.com
www.clearbags.com

Clockwork Apple, NYC
32b Gansevoort St.
New York, NY 10014
USA
646.206.3561

Coast Litho
848 60th St.
Oakland, CA 94608
USA
510.654.7336

Cognition Audioworks
1096 Queen St. #23
Halifax, NS B3H2R9
Canada
www.cognitionaudioworks.com

ColorGraphics
1421 S. Dean St
Seattle, WA 98144
USA
206.682.7171
www.colorgraphics.com

ColorNet Press
2216 Federal Ave.
Los Angeles, CA 90064
USA
310.477.0407
www.colornetpress.com

Combination No. 10
www.gutbrainsound.com

Confetti
Av. Eng. Eusébio Stevaux, 2472
Interlagos 04696-000
São Paulo
Brazil
55.11.5696.3600

Corporate Packaging
781 Beta Dr.
Cleveland, Ohio 44143
USA
440.646.1844

Cousin Silas
moderndance@btinternet.com

Covenant Printing
3323 Princeton Dr. NE
Albuquerque, NM 87107
USA
505.224.1237

Creative Bag Co., Ltd.
975 Pacific Gate, Units 1-6
Mississauga, Otario L5T 2A9
Canada
800.565.5554
www.creativebag.com

Dave Cupp
2374 Banning Rd.
Cincinnati, OH 45239
USA
513.681.6105

Custom Formed Products
8205 Washington Church Rd.
Dayton, OH 45458
USA
937.312.9830

Darby Printing & Litho
80 Readington Rd.
Branchburg, NJ 08876
USA
908.231.8883
www.citilitho.com

Dark Audio Project
www.darkaudioproject.com

Day Moon Press
3320 Beacon Ave. S
Seattle, WA 98144
USA
206.721.0064

D. E. Baugh
Indianapolis, IN
USA
800.942.4834
www.debaugh.com

Dick Blick Art Materials
P.O. Box 1267
Galesburg, IL 61402-1267
USA
800.828.4548
www.dickblick.com

Die Bene Tleilax
www.tleilaxu-culture.org

Digipak
www.digipak.com

Digital Banana
2904 W. Clay St.
Richmond, VA 23220
USA
804.353.7292
www.dbanana.com

Digital Imaging Technologies
27 Kent St., Ste. 108
Ballston Spa, NY 12020
USA
518.885.4400
www.digimtech.com

Disk Faktory
17173-A Gillette Ave.
Irvine, CA 92614
USA
949.477.1700
www.diskfaktory.com

Diversified Graphics
1700 Broadway NE
Minneapolis, MN 55413
USA
612.331.1111
www.dgi.net

DMC
Avenue Ledru Rollin
75012 Paris
France
33.1.49.28.00
www.dmc.com

Domtar
www.domtar.com

Dynagraphics
300 NW 14th Ave.
Portland, OR 97209
USA
503.228.9453
www.dynagraphics.com

Envelopemall.com
2028 W. Fulton
Chicago, IL 60612
USA
800.632.4242
www.envelopemall.com

Epson America Inc.
3840 Kilroy Airport Way
Long Beach, CA 90806
USA
562.981.3840
www.epson.com

Sara Essex
New Orleans, LA
USA
504.523.6649
www.saraessex.com

Everett Graphics
1680 Booth Ave.
Coquitlam, British Columbia V3K 1B9
Canada
604.818.4525

Evident Crime Scene Products
www.evidentcrimescene.com

Fabricland Interiors
www.fabricland.com

Ferrara Pan
Forest Park, IL
USA

Field Print
9 Hutton St. Industrial Estate
Boldon Colliery
Newcastle-upon-Tyne, NE35 9LW
UK

Fire Mountain Gems
One Fire Mountain Way
Grants Pass, OR 97526-2373
USA
www.firemountaingems.com

Fit to Print
200 Wales St.
Abington, MA 02351
USA
781.871.0620

Franklin Southland
3212 Seventh St.
Metairie, LA 70002
USA
504.833.6355
www.franklinsouthland.com

Freestyle Photographic Supplies
www.freestylephoto.biz

Fridur
ig_enigma@hotmail.com

Fruit of the Loom
1 Fruit of the Loom Dr.
Bowling Green, KY 42103
USA
270.781.6400
www.fruit.com

G2 Graphic Service
5510 Cleo Ave.
North Hollywood, CA 91601
USA
818.623.3100
www.g2online.com

G.A.C./Cenveo Seattle
832 S. Fidalgo St.
Seattle, WA 98108
USA
206.767.4190
www.cenveo.com

Giuseppe Rapisarda
www.rapisarda.org

Glenmore Printing
150-13751 Mayfield Pl.
Richmond, British Columbia V6V 2G9
Canada
604.273.6323
www.glenmoreprinting.com

Golden Impressions
1520 NW 17th St.
Portland, OR 97209
USA
800.621.8878

Graphic Press
6100 S. Malt Ave.
Los Angeles, CA 90040
USA
323.726.6100
www.graphicpress1.com

Grafix
Bulevar Vojvode Mišića 17
11000 Beograd
Serbia and Montenegro
381.11.3067.960
www.grafix.co.yu

Andrew Greene
agreene1@si.rr.com

Mike Hallenbeck
http://juniorbirdman.com/archive

Harvey Lloyd Screens
Unit G, Durgates Industrial Estate
Wadhurst, East Sussex
TN5 6DF London
UK
44.1892.783.800
www.harveylloydscreens.co.uk

Harvey Press
246 Harbor Circle
New Orleans, LA 70126
USA
504.246.8474
www.harveypress.com

Haverkamp Printing
Kwadijkerkoogweg 1
1442 LA Purmerend
Postbus 82
1440 AB Purmerend
0299.413.413
www.haverkampprinting.nl

HBI
10 East 53rd St.
New York, NY 10022-5299
USA

Hobby Lobby
7707 SW 44th St.
Oklahoma City, OK 73179
USA
www.hobbylobby.com

Horrendous
www.benjaminhorrendous.co.uk

Hirsch GmbH
Brückenfeldstraβe 54,
75015 Bretten
Germany
49.7252.94600
www.hirschdruck.de

Identity
Unit 30, Eldon Way, Paddock Wood
Tonbridge, Kent
TN12 6BE London
UK
44.1892.837.989

Imaging Bureau
4545 Cambridge Rd.
Fort Worth, TX 76155
USA
www.imagingbureau.com

Independent Can Company
Belcamp, MD
USA

JB Graphics
5500 East 5th St. NW
USA
505.341.0338

Jenco Productions
401 South J St.
San Bernardino, CA 92410
USA
909.381.9453
Fax 909.381.2582

Jennifer Papers
406 Fulton St.
Troy, NY 12180
USA
518.272.4572

Jesse James and Company, Inc.
615 N. New St.
Allentown, PA 18102
USA
610.435.7899
www.jessejamesbutton.com

Jet Lithocolor, Inc.
1500 Centre Circle
Downers Grove, IL 60515
USA
630.932.9000
www.jetlitho.com

JKM Ribbon
431 Commerce Ln., Ste. B
West Berlin, NJ 08091
USA
800.767.3635
www.jkmribbon.com

Jo-Ann Fabrics & Crafts
www.joann.com

Jornik/Sunrise Business Products
USA
866.407.3511
www.sun-rise.com

Kate's Paperie
140 W. 57th St.
New York, NY 10019
USA
212.459.0700

Kolo
www.kolo-usa.com

Kreinik Metallics
www.kreinik.com

Lake County Press
98 Noll St.
Waukegan, IL 60085
847.336.4333

Lavezzo Gráfica e Editora
Rua Anhaguera, 667
Barra Funda
01135-000 São Paulo
Brazil
3392.2555
Fax 3392.2832
www.lavezzo.com.br

Leewood Press
564 Sixth Street
San Francisco, CA 94103
USA
415.701.7017

James Leland
USA
323.896.6659
www.jamesleland.com
james@jamesleland.com

Louey Rubino Design
2525 Main St., #204
Santa Monica, CA 90405
USA
310.396.7724
www.loueyrubino.com

MacDonald Photography
22W540 Poss St.
Glen Ellyn, IL 60137
USA
630.790.9519
Fax 630.790.2188
www.macpix.com
brian@macpix.com

Terry Marks
USA
620.628.6427
www.tmarksdesign.com
terry@tmarksdesign.com

Matrix Imaging
118 W. North St.
Indianapolis, IN 46204
USA
317.635.4756
www.matrixdigitalphoto.com

Metropolitan Fine Printing
1435 E. Pender St.
Vancouver, British Columbia V5L 1V7
Canada
866.254.4201
www.metprinters.com

Michaels
www.michaels.com

Millennium Graphics
79 Astor Ave.
Norwood, MA 02062
USA
781.762.3525
www.mgraphics.net

Mobile
mobile012@hotmail.com

Mondadori Electa SpA
Via Trentacoste 7
20134 Milan
Italy
39.02.21.56.31
Fax 539.02.26.41.31.21

Moon
www.burningemptiness.fr.st

Mutual Tool & Die, Inc.
937.268.6713

Mystified
autocad13@hotmail.com

Joel Nakamura, illustrator
USA
505.989.1404
jonaka@nm.net
www.joelnakamura.com

Nava Press
98 via Breda
20126 Milan
Italy
39.02252991
Fax 39.02576205

Nectarphonic
www.elevenshadows.com/nectar

Nichole Sloan Photography
109 College St.
McDonough, GA 30253
USA
888.957.2232
www.nicholesloan.com

Greta Nintzel
www.gretagurl.com

David Nix
www.davidnix.co.uk

Office Depot
800.GO.DEPOT
www.officedepot.com

Old Time Candy Company
25222 Sprague Rd.
Olmsted Falls, OH 44138
USA
440.243.2355
www.oldtimecandy.com

Ole Peterson
lizole@comcast.net

One Heart Press
1616 16th St.
San Francisco, CA 94103
USA
415.861.1616
www.oneheartpress.com

O'Neil Printing
366 North 2nd Ave.
Phoenix, AZ 85003
USA
602.258.7789
www.oneilprint.com

Packaging Services Corporation
26100 Pinehurst
Madison Heights, MI 48071-0945
USA
800.328.7799

Palacek
P.O. Box 225
Richmond, CA 94808
USA
800.274.7730
www.palecek.com

Paper Mart
5361 Alexander St.
Los Angeles, CA 90040
USA
800.745.8800
www.papermart.com

Paper N' Inc.
400 Oyster Point Blvd., Ste. 114
San Francisco, CA 94080
USA
650.875.7720

Panayiotis Kokoras
www.panayiotiskokoras.com

Patented Printing
1630 E. Second St.
Dayton, OH 45403
USA
800.799.0010
www.patentedprinting.com

Pat Reagh Printing
96A Bloomfield Rd.
Sebastapol, CA 95472
USA
707.829.6805

Maggi Payne
www.maggipayne.com

Penmor Lithographers
8 Lexington St.
P.O. Box 2003
Lewiston, ME 04241
USA
800.339.1341
www.penmor.com

Penfold Buscombe
20 Baker St.
Banksmeadow NSW 2019
Australia
61.2.8333.6555

Pennsylvania Dutch Candies
1250 Slate Hill Rd.
Camp Hill, PA 17011
USA
866.736.6388
www.padutchcandies.com

Peschke Druck
Schatzbogen 35
81829 München
Germany
49.89.427700
www.peschkedruck.de

Planes Overhead
www.leaftone.com

Porkopolis
P.O. Box 3529
Cincinnati, OH 45201
USA

Postcard Press
18732 Crenshaw Bvld.
Torrance, CA 90504
USA
800.957.5787
www.postcardpress.com

Richard Poynter
Lyndhurst, Westland Green
Little Hadham, Herts
SG11 2AF London
UK
44.1279.842.395

Precision Laser Services
www.precisionlaser.com

PrintExchange
1009 Broad Ripple Ave., Ste. E
Indianapolis, IN 46220
USA
317.590.0868

Printers Square
836 Candia Rd.
Manchester, NH 03109
USA
603.623.0802
www.psquare.com

PrintingForLess.com
211 E. Geyser St.
Livingston, MT 59047
USA
800.930.6040
www.printingforless.com

Proforma Mactec Solutions
484 Lake Park Ave. #29
Oakland, CA 94610
USA
510.534.5784

Progress Packaging Ltd.
20 Tangiers Rd.
Downsview, ON M3J 2B2
Canada
www.luv2pak.com

Publikum
Slavka Rodiće 6
11090 Beograd
Serbia and Montenegro
381.11.232.2201
www.publikum.co.yu

Mike Pursley
mike_pursley@hotmail.com

Quality Printing
1047 Broadway
Anderson, IN 46012
USA
800.771.1148
www.quality-printing.com

Quebecor World George Rice & Sons
2001 N. Soto St.
Los Angeles, CA 90032
USA
323.223.2020
www.quebecorworldinc.com

Radex Inc.
www.radexinc.com

Relevo Araujo
Rua Javaés 136
Bom Retiro
São Paulo - SP
Brazil
11.3331.3100
www.relevoaraujo.com.br

Restoration Hardware, Inc.
3670 Galleria
Edina, MN 55435-4220
USA
952.926.5557

Rimage Corporation
7725 Washington Ave. S
Minneapolis, MN 55439
USA
800.445.8288
www.rimage.com

Roadrunner Press
2320 W. Magnolia Blvd.
Burbank, CA 91506
USA
818.843.8722

Rob Brinson Studio
887-B W. Marietta St. NW
Atlanta, GA 30318
USA
404.874.2497
www.robbrinson.com

David Robin
1123 Broadway, Ste. 519
New York, NY 10010
USA
212.691.0088
www.davidrobin.com

Roswell Bookbinding
2614 N. 29th Ave.
Phoenix, AZ 85009
USA
602.272.9338
www.roswellbookbinding.com

R.P. Collier
trundlebox.iuma.com

RTO Group
170 Post Rd.
Fairfield, CT 06430
USA
203.254.9544
www.rtogroup.com

Rubber Stampede
Whittier, CA
USA
www.deltacrafts.com/RubberStampede

John Salcido
juandabaptis@hotmail.com

Sam's Club
www.samsclub.com

Satyr Oz
satyroz@hotmail.com

Schneider Söhne GmbH & Co KG
Gehrnstr. 7-11
D- 76275 Ettlingen
Germany
49.72.43730
www.schneidersoehne.de

Brian Schorn
brian@circulus.us

Cameron Sears
www.home.primus.com.au/csears

Siewers Lumber & Millwork
1901 Ellen Rd.
Richmond, VA 23230
USA
804.358.2103
www.siewers.com

Shadi + Company
675 Hudson, Ste. 5N
New York, NY 10014
USA
212.463.8782
www.shadiandcompany.com

Signalbleed
www.geocities.com/signalbleed

Sir Speedy
www.sirspeedy.com

Siska Inc.
P.O. Box 921
Saddle Brook, NJ 07663
USA
800.393.5381
www.siska.com

Specialty Bottle LLC
5215 5th Ave. S
Seattle, WA 98108
USA
206.340.0459
www.specialtybottle.com

Specialty Box & Packaging Co., Inc.
1040 Broadway
Albany, NY 12204
USA
800.493.2247
www.specialtybox.com

Spicers Papers
12310 E. Lauson Ave.
Santa Fe Springs, CA 90670
562.981.1990
www.spicers.com

Staton Wholesale
4552 Simonton Rd.
Dallas, TX 75244
USA
800.888 8888
www.statonwholesale.com

Staples
www.staples.com

State Line Wholesale
800.858.6966

Steve Woods Printing Co.
2205 E. University
Phoenix, AZ 85034
USA
888.484.2448
www.stevewoodsprinting.com

Storelite leuchtfarben
Speicherstrasse
P.O. Box 147
CH 9053 Teufen
Germany
41.71.3.357373
www.rctritec.com

Dan Susnara
7806 S. Kilpatrick
Chicago, IL 60652
USA
773.735.5792

Target Corporation
www.target.com

Taylor Box Company
293 Child St.
Warren, RI 02885
USA
401.245.5900

Tat-Gun
smpqh@yahoo.com

Taurus Bookbindery
2748 Ninth St.
Berkeley, CA 94710
USA
510.548.2313

TAYO
Rod. Régis Bittencourt
Km 274 nº 4501/Jd. 3 Marias
Taboão da Serra 06793-100
São Paulo
Brazil

TCHANT
mcquaz@hotmail.com

The Ace Group, Inc.
149 W. 27th St.
New York, NY 10001
USA
212.255.7846
www.acegroup.com

The Actualizers, Inc.
250 Park Ave. S, Ste. 201
New York, NY 10003
USA
212.477.4300
www.actualizers.com

The Chocolate Gecko
540 Delaware Ave.
Albany, NY 12209
USA
518.426.0866
www.chocolategecko.com

The Computer Group, Inc.
4455 Reynolds Dr.
Hilliard, OH 43026-1261
USA
800.446.4076
www.tcgroup.net

The Copy Co.
616 6th Ave. S
Seattle, WA 98114
USA
206.622.4050

The Paper Company
10 Sams Point Road
Beaufort, SC 29907
USA
800.449.1125
www.papercompany.com

Bill Timmerman
USA
602.420.9325
wltimm@cox.net

Tin R.P.
www.tindotrp.fr.st

Tiskarna TIPOS Ljubljana Slovenija
Vojkova 58
Ljubljana 1000
Slovenija

Towsley's, Inc.
1424 Dewey St.
Manitowoc, WI 54221
800.960.1055

Union-Hoermann Press
2175 Kerper Blvd.
Dubuque, IA 52001
USA
563.582.3631

Union Press
1723 W. 8th St.
Wilmington, DE 19805
USA
302.652.0496

Uline
800.295.5510
www.uline.com

Unioninvestplastika
Semizovac bb
71000 Sarajevo
Bosnia
387.33.453.563

US Plastics Corp.
1390 Neubrecht Rd.
Lima, OH 45801-3196
USA
800.809.4217
www.usplastic.com

Wayzata Bay Spice Company
22643 Jessa Place
Rogers, MN 55374
USA
763.428.5851
www.wbspice.com

Werkstatt Höeflich
Enhuberstrasse 6-8
D-80333 München
Germany

Whatcom Seed Company
P.O. Box 40700
Eugene, OR 97404
USA
http://seedrack.com

W.C. Sims Co.
3845 W. National Rd.
Springfield, OH 45504
USA
937.325.7035
www.wcsims.com

Whitehall
www.nartworld.com

Woodwright and Lumber Company
937.275.7242

York Graphic Services
3650 W. Market St.
York, PA 17404
USA
717.505.9701
www.ygsc.com

Yupo Corporation America
800 Yupo Ct.
Chesapeake, VA 23320
USA
www.yupo.com

Zone 5
8 Corporate Circle
Albany, NY 12203
USA
518.456.8312
www.zone5.com

Zooom Printing LLC
2010 E. Franklin St.
Richmond, VA 23223
USA
www.zooomprinting.com

Zucker Feather Products
P.O. Box 331, 28419 Hwy. 87
California, MO 65018
USA
www.zuckerfeathers.com

DIRECTORY OF CONTRIBUTORS

Adobe Systems Incorporated
345 Park Ave.
San Jose, CA 95110
USA
408.536.6000
www.adobe.com
p. 161

Alexander Isley Inc.
9 Brookside Pl.
Redding, CT 06896
USA
203.544.9692
Fax 203.544.7189
www.alexanderisley.com
aline@alexanderisley.com
p. 106

Appleton Coated
569 Carter Ct.
Kimberly, WI 54136
USA
800.663.1813 (direct)
Fax 920.968.3950
www.utopiapaper.com
fgoldinger@appletoncoated.com
p. 178

Art & Anthropology
2850 Welton St.
Denver, CO 80205
USA
303.308.0453/303.522.4380
Fax 720.226.0531
www.artandanthropology.com
p. 104

ATTIK Design Inc.
445 Bush St., 3rd Fl.
San Francisco, CA 94108
USA
415.989.6401
www.attik.com
p. 150

Baesman Printing Corporation
4477 Reynolds Dr.
Hillard, OH 43206
USA
614.771.2300
www.baesman.com
p. 120

Belyea
1809 Seventh Ave.
Seattle, WA 98101
USA
206.682.4895
Fax 206.623.8912
www.belyea.com
info@belyea.com
p. 164

Blue River
The Foundry, Forth Banks
Newcastle upon Tyne, NE1 3PA
UK
44.191.261.0000
Fax 44.191.261.0010
www.blueriver.co.uk
design@blueriver.co.uk
p. 66

Brian Biggs
P.O. Box 25922
Philadelphia, PA 19128
USA
www.MrBiggs.com
brian@MrBiggs.com
p. 170

Blockdot, Inc.
4153 Commerce St.
Dallas, TX 75226
USA
214.823.0500
Fax 214.823.0535
www.blockdot.com/www.kewlbox.com
info@blockdot.com
p. 172

Blu Concept Inc.
103-1104 Hornby St.
Vancouver, BC V6Z 1V8
Canada
604.872.2583
Fax 604.872.2588
www.bluconcept.com
rik@bluconcept.com
p. 68

Denise Bosler, illustrator
704 Old Swede Rd.
Douglassville, PA 19518
USA
610.324.6915
www.bosler.com
illustration@bosler.com
p. 36

Capsule
10 S. Fifth St., Ste. 645
Minneapolis, MN 55402
USA
612.341.4525
Fax 612.341.4577
www.capsule.us
aaronkeller@capsule.us
p. 122

Carmichael Lynch Thorburn
800 Hennepin Ave.
Minneapolis, MN 55403
USA
612.375.8201
www.clthorburn.com
p. 178

ceft & company
52-54 Walker St., 4th Fl.
New York, NY 10013
USA
www.ceftandcompany.com
p. 46

Curb-Crowser
800 Washington Ave. N, Ste. 322
Minneapolis, MN 55401
USA
612.252.2344
Fax 612.252.2343
www.curb-crowser.com
tracie@curb-crowser.com
p. 58; 100

Cyr Studio
P.O. Box 795
Stroudsburg, PA 18360
USA
Tel/Fax 570.420.9673
www.cyrstudio.com
lisa@cyrstudio.com
p. 162

Lloyd Dangle
P.O. Box 21097
Oakland, CA 94602
USA
www.lloyddangle.com
www.troubletown.com
lloyd@troubletown.com
p. 170

Double Image Studio
217B W. 7th St.
Richmond, VA 23224
USA
804.232.5500
Fax 804.232.5567
www.doubleimagestudio.com
mail@doubleimagestudio.com
p. 22

Douglas Joseph Partners
11812 San Vicente Blvd., Ste. 125
Los Angeles, CA 90049
USA
310.440.3100
Fax 310.440.3103
www.djpartners.com
info@djpartners.com
p. 166

emeryfrost, Sydney
Level 1, 15 Foster St.
Surry Hills, NSW 2010
Australia
61.2.9280.4233
Fax 61.2.9280.4266
p. 28

emeryFrost, Melbourne
80 Market St.
Southbank, VIC 3006
Australia
61.3.9699.3822
Fax 61.2.9690.7371
www.emeryfrost.com
info@emeryfrost.com
p. 28

Eureka
1 Sorrel Dr.
Wilmington, DE 19803
USA
302.477.9224
Fax 302.477.1771
www.abouteureka.com
lisa@abouteureka.com
p. 73

Fan Works Design, LLC
2505 Hanover Ave,
Richmond, VA 23220
USA
804.353.3060
Fax 804.353.3063
www.fanworksdesign.com
info@fanworksdesign.com
p. 90; 118

Finchworks
P.O. Box 88434
Los Angeles, CA 90009
USA
310.643.9286
Fax 310.643.0246
frandal@finchworks.com
www.finchworks.com
p. 16

Folie a Trois/Black Pixel
Đure Đakovića 5
11000, Belgrade
Serbia and Montenegro
381.64.18.18.350
www.the-mighty.com
office@the-mighty.com
p. 174

FrankSturgesReps
USA
740.369.9702
www.sturgesreps.com
frank@sturgesreps.com
p. 120

Fusionary Media, Inc.
820 Monroe Ave. NW, Ste. 212
Grand Rapids, MI 49503
USA
616.454.2357
Fax 616.454.6827
www.fusionary.com
info@fusionary.com
p. 80

GJP Advertising
154 Pearl St.
Toronto, Ontario M5H 1L3
Canada
416.979.7999
www.gjpadvertising.com
p. 69

Claudia Goetzelmann, photographer
2443 Fillmore St.
San Francisco, CA 04115
USA
415.305.7425
www.claudiagoetzelmann.com
claudia@claudiagoetzelmann.com
p. 39; 70; 74

Dave Gordon
USA
917.620.3089
www.illustrationranch.com
p. 170

Susan Gross
P.O. Box 219
Boonville, CA 95415
USA
707.895.3938
Fax 707.895.3933
www.SusanGross.com
Susan@SusanGross.com
p. 170

H
1055 St. Charles Ave,, Ste. 300
New Orleans, LA 70130
USA
504.522.6300
Fax 504.524.6359
www.thinkH.com
info@thinkH.com
p. 20; 116

Hand Made Group
Via Sartori, 16
STIA (AR)
Italy
39.0575.582083
Fax 39.0575.582083
www.hmg.it
info@hmg.it
p. 48; 54; 113

Harvard School of Design
Department of Urban Design
USA
www.harvard.edu
p. 176

Hatch Show Print
316 Broadway
Nashville, TN 37201
USA
615.256.2805
Fax 615.254.5202
www.hatchshowprint.com
hatchshowprint@bellsouth.net
p. 178

hat-trick design
3rd Fl., 3 Morocco St.
London, SE1 3HB
UK
44.20.7403.7875
Fax 0.20.7403.8926
www.hat-trickdesign.co.uk
info@hat-trickdesign.co.uk
p. 76

Steve Holmes
USA
415.331.9004
www.energidesign.com
p. 160

Hornall Anderson Design Works LLC
1008 Western Ave., Ste, 600
Seattle, WA 98104
USA
206.467.5800
Fax 206.467.6411
www.hadw.com
info@hadw.com
p. 102; 114

Huber&Co Design
Kobellstrasse 8
D-80336 Muenchen
Germany
49.89.42.376.12
Fax 49.89.42.376.14
www.huberundco.com
mail@huberundco.com
p. 18; 96

Diana Marye Huff
USA
805.646.5492
www.dianahuff.com
p. 52

Sterling Hundley
3920 Doeskin Dr.
Apex, NC 27539
USA
804.306.9536
www.sterlinghundley.com
p. 12

Ico Design Consultancy Limited
75-77 Great Portland St.
London W1W 7LR
UK
44.207.323.1088
Fax 44.207.323.1245
www.icodesign.co.uk
niall.henry@icodesign.co.uk
p. 26

IE Design + Communications
422 Pacific Coast Hwy.
Hermosa Beach, CA 90254
USA
310.376.9600
Fax 310.376.9604
www.iedesign.com
ted@iedesign.net
p. 121

Independent Opposition
USA
www.independentopposition.com
www.mattfrantz.com
matt@mattfrantz.com
p. 168

Innovative
1435 N. Meridian St.
Indianapolis, IN 46202
USA
317.686.6086
Fax 317.686.6096
www.innovativei.com
conrad@innovativei.com
p. 112

Iron Blender Studios
P.O. Box 1803
Westfield, MA 01086
USA
413.572.5584
Fax 413.513.9640
www.ironblender.com
wendy@ironblender.com
p. 98

KBDA
2558 Overland Ave.
Los Angeles, CA 90064
USA
310.287.2400
Fax 310.287.0909
www.kbda.com
kim@kbda.com
p. 94; 103

Larson-Juhl
3900 Steve Reynolds Blvd.
Norcross, GA 30093
USA
www.larsonjuhl.com
p. 147

Lynn Cyr Design
7 Fannie Way
Franklin, MA 02038
USA
508.533.4526
www.lynncyr.com
lynn@lynncyr.com
p. 72

MAGMA [Büro für Gestaltung]
Bachstr. 43
76185 Karlsruhe
Germany
49.721.92919.70
Fax 49.721.92919.80
www.magma-ka.de
info@magma-ka.de
p. 134

Magnet Reps
3450 Vinton Ave.
Los Angeles, CA 90034
USA
866.390.5656
Fax 310.876.7199
www.magnetreps.com
art@magnetreps.com
p. 156

Michael Osborne Design
444 De Haro St., Ste. 207
San Francisco, CA 94107
USA
415.255.0125
Fax 415.255.1312
www.modsf.com
info@modsf.com
p. 77

Mirko Ilić Corporation
207 East 32nd St.
New York, NY 10016
USA
212.481.9737
Fax 212.481.7088
www.mirkoilic.com
studio@mirkoilic.com
p. 132; 142; 174

Modern Dog Design Co.
7903 Greenwood Ave. N
Seattle, WA 98103
USA
206.789.7667
Fax 206.789.3171
www.moderndog.com
bubbles@moderndog.com
p. 30

Monster
www.monsterillo.com
p. 170

Motive Design Research
2028 Fifth Ave.
Seattle, WA 98121
USA
206.374.8761
Fax 206.374.8763
www.altmotive.com
info@altmotive.com
p. 62

Mucca Design
568 Broadway, Ste. 604A
New York, NY 10012
USA
212.965.9821
www.muccadesign.com
p. 160

Nassar Design
11 Park St.
Brookline, MA 02446
USA
617.264.2862
Fax 617.264.2861
n.nassar@verizon.net
p. 176

Bo Nielsen
www.skinnyfish.net
info@skinnyfish.net
p. 160

Orlando Facioli Design
Rua São carlos do Pinhal, 152/92
São Paulo SP 01333-000
Brazil
11.55.3262.5204 or 11.55.8145.0660
www.orlandofacioli.com.br
orlando@orlandofacioli.com.br
p. 50; 78; 108

Bud Peen Illustration & Design
565 Santa Ray Ave.
Oakland, CA 94610
USA
510.465.8302
www.budpeen.com
p. 170

Plainspoke
18 Sheafe St.
Portsmouth, NH 03801
USA
603.433.5969
Fax 603.433.1587
www.plainspoke.com
matt@plainspoke.com
p. 24; 148

Planet 10
1238 N. Pennsylvania St.
Indianapolis, IN 46033
USA
317.636.7838
www.planet10.net
p. 156

PLAZM
P.O. Box 2863
Portland, OR 97208
USA
503.528.8000
Fax 503.528.8092
www.plazm.com
info@plazm.com
p. 38; 136

Principle, Inc.
USA
877.522.1487
Fax 418.948.8998
www.designbyprinciple.com
pamela@designbyprinciple.com
p. 147

Mario Queiroz
Alameda Franca, 1166
Jardim Paulistano 01422-000
São Paulo
Brazil
11.553063.5787
www.marioqueiroz.com.br
p. 78

rabih hage
69-71 Sloane Ave.
London SW3 3DH
UK
44.20.7823.8288
Fax 44.20.7823.8258
www.rabih-hage.com
mail@rabih-hage.com
p. 76

Real Art Design Group, Inc.
232 E. Sixth St.
Dayton, Ohio 45402
USA
937.223.9955
Fax 937.223.3013
www.realartusa.com
info@realartusa.com
p. 92; 110

Red Canoe
347 Clear Creek Trail
Deer Lodge, TN 37726
USA
423.965.2223
Fax 423.965.1005
www.redcanoe.com
studio@redcanoe.com
p. 52

Red Nose Studio
Greenfield, IN
USA
Tel/Fax 317.467.9105
www.rednosestudio.com
rednosestudio@mac.com
p. 156

Refinery Design Company
2001 Alta Vista St.
Dubuque, IA 52001
USA
563.584.0172
Fax 563.557.8850
www.refinerydesignco.com
refinery@refinerydesignco.com
p. 40

Riordon Design
131 George St.
Oakville, Ontario L6J 3B9
Canada
905.339.0750
Fax 905.339.0753
www.riordondesign.com
ric@riordondesign.com
p. 88; 144

Roberto de Vicq de Cumptich
1326 Madison Ave.
New York, NY 10128
USA
212.289.2369
www.bemboszoo.com
p. 88; 144

Rome & Gold Creative
1606 Central Ave. SE, Ste. 102
Albuquerque, NM 87106
USA
505.897.0870
Fax 505.843.7500
www.rgcreative.com
info@rgcreative.com
p. 60; 64

Rule29
821 Kindberg Ct.
Elburn, IL 60119
USA
630.365.5420
Fax 630.365.5430
www.rule29.com
justin@rule29.com
p. 14; 86

Salvato, Coe & Gabor Design
2015 W. 5th Ave.
Columbus, OH 43212
USA
614.488.3131
www.scgdesign.com
p. 120

Sayles Graphic Design
3701 Beaver Ave.
Des Moines, IA 50310
USA
515.279.2922
Fax 515.279.0212
www.saylesdesign.com
sheree@saylesdesign.com
p. 146

Isabel Samaras
USA
www.devilbabe.com
izzycat@aol.com
p. 170

John Sinal Photography
2040 E. 6th Ave.
Vancouver, British Columbia V5N 1P9
Canada
604.669.1301
p. 68

Marcos Sorensen
USA
415.816.8668
www.astrocat.com
msorensen@astrocat.com
p. 170

Spiral Design Studio, LLC
915 Broadway
Albany, NY 12207
USA
518.432.7976
Fax 518.462.6625
www.spiraldesign.com
info@spiraldesign.com
p. 56; 158

Starshot GmbH & Co KG
Malsenstrasse 84
80638 München
Germany
0.89.159.866.0
Fax 89.159.866.88
www.starshot.de
harmsen@starshot.de
p. 130

Michiko Stehrenberger
USA
206.495.0844
www.michiko.com
gallery@michiko.com
p. 170

Storm Editions, Inc.
ALT Pick magazine
1133 Broadway, Ste. 1408
New York, NY 10011
USA
212.675.4176
altpickmagazine.com
altpick@altpick.com
p. 138

StrawberryFrog
Tesselschadestraat 13
1054 ET
Amsterdam
The Netherlands
31.20.530.0400
Fax 31.20.5300.499
www.strawberryfrog.com
froggy@strawberryfrog.com
p. 34

Gordon Studer
1566 62nd St.
Emeryville, CA 94608
USA
510.655.4256
www.gordonstuder.com
gstuder@rcn.com
p. 170

STVARNIK
Resljeva 35
1000 Ljubljana
Slovenija
00386.01.4347.348
stvarnik.doo@siol.net
p. 128

the[Box]
421 E. Franklin St., #250
Richmond, VA 23219
USA
804.343.1888
www.theboxcreative.com
p. 22

The Pushpin Group, Inc.
55 E. 9 St., 1G
New York, NY 10003
212.529.7590
Fax 212.529.7631
www.pushpininc.com
p. 140

Tihany Design
135 W. 27th St.
New York, NY 10001
USA
212.366.5544
Fax 212.366.4302
www.tihanydesign.com
mail@tihanydesign.com
p. 132

Turner Duckworth, London
Voysey House, Barley Mow Passage
London, W4 4PH
UK
44.20.8994.7190
Fax 44.20.8994.7192
www.turnerduckworth.com
moira@turnerduckworth.co.uk
p. 32

Turner Duckworth, San Francisco
831 Montgomery St.
San Francisco, CA 94133
USA
415.675.7776
Fax 415.675.7778
www.turnerduckworth.com
joanne@turnerduckworth.com
p. 32

Trio and Fabrika
Alipašina 29
71000 Sarajevo
Bosnia and Herzegovina
387.33.253.900
Fax 387.33.253.900
www.fabrika.com
fabrika@fabrika.com
p. 142

Vinton Studios
1400 NW 22nd Ave.
Portland, OR 97210
USA
503.225.1130
Fax 503.226.3746
www.vinton.com
askusanything@vinton.com
p. 38

Vinton Studios
1100 Glendon Ave., 17th Fl.
Los Angeles, CA 90024
USA
310.689.7222
Fax 310.689.7244
LA@vinton.com
p. 38

Brian Wilder Photography
USA
617.464.2066
www.brianwilder.com
brian@brianwilder.com
p. 24

Michael Wertz
USA
510.663.5860
Michael@wertzateria.com
p. 170

James A. Winters
2940 16th St., #104
San Francisco, CA 94103
USA
415.786.7893
www.jimwinters.com
p. 170

ABOUT THE AUTHOR

Lisa L. Cyr is an artist, author, and national lecturer. Her clients include advertising agencies, design firms, and publishers. She speaks actively about successful promotional strategies, marketing opportunities, and entrepreneurial endeavors at professional organizations, universities, and industry conferences and events. In addition to her speaking engagements, Cyr writes for many of the industry trade publications including *Communication Arts, Step Inside Design, HOW, ID, Alt Pick, Applied Arts*, and others. Her articles range from revealing issues that face the industry to featuring top talent in the business. Her recent books, *The Art of Promotion, Brochure Design That Works*, and *Graphic Design That Works*, feature top national and international promotional work with sidebars that go beyond the basics to explore strategic and innovative thinking. A graduate of Massachusetts College of Art (BFA) and Syracuse University (MA), Cyr has exhibited her creative work both nationally and internationally. Her work is also in the permanent collection of the Museum of American Illustration. Cyr is an artist member of the Society of Illustrators, NYC. She works in partnership with her husband, Christopher Short, a graphic illustrator and 3D animator. Cyr has designed a traveling lecture titled *Creatively Speaking* to accompany this book. Interested organizations and universities can visit www.cyrstudio.com for more details.